Romantic Relationships ~
The Greatest Arena for Spiritual & Emotional Growth

*Codependent Dysfunctional Relationship Dynamics
& Healthy Relationship Behavior*

By **Robert Burney**
Author of
Codependence *The Dance of Wounded Souls*

A thirteen part series of articles titled Dysfunctional Relationship Dynamics & Healthy Relationship Behavior was originally published online on the Inner Child/Codependency Recovery page that I then edited for Suite101.com Directory - although bits and pieces of the articles had been part of articles and web pages published previously. That series of articles has been incorporated into this book.

Cover image by Ness Butler

ISBN-10: 1478189886
ISBN-13: 978-1478189886
Published in September 2012 as Print on Demand Trade Paperback through CreateSpace
by Joy to You & Me Enterprises
PO Box 235401
Encinitas, California 92023

First Edition
Printed in United States of America

Dedication

Dedicated to my partner, friend, lover, teacher, muse, and wife Susan Hinesley. You are a gorgeous, wise, brilliant, sexy, amazing woman with a heart of gold and a Radiant Spirit!!! Thank you for being willing to explore emotional intimacy with me for the last 7 years. Thank you for sharing your body, mind, heart, and soul with me. It has been a really exciting adventure that I do treasure.

"It is in taking responsibility and working through issues that the True magic of emotional intimacy can flower. The sacred magic that is Love is worth the effort.

Two people consciously working together can be a very beautiful experience." - Chapter 1

"To be willing to be conscious and emotionally honest with ourselves is a courageous act of faith that will allow us to progressively increase the number of moments in each day that we have the ability and freedom to be happy and Joyous in the now. To find another being who is willing to join us in this adventure, and to explore True emotional intimacy with us, is a priceless gift to be cherished and treasured." - Chapter 12

Table of Contents

Author's Foreword

"Perspective is a key to Recovery. I had to change and enlarge my perspectives of myself and my own emotions, of other people, of God and of this life business. Our perspective of life dictates our relationship with life. We have a dysfunctional relationship with life because we were taught to have a dysfunctional perspective of this life business, dysfunctional definitions of who we are and why we are here.

It is kind of like the old joke about three blind men describing an elephant by touch. Each one of them is telling his own Truth, they just have a lousy perspective. Codependence is all about having a lousy relationship with life, with being human, because we have a lousy perspective on life as a human." - Codependence: The Dance of Wounded Souls

Our perspective of love and romance dictates our relationship with love and romance - and that has been the problem, that has been why we have had a lousy relationship with love and romance. We were set up to feel like failures in romantic relationships by the dysfunctional perspectives and expectations of love and romance we learned growing up. There is no happily-ever-after that we can reach when we find our prince or princess. As an adult you obviously know that intellectually - but emotionally you are still looking for it because it is what we were taught as children, it is part of the foundation programming that determines how we relate to life. On some level you are probably judging your self because you haven't reached happily-ever-after.

As I state on my website in the section on Romantic Relationships, "The thing that is so important about the issue of Romantic Relationships is to realize how we were set up to "fail" in romance - to really get it on a gut level, so that we can forgive ourselves." It is very important to start realizing how we were set up, so that we can change our attitudes, definitions, and expectations of romantic relationships into ones that are more functional - into ones that can help us start to learning how to approach love and romance in healthier ways.

Once we start letting go of feeling responsible for something we were powerless over, letting go of the false guilt and toxic shame about our "mistakes" and "failures" in romance - then we can start to learn how to take healthy risks and make better choices. It is better to love and lose then never love - but we need to change what we are expecting from love and romance in order to even have a chance of being able to start learning how to have an interdependent relationship that can work for us.

When I am speaking I sometimes say, "There are things that I have written in ways that I like so much that I quote myself." One of the main sayings of mine that I quote - and have used in my writing and speaking for years - is, "Romantic relationships are the greatest arena for Spiritual and emotional growth available to us." In making that statement I am stating a Truth that it is vital to awaken to if you want to have a chance to have a romantic relationship that works for you and a partner.

So, it was pretty easy when I started putting this book together to pick a title. **Romantic Relationships ~ The Greatest Arena for Spiritual & Emotional Growth** was a natural. The subtitle - *Codependent Dysfunctional Relationship Dynamics & Healthy Relationship Behavior* - speaks to some areas it is important to focus upon. First it is important to realize that our patterns in relationship, especially romantic relationships - although normal in a dysfunctional society - are not normal, natural interaction patterns, they are dsyfunctional inter-reaction patterns caused by codependency, by our childhood emotional wounding and intellectual programming. Secondly it is vital to start learning how to behave in healthy loving ways in relationships so that we can give our self the gift of being available for a romantic relationship that can be a great adventure with someone else who is working on learning how to be healthy in their relationship with self and others.

This book is a primarily a compilation of writings from my website that I have edited, rewritten and expanded upon to fit together in this work. The first half of the book - Part 1 & 2 - are built around a 13 article series that I originally wrote for an internet directory (although many of those article were based upon or grew out of articles and web pages published previously on my website Joy2MeU.com.) That series, entitled Dysfunctional Relationship Dynamics - Healthy Relationship Behavior was published as an e-book by that internet directory some years ago. I have extensively rewritten and expanded the articles that made up that series and added 7 more articles from my website which have also been edited and in some cases expanded - so that the content of these two parts of this book are a much expanded body of work from the earlier one.

Within some of the chapters of this book I quote other articles that are on my website. The title of those articles will be noted - and if you wanted to explore them further you could go to the site index page of my website: http://Joy2MeU.com/Siteindex.htm At the beginning of almost every chapter is a quote from my book *Codependence: The Dance of Wounded Souls* - and all quotes in italic within the content are also from *The Dance* - with the exception of Chapter 39 (something that is explained in that chapter.)

I think that you will find the information that I share in these pages helpful in more clearly understanding why you have had problems in romantic relationships. Hopefully reading this book can help you to forgive your self for something that is not your fault. It is not your fault you have had had your heart broken - that you have had problems in romantic relationships. It is not because there is something wrong with who you are. You were set up to fail in romantic relationships. Your relationship with your self, with your own gender and sexuality, with the concepts of love and romance, got all messed up in your childhood - which is why you have had a lousy relationship with romantic relationship.

You can change that reality. You can learn to be more loving to your self and open to the possibility of having a loving interdependent relationship with another person. Loving is the greatest adventure available to us - give your self a change to experience how wonderful it can be by being willing to do the work to change your programming and heal your emotional wounds. It is very much worth it to learn to love - and reading this book could be a huge step in helping you to become capable of having a healthier romantic relationship.

Part One ~ Codependent Relationship Dynamics

Dysfunctional Beliefs about Romance & Love

Chapter 1 - Dysfunctional Definition of Love
Toxic Love - the dysfunctional, addictive, cultural norm

"As long as we believe that someone else has the power to make us happy then we are setting ourselves up to be victims" - *Codependence: The Dance of Wounded Souls*

One of the biggest problems with relationships in this society is that the context we approach them from is too small. We were taught that getting the relationship is the goal.

It starts in early childhood with Fairy Tales where the Prince and the Princess live happily-ever-after. It continues in movies and books where "boy meets girl" "boy loses girl" "boy gets girl back" - the music swells and the happy couple ride off into the sunset. The songs that say "I can't smile without you" "I can't live without you" "You are my everything" describe the type of love we learned about growing up: toxic love - an addiction with the other person as our drug of choice, as our Higher Power.

Any time we set another human being up to be our Higher Power we are going to experience failure in whatever we are trying to accomplish. We will end up feeling victimized by the other person or by our self - and even when we feel victimized by the other person we blame our self for the choices we made. We are set up to fail to get our needs met in Romantic Relationships because of the belief system we were taught in childhood and the messages we got from our society growing up.

There is no goal to reach that will bring us to happily-ever after. We are not incomplete until we find our soul mate. We are not halves that cannot be whole without a relationship.

True Love is not a painful obsession. It is not taking a hostage or being a hostage. It is not all-consuming, isolating, or constricting. Believing we can't be whole or happy without a relationship is unhealthy and leads us to accept deprivation and abuse, and to engage in manipulation, dishonesty, and power struggles. The type of love we learned about growing up is an addiction, a form of toxic love.

Here is a short list of the characteristics of Love vs. toxic love (compiled with the help of the work of Melody Beattie & Terence Gorski.)

1. **Love** - Development of self first priority.
Toxic love - Obsession with relationship.

2. **Love** - Room to grow, expand; desire for other to grow.
Toxic love - Security, comfort in sameness; intensity of need seen as proof of love (may really be fear, insecurity, loneliness)

3. **Love** - Separate interests; other friends; maintain other meaningful relationships.

Toxic love - Total involvement; limited social life; neglect old friends, interests.

4. **Love** - Encouragement of each other's expanding; secure in own worth.
Toxic love - Preoccupation with other's behavior; fear of other changing.

5. **Love** - Appropriate Trust (i.e. trusting partner to behave according to fundamental nature.)
Toxic love - Jealousy; possessiveness; fear of competition; protects "supply."

6. **Love** - Compromise, negotiation or taking turns at leading. Problem solving together.
Toxic love - Power plays for control; blaming; passive or aggressive manipulation.

7. **Love** - Embracing of each other's individuality.
Toxic love - Trying to change other to own image.

8. **Love** - Relationship deals with all aspects of reality.
Toxic love - Relationship is based on delusion and avoidance of the unpleasant.

9. **Love** - Self-care by both partners; emotional state not dependent on other's mood.
Toxic love - Expectation that one partner will fix and rescue the other.

10. **Love** - Loving detachment (healthy concern about partner, while letting go.)
Toxic love - Fusion (being obsessed with each other's problems and feelings.)

11. **Love** - Sex is free choice growing out of caring & friendship.
Toxic love - Pressure around sex due to insecurity, fear & need for immediate gratification.

12. **Love** - Ability to enjoy being alone.
Toxic love - Unable to endure separation; clinging.

13. **Love** - Cycle of comfort and contentment.
Toxic love - Cycle of pain and despair.

Love is not supposed to be painful. There is pain involved in any relationship but if it is painful most of the time then something is not working.

There is nothing wrong with wanting a relationship - it is natural and healthy. There is nothing wrong with wanting a relationship that will last forever - expecting it to last forever is what is dysfunctional. Expectations set us up to be a victim - and cause us to abandon ourselves in search of our goal.

If we can start seeing relationships not as the goal but as opportunities for growth then we can start having more functional relationships. A relationship that ends is not a failure or a punishment - it is a lesson.

As long as our definition of a successful relationship is one that lasts forever - we are set up to sabotage the relationship or sacrifice our self. As long as we believe that we have to have the other in our life to be happy, we are really just an addict trying to protect our supply - using another person as our drug of choice. That is not True Love - nor is it Loving.

Chapter 2 - Power Struggle
"A relationship is not a game with of winners and losers"

"One of the core characteristics of this disease of Codependence is intellectual polarization - black and white thinking. Rigid extremes - good or bad, right or wrong, love it or leave it, one or ten. Codependence does not allow any gray area - only black and white extremes.

Life is not black and white. Life involves the interplay of black and white. In other words, the gray area is where life takes place. A big part of the healing process is learning the numbers two through nine - recognizing that life is not black and white."

"If we are reacting out of what our emotional truth was when we were five or nine or fourteen, then we are not capable of responding appropriately to what is happening in the moment; we are not being in the now." - Codependence: The Dance of Wounded Souls

I heard someone at a CoDA meeting this week talk about a truly revolutionary concept that their codependence counselor introduced into a session with her and her husband one day. She and her husband were in a hot and heavy argument when the counselor interrupted to ask, "Do you want to be happy or do you want to be right." She said that it was a question that they had to consider for a while because being right was awful important to them both.

It is normal for relationships in this society to deteriorate into power struggles over who is right and who is wrong. That is because we grew up in a dysfunctional society that taught that it was shameful to be wrong. We got the message that our self-worth depends on not making mistakes, on being perfect - that it caused our parents great emotional pain (or they caused us great emotional or physical pain) when we made a mistake, when we were wrong.

Codependence is an emotional defense system that is set up to protect the wounded inner child within us from the shame of being exposed as unlovable and unworthy, as stupid and weak, as a loser and failure, as whatever it was that we got the message was the worst thing to be. We were taught to evaluate whether we had worth in comparison to others. Smarter than, prettier than, faster than, richer than, more successful than, thinner than, stronger than, etc., etc. In a codependent society the only way to feel good about self is to look down on someone else. So we learned to judge (just like our role models did) others in order to feel good about ourselves. Being "right" was one of the most important ways to know that we had worth.

When a codependent feels attacked - which is any time it seems as if someone is judging us - it can be with a look or a tone of voice or just that someone doesn't say something, let alone when someone actually says something to us that could be interpreted as meaning that we weren't doing something right - the choices we are faced with are to blame them or blame ourselves. Either they are right - in which case it proves that we are the stupid loser that the critical parent voice in our head tells us we are - or they are wrong in which case it is time to attack them and prove to them the error of their ways.

In most relationships where the people have been together for a few years they have already established entrenched battle lines around painful emotional scars where they push each others buttons. All one person has to do is use a certain tone of voice or have a certain look on their face and the other person pulls out and loads the big guns. One person is readying their answer in their head to what they "know" the other is going to say before the other even has a chance to say it. The battle begins and neither one of them actually listens to what the other is saying. They start pulling out their lists of past hurts to prove their point of how each other is "doing" horrible things to them. The battle is on to see who is right and who is wrong.

And that is not even the right question.

The type of questions we need to be asking are: "What button just got pushed?" "Why am I reacting so strongly to this?" "How old do I feel right now?" "In what way does what is happening feel like something that happened in my childhood" "How does this remind me of the way my paents acted or treated me?"

We attract into our lives those people who will perfectly push our buttons for us. Who fit our particular issues exactly. When we are looking at life as a growth process then we can learn from these lessons. If both people in a relationship are willing to look at what is underneath the dynamics that are happening - then some magical, wonderful intimacy can result. As long as we are reacting unconsciously to the past, then we will blame and argue about who is right and who is wrong.

A relationship is a partnership, an alliance, not some game with winners and losers. When the interaction in a relationship becomes a power struggle about who is right and who is wrong then there are no winners.

Chapter 3 - Inter-reacting & blaming
The Codependent Dance of Romance

"We have a feeling place (stored emotional energy), and an arrested ego-state within us for an age that relates to each of those developmental stages. Sometimes we react out of our three-year-old, sometimes out of our fifteen-year-old, sometimes out of the seven-year-old that we were.

If you are in a relationship, check it out the next time you have a fight: Maybe you are both coming out of your twelve-year-olds. If you are a parent, maybe the reason you have a problem sometimes is because you are reacting to your six-year-old child out of the six-year-old child within you. If you have a problem with romantic relationships maybe it is because your fifteen-year-old is picking your mates for you." - *Codependence: The Dance of Wounded Souls*

At the CoDA meeting I am the secretary of here locally, one of the people sharing last week made one of those perfect Freudian slips while sharing. She talked about inter-reacting with someone. That is codependency: two people inter-reacting, each reacting out of their emotional wounds and childhood programming.

If we are inter-reacting, we are incapable of being honest in relating to other people. If we are not seeing ourselves with any clarity and emotional honesty, then we cannot see the other person with clarity - let alone the relationship. No true communication can take place between two people who are reacting to the past instead of being present in the moment - inter-reacting. (I like that word. ;-)

And of course, the type of relationship this dynamic impacts the most is romantic. As I say elsewhere in my writing: romantic relationships are the greatest arena for Spiritual and emotional growth available to us - because they are the relationships that mean the most to us, that we have the most at stake emotionally. It is in romantic relationships that our buttons are pushed - that our deepest wounds are triggered. It is in romantic relationships that our core fear of intimacy is activated. And the problem with far too many romantic relationships - which of course, includes marriages - is that they are inter-reactions, not interactions.

When we look to a romantic relationship to make us happy and give us worth, we give another person the power to make us feel good about ourselves, to feel worthy and lovable. The person who we have given that power to, usually becomes the person to blame when we do not feel good.

The prince or princess who was going to rescue us becomes the villain who is abusing / oppressing / smothering / abandoning us. The type of love that we learned growing up in dysfunctional societies is toxic love. That codependent, addictive toxic variety of love involves giving another person power over our self esteem - empowering another wounded human being to be our higher power who determines if we have worth. It is a set up to end up feeling like a victim - with the other person as the villain, or our own perceived shameful defectiveness making us the villain who deserves to be abused.

We are subconsciously programmed and emotionally set up in early childhood (by fairy tales which are later reinforced by books, movies, songs, etc.) to believe that a romantic relationship will lead us to "happily ever after." This makes us feel like failures when it does not happen. Because we feel like failures and are codependent, we go to one of the extremes: we try harder to change or please the other person, to earn their love, to make them available; or we blame. (And trying harder is really about blaming ourselves, thinking that it is our fault, that we are not doing it "right.")

There is no happily ever after in this lifetime, in these bodies - it is a misconception, a misinterpretation of Metaphysical levels of reality. Knowing that consciously, intellectually, does not help us stop feeling like a failure. It is vital to heal our emotional wounds and forgive ourselves for expecting life - and romance - to be something it is not.

We were set up to feel like failures in romantic relationships by dysfunctional societal beliefs. Feeling like a failure is emotional - buying into the belief in failure is mental: two different levels of our being. It is very important in recovery to start being able to practice discernment in relationship to our own inner process. A major component in becoming empowered to take responsibility for being co-creators of our life experience is being able to recognize when our feelings are a direct result of the beliefs we are empowering. Becoming conscious of how our subconscious programming from childhood is still affecting us today is the only way we can change that programming. Consciousness can lead to empowerment when we are willing to focus on the things we do have the power to change - and own our power to make choices instead of being the victim of dysfunctional programming.

The intellectual paradigm we are empowering to define our lives determines our perspective of life and our emotional reactions.

> "One of the biggest problems with relationships in this society is that the context we approach them from is too small. If getting the relationship is the goal, we will end up being the victim. If we can start seeing relationships not as the goal but as opportunities for growth then we can start having more functional relationships. A relationship that ends is not a failure or a punishment - it is a lesson. As long as our definition of a successful relationship is one that lasts forever - we are set up to fail. There is nothing wrong with wanting a relationship that will last forever, expecting it to last forever is what is dysfunctional." - Romantic Relationships and Valentine's Day

When the intellectual paradigm which we are allowing to define our lives - the context in which we are relating to life / love / romance - is based upon the belief that if we do it "right" - or find the "right person" we will reach the destination of "happily ever after," we are set up to feel like failures when we are not magically transformed by a relationship.

When we blame it all on our self we are not seeing things clearly. When we blame it all on the other person we are not seeing things clearly. When we are inter-reacting and blaming, we aren't being fair to our self or the other person.

Chapter 4 - Set up to feel like failures
"Is the way you view love working to make you happy"

"Recovery is not a dance of right and wrong, of black and white - it is a dance of integration and balance. The questions in Recovery are: Is it working for you? Is the way you live your life working to meet your needs? Is the way you are living your life bringing you some happiness?" - Codependence: The Dance of Wounded Souls

Failure and success, winning and losing, right and wrong are part of the polarized belief system - the black and white thinking - that is the foundation, and cause, of codependency. Anyone who is thinking in terms of failure and success according to dysfunctional, delusional definitions is being codependent. They are exhibiting the programming - the brain washing - that results from growing up in a codependent culture.

When we believe in the deepest levels of our being, at the core of our programming, that we have to have a romantic relationship to be whole, to be happy and fulfilled in life, we are making that dream / delusion our higher power which determines if we have worth - which is a set up to feel like a failure. And because failure, being wrong, is considered shameful - a sign of unworthiness, of being defective - we end up putting a great deal of energy into blaming and/or denial. (Blaming is a manifestation of denial - and is only possible because of a polarized belief system.)

When our self esteem is dependent upon reaching "happily ever after," we are set up to give away power over how we feel about our self to a delusion, a fairy tale. We look outside of ourselves and see other codependents - who were taught to keep up appearances and wear masks - who seem to have reached happily ever after.

> "We are trained in childhood to be emotionally and intellectually dishonest. Through both direct messages and watching our role models. We learned that it was very important to keep up appearances - to wear a mask. . . We got told that it was not okay to speak our truth. There was an old song I always thought described how I saw people interacting, that went something to the effect "The games people play now, every night and every day now, never saying what they mean - never meaning what they say."" - The Condition of Codependency

We feel like something is wrong with us because other people seem to be happy and successful and we feel like failures. We judge how **we feel on the inside** against how **they look on the outside**. And when those people that we put up on pedestals as having it made, prove to be human - get arrested, get a divorce, commit suicide, etc. - we are shocked (and usually secretly pleased) but we go right back to judging our self in comparison to someone else whose life **looks** better than ours **feels**.

As magical thinking children we were brainwashed / programmed to believe that love will magically transport us to happily-ever-after. We had that delusion reinforced by songs and books and movies. We are constantly being bombarded with advertising that uses our desire to be loved "happily ever after" to manipulate us into spending money on the magical ingredient that is missing - the right beer / car / clothes / makeup / medication / whatever - that will transform our lives.

It is a false belief, a dysfunctional concept, that sets us up to feel such desperate need for our dream to come true. When our feelings of self worth are dependent upon an illusion, we will put a great deal of energy into convincing our self that the dream has come true. Our investment in the fantasy, the dream, is what can make it so hard to let go of a relationship.

> "It is letting go of the dream, the idea / concept, of the relationship that causes the most grief in every relationship break up that I have ever worked with. We give power and energy to the mental construct of what we want the relationship to be and cannot even begin to see the situation and the other person clearly.
>
> Far too often - because of the concept of toxic / addictive love we are taught in this society - it is the **idea** of the other person that we fall in love with, not the actual person. It is so important to us to cast someone in the role of Prince or Princess that we focus on who we want them to be - not on who they really are. In our relationship with our self, we attach so much importance to getting the relationship that we are dishonest with ourselves - and with the other person - in order to manifest the dream / concept of relationship that will fix us / make our life worthwhile. Then we end up feeling like a victim when the other person does

not turn out to be the person we wanted." - The True Nature of Love - part 4, Energetic Clarity

What makes relationship break ups so difficult in a codependent society is not the pain of the romance ending - although there is certainly a lot of pain and grief about such endings - it is the shame that our disease beats us up with for: being "failures;" or for being unworthy and unlovable; or for being so "stupid" as to make such a "wrong" choice. Very often we hang onto a relationship long after it is empty and dead because we feel that ending it will prove that we were "wrong" - or that something is wrong with us. This is especially true in instances where our family or friends warned us that the person wasn't good for us - then we have a great deal of ego investment in proving them wrong. This kind of attempt to avoid "failure" - to avoid admitting "defeat" - has caused many a person to stay in relationships that were abusive long after they knew it was hopeless.

The subconscious programming is so strong that it overrides common sense, intellectual knowledge, and conscious awareness - and keeps us putting a great deal of energy into rationalizing and denying reality. It is that subconscious programming - which can not be substantially changed without becoming emotionally honest, which includes releasing the repressed grief energy from childhood - that makes us powerless to live life in any way except reacting to the extremes of codependency. It is powerlessness over that programming that has caused us to be our own worst enemies.

"I spent most of my life being the victim of my own thoughts, my own emotions, my own behaviors. I was consistently picking untrustworthy people to trust and unavailable people to love. I could not trust my own emotions because I was incapable of being honest with myself emotionally - which made me incapable of Truly being honest on any level.

I had to become willing and open and honest enough to start becoming conscious of the dysfunctional attitudes, the dysfunctional perspectives."

It is a sad reality that codependents spend their lives living in reaction to their childhood wounding. Whether we are trying to earn our parents love and respect by being what they wanted us to be, or going to the other extreme rebelling against them, we are living in reaction to childhood - we are not living our own lives. Many women, and men, have stayed in marriages - that they knew were a mistake on their wedding day - for 20 or 30 or 40 years because they were trying to prove their parents wrong, or trying to avoid the shame of "failing."

As long as we are reacting to some arbitrary, absolute standard - a marriage that lasts is a success, one that ends is a failure - we are set up to live our lives in reaction. We are set up to feel like a failure, or to blame someone or something for how we live our lives. We are set up to feel like a victim. It is only by seeing our self and reality with more clarity that we can start to own our power to make choices instead of reacting. We become empowered to take responsibility for being a co-creator in our lives by owning our power to make choices.

Until we start becoming conscious of the power of this subconscious intellectual and emotional programming, we are powerless to do anything in our life except react.

We do not have the ability to respond - response ability - if our choices are limited to right and wrong according to some arbitrary, dysfunctional cultural beliefs.

> *"We must start recognizing our powerlessness over this disease of Codependence.*
> *As long as we did not know we had a choice we did not have one.*
> *If we never knew how to say "no," then we never really said "yes."*
> *We were powerless to do anything any different than we did it. We were doing the best we knew how with the tools that we had. None of us had the power to write a different script for our lives."*

Anyone who stays in a marriage because they do not believe they have a choice to leave it, is not making a choice to stay. We can only Truly commit to a course of action by owning that we have a choice in the matter. Staying because we "have to" / it is "wrong" to leave, is not a choice. Staying for the sake of the children - or to spare the children the pain of a divorce - is also dysfunctional and a set up to feel like a victim with no choices.

What makes many divorce experiences feel like "disasters" is not the end of the relationship - it is the blaming that goes on to keep from feeling the shame of being a "failure." It is the battle over who is "right" and who is "wrong" that causes so much emotional trauma. It is trying to identify - and punish - the villain, that makes divorce lawyers rich and emotionally wounds the children who get caught in the middle of this codependent dance of blame and shame, of right and wrong.

On the day I was finishing this piece of writing some years ago, a man I had never met before came to our CoDA meeting. In the course of sharing, he started to talk about his parents. This man was probably around 50, and was going to visit his parents the next day. He started crying - struggling mightily to control his emotions, gulping shallow breaths and holding them as his body quivered. He choked out that he wished his parents hadn't behaved so horribly in his childhood.

He recounted how his mother had said to him recently, "Oh, but our family wasn't dysfunctional. Your father and I stayed together." He cried as he said in a strangled voice, "That was a big part of the problem."

Children are damaged just as much by parents who stay together in a dysfunctional marriage as children whose parents divorce. Sometimes it is even more damaging in the long run because the delusion that the family was successful is so strong that it makes it hard for the adult children to understand why they have lived their lives so dysfunctionally - after all, they came from a happy family. The happy family myth was the higher power the parents sacrificed themselves to maintain. Keeping up appearances to avoid shame, to avoid "failure." Parents who stay together for "the children's sake," or to keep up appearances, are disasters as role models for what a romantic relationship looks like.

> *"What we traditionally have called normal parenting in this society is abusive because it is emotionally dishonest. Children learn who they are as emotional beings from the role modeling of their parents. "Do as I say not as I do," does not work with children. Emotionally dishonest parents cannot be emotionally healthy role models, and cannot provide healthy parenting."*

It is vital to start recognizing how our childhood programming has set us up to live our lives dysfunctionally - and how it has set us up to expect romantic relationships to be something they are not. To paraphrase the quote from my book at the beginning of this chapter: "Is the way you view romance bringing you happiness" "Is the way you view love working to make you happy"

We need to become aware of the dysfunctional programming before we can start to learn how to have more functional relationships - before we can start to learn and practice healthy relationship behavior.

It is not your fault that your heart has been broken in relationships!

It is not your fault that you have lived your life the way you have - that you have approached relationships in a way that doesn't work!

You have not felt like failures in relationship because there is something wrong with who you are!

We were set up by our childhood programming and experiences to have a dysfunctional relationship with the concepts of love and romance. The thing that is so important about the issue of Romantic Relationships is to realize how we were set up to "fail" in romance - to really get it on a gut level - so that we can forgive ourselves. Once we start letting go of feeling responsible for something we were powerless over, letting go of the false guilt and toxic shame about our "mistakes" and "failures" in romance - then we can start to learn how to take healthy risks. Loving and losing **is** much better than never loving at all - once we start seeing romance, love, and relationships in a more realistic way, once we stop expecting them to be something they are not.

Romantic Relationships are the most powerful, meaningful, traumatic, painful, explosive, heart wrenching single topic for most people. Our hearts have been broken because we were taught to do the Dance of Love in a dysfunctional way/to the wrong music. Our hearts have been broken! And then they were broken again.

It is not your fault. It is not your fault! IT IS NOT YOUR FAULT!

It was a set up. You were set up. We were set up.

Chapter 5 - Different Programming for men & women
Set up by dysfunctional beliefs & dishonest role models

"We were taught that life is about destinations, and that when we get to point x - be it marriage or college degree or fame and fortune or whatever - we will live happily ever after.

That is not the way life works. You know that now, and probably threw out that fairy tale ending stuff intellectually a long time ago. But on some emotional level we keep looking for it because that is what the children in us were taught. We keep living life as if it is a dress rehearsal for "when our ship comes in." For when we really start to live. For when we get that relationship, or accomplishment, or money that will make us okay, that will fix us." - Codependence: The Dance of Wounded Souls

The programming from our childhood causes both men and women to be set up to feel like failures if they do not reach a destination where they find "happily ever after." It is women however, who traditionally were brainwashed to believe that their self worth is dependent upon reaching the destination that involves a romantic relationship. Traditionally women in this society were taught to be codependent upon their relationships with men, while men were taught to be codependent - that is, take their self definition and self worth from - what they do. Additionally, men were taught to be shut down to their emotions.

"In this society, in a general sense, the men have been traditionally taught to be primarily aggressive, the "John Wayne" syndrome, while women have been taught to be self-sacrificing and passive. But that is a generalization; it is entirely possible that you came from a home where your mother was John Wayne and your father was the self-sacrificing martyr. . . . . . .

When the role model of what a man is does not allow a man to cry or express fear; when the role model for what a woman is does not allow a woman to be angry or aggressive - that is emotional dishonesty."

Both men and women had their relationships with their own emotions twisted and distorted by the messages and role modeling of a dysfunctional, emotionally dishonest, patriarchal culture.

The traditional societal standards for appropriate female behavior included the belief that it was not appropriate (not "lady like") for a woman to be angry or assertive - which not only makes it virtually impossible to set boundaries but also precludes real emotional intimacy. It is not possible to be emotionally honest and intimate in relationship to anyone with whom it is not okay to be angry. True emotional intimacy requires sharing all of our emotions. Someone who does not have permission to own anger is forced to use other methods to try to get their needs met, learns to manipulate in emotionally dishonest ways - crying when they are angry, or using sex manipulatively to gain power in a relationship, for instance.

And, though the traditional societal standards set men up to be "John Wayne" and women to be self-sacrificing martyrs, this role was in reality reversed in many families due to the reactive extremes of codependency. In other words, some men who hated the abusive behaviors of their father / male role models would react to the other extreme, would suppress their own anger and become more passive and martyr like - and would then usually end up marrying a woman who was like their father. While a woman who could not stand the "doormat" role modeling of her mother, would become the angry abusive one in a relationship with a man who would be the doormat. Twisting things even further, in most cases, though the roles were reversed within the relationship inter-reaction, the couple would then try to look "normal" out in society - in other words, they would attempt to keep up appearances and be seen by others as a "normal" couple. Normal in this dysfunctional society meaning the man was the boss and the woman was his helpmate.

That is the traditional view of a male - female relationship: the male has worth because he does (brings home the bacon), and the woman has worth because she serves the male. The traditional context for family values and marriage in this society is patriarchal supremacy with women and children treated as property.

Men got the message from societal role models that it was not "manly" to be emotionally vulnerable. Someone who cannot be emotionally vulnerable is truly incapable of any level of emotional intimacy.

"An incident happened when I was about 11 that I didn't understand until several years into recovery. At my grandmothers funeral I started crying hysterically and had to be taken out of the funeral home. I wasn't crying because my grandmother had died - I was crying because I had seen my uncle cry. It was the first time in my life I had seen a man cry and it opened the floodgates of all the repressed pain I was carrying. Of course, I went right back to repressing after that because I still hadn't seen my father cry and he was my role model.

The belief that it is unmanly to cry or express fear is part of the prototype for what a man is supposed to be in our society. Most men are programmed to keep their emotions (except for anger) bottled up in a concrete bunker inside of themselves because that is what they learned from society and from their role models." - Wounded Parents - the tragic legacy of dysfunctional families

Both men and women were set up to not know how to be healthy in romantic relationships, but it was women who got the message their worth as a being was tied up in getting to a destination that included a relationship. It is normally women who seek counseling because their self esteem is invested in the relationship. It is not possible to work out problems in a relationship without dealing with emotions - and a man is taught not to deal with emotions. A man focuses on the work that his self worth comes from and ignores problems in the relationship, and/or blames the woman for them. It is a double set up for women in this dysfunctional, emotionally dishonest society.

"It is a double set up for women in this society. First of all the men were taught that it was not okay to be emotional and that what makes them successful as a man is what they produce - and then women were taught that they needed to be successful in romantic relationships with emotionally unavailable men in order to be successful as a woman. What a set up!

It is not women's fault. It is also not men's fault. It is a set up." - The Heart Break of Romantic Relationship - part 2

Men were programmed to be emotional cripples whose only acceptable emotional outlet was anger, and women were brainwashed to feel they had worth only in relationships to men. Truly a set up! Women were brain washed into defining themselves so completely in relationship to men that they give up their name for their husband's name. (Of course, the name they give up was their fathers - a symbolic transfer of ownership.)

Men are defined - and determine their worth - by what they do, their work, fulfilling their role as provider. A man can be a lousy father and husband - can be a really unpleasant and nasty human being - and still be considered successful and worthy of admiration in our dysfunctional society if he makes a lot of money. And if he is successful enough then he can get himself a trophy wife to prove it - leaving the wife that put up with him for years feeling like a failure.

Marriage has not been a full partnership, a Sacred Union, for most women in this society. It has historically been a form of indentured servitude. It is probably an appropriate irony that marriage is referred to as an institution - since in modern day usage that term is most often used to refer to places where people are locked up.

> "Modern civilizations - both Eastern and Western - are no more than a generation or two removed from the belief that children were property. This, of course, goes hand in hand with the belief that women were property." - Inner child healing - Why do it?

The traditional context for family values and marriage in this society is patriarchal supremacy - though changes that started manifesting in the 1960s have altered the traditional programming. There is much good that has come out of those changes but there has also been negative effects.

> "The Women's Movement caused many great and wonderful changes in society that have allowed women to start owning their individual worth and dignity - and has helped women to start seeing themselves as more than just extensions of men. Like any change that takes place however, there were both positive and negative affects. One of the negative affects of the Feminist Movement for many women is that they now feel that they are dependent on both relationship and career for their self worth. Many women feel that unless they are both successful in career, and in a romantic relationship, they are failures - because they are still reacting to the programming to look externally for self worth.
>
> The even more devastating negative affect of the Women's movement in my perspective, is that women who inherently are most heart connected because of their ability to give birth - have been given the right to compete with men who have never been heart connected in an economic system that does not honor the heart. In other words, women have won the dubious right to be more like men - in the emotionally dishonest, human doing prototype of traditional accepted male behavior." - Old tapes / traditional beliefs and gender roles for men and women

We were set up by dysfunctional beliefs and emotionally dishonest role models to have a dysfunctional relationship with romance and love. We were set up to have dysfunctional relationships with our self - with our own emotions, gender, bodies, and sexuality by the emotionally dishonest, shame based cultural beliefs we grew up with - and the wounded role models that were our higher powers in childhood. It is no wonder we have problems with romantic relationships.

> "Men and women are not from different planets. Anyone who is trying to explain male - female relationships without taking into account the impact that culturally programmed emotional dishonesty, generational shame about sexuality, and centuries of patriarchal supremacy have had on how human beings relate to

their own gender and sexuality - let alone to romantic relationships - is focusing on symptoms. It is not possible to bring about fundamental change or true understanding by focusing on symptoms. Just as it is not possible to understand our romantic relationship patterns without starting to see how our childhood wounding and programming was causal in producing those patterns." - Men and Women are from the same planet

What is so important to realize is that it is not our fault - and it is possible to change how we are relating to our self, to love and romance by pursuing our codependency recovery / inner child healing.   There is nothing wrong with who we are - with our True Self - it is our relationship with our self and romantic relationships that got messed up in childhood, and we do have the power to change how we are relating to our self and to romantic relationships. There is a way out - that is the good news.

Chapter 6 - Codependent & Counterdependent Behavior
Dependent vs Fiercely Independent

"I spent most of my life doing the Serenity prayer backwards, that is, trying to change the external things over which I had no control - other people and life events mostly - and taking no responsibility (except shaming and blaming myself) for my own internal process - over which I can have some degree of control. Having some control is not a bad thing; trying to control something or somebody over which I have no control is what is dysfunctional." - Codependence: The Dance of Wounded Souls

Attempts to control are a reaction to fear. It is what we do to try to protect ourselves emotionally. Some of us (classic codependent behavior) tried to control through people pleasing, being a chameleon, wearing a mask, dancing to other people's tunes. Some of us (classic counterdependent behavior) protected ourselves / tried to be in control by pretending that we didn't need other people. Either way we were living life in reaction to our childhood wounds - we were not making clear, conscious choices. (If our choice is to be in an abusive relationship or not to be in a relationship at all, that is not a choice - that is reacting between two extremes that are symptoms of our childhood wounds.)

Both classic codependent and classic counterdependent behaviors are part of the condition / disease of codependency in my definition. They are just two different extremes in the spectrum of behavioral defense systems that the ego adapts in early childhood. The ways in which we got hurt the most in childhood felt to our egos like a threat to survival, and it built up defenses to protect us.

While the classic codependent had their sense of self crushed (it is 'self' destroying to feel that love is conditional on pleasing others, living up to the expectations of others - even if our parents never raised their voices to us) in childhood to the extent that confrontation (owning anger, setting boundaries, taking the chance of hurting someone, etc.) feels life threatening, so the classic counterdependent feels like vulnerability (intimacy, getting close to / being dependent on other people) is life threatening.

Both the classic counterdependent and codependent patterns are reactive codependent traits that are out of balance and dysfunctional. We do need other people - but to allow our self worth to be determined in reaction to other people is giving power away and setting ourselves up to be victims. It is very important to own that we have worth as the unique, special being that each of us is - not dependent on how other people react to us.

This is a very difficult process for those of us who have classic 'codependent' patterns of trying very hard to get other people to like us, of feeling that we are defined by how others think of us and treat us, of being people pleasers and martyrs. Classic codependent behavior involves focusing completely on the other (when a codependent dies someone else's life passes in review.) Having no self except as defined in relationship to the other. This is dishonest and dysfunctional. It sets us up to be victims - and causes one to not only be unable to get one's needs met, but to not even be aware that it is all right to have needs.

A classically codependent person, when asked about themselves, will reply by talking about the other. Obviously, before someone with this type of behavioral defense can experience any self-growth, they have to first start opening up to the idea that they have a self. The process of owning self is frustrating and confusing. The concept of having boundaries is foreign and bewildering. It is an ongoing process that takes years. It unfolds in stages. There is always another level of the onion to peel. So, for someone whose primary pattern is classically codependent, the next level of growth will always involve owning self on some deeper level. A very important part of this process is owning the right to be

Classic counterdependent behavior focuses completely on the self and builds huge walls to keep others out. It is hard for those of us who exhibit classically counterdependent behavior patterns to even consider that we may be codependent. We have lived our lives trying to prove that we don't need others, that we are independent and strong. The counterdependent is the other extreme of the spectrum. If our behavior patterns have been primarily counterdependent it means that we were wounded so badly in childhood that in order to survive we had to convince ourselves that we don't need other people, that it is never safe to get close to other people.

Each of us has our own spectrum of behavioral defenses to protect us from being hurt emotionally. We can be codependent in one relationship and counterdependent in another - or we can swing from co to counter - within the same relationship. Often, someone who is primarily counterdependent will get involved with someone who is even more counterdependent and then will act out the codependent role in that particular relationship - the same can happen with two people with primarily codependent patterns.

Both the classic codependent patterns and the classic counterdependent patterns are behavioral defenses, strategies, design to protect us from being abandoned. One tries to protect against abandonment by avoiding confrontation and pleasing the other - while the second tries to avoid abandonment by pretending we don't need anyone else. Both are dysfunctional and dishonest.

Chapter 7 - Come Here, Go Away
"boring and incredibly painful repeating patterns"

"We are all carrying around repressed pain, terror, shame, and rage energy from our childhoods, whether it was twenty years ago or fifty years ago. We have this grief energy within us even if we came from a relatively healthy family, because this society is emotionally dishonest and dysfunctional.

When someone "pushes your buttons," he/she is activating that stored, pressurized grief energy. She/he is gouging the old wounds, and all of the newer wounds that are piled on top of those original wounds by our repeating behavior patterns." -
Codependence: The Dance of Wounded Souls

As long as we haven't healed our childhood wounds then there are a lot more than two people involved in our relationships. There may only be two people in the room - but the room is also full of the ghosts of all of our past emotional wounds. Until we start clearing our emotional process of the buttons/triggers that throw us into the past, we are not capable of being honest in the now. When we react in the now out of old wounds and old tapes we are being emotionally dishonest with ourselves and our partners.

The way one dynamic in a dysfunctional relationship works is in a "come here" - "go away" cycle. When one person is available the other tends to pull away. If the first person becomes unavailable the other comes back and pleads to be let back in. When the first becomes available again then the other eventually starts pulling away again. It happens because our relationship with self is not healed. As long as I don't love myself then there must be something wrong with someone who loves me - and if someone doesn't love me than I have to prove I am worthy by winning that person back. On some level we are trying to earn the love of our unavailable parent(s) to prove to ourselves that we are worthy and lovable.

What is normal and natural in many romantic relationships in this society is for a person whose primary fear is abandonment to get involved with someone whose primary fear is being smothered / losing self. The person with abandonment fears reacts to shows of independence on the part of the other as if the other were abandoning them. That causes them to become more needy and clinging - which causes the other person to pull away - which causes the first person to cling more - which causes the other to pull away more. Eventually the person with abandonment fears gets angry and disgusted and pulls back into themselves - which to the other makes it safe to come back and plead to be let back in. And after a short honeymoon period the dance can start all over again.

"Wait a minute!" you are probably saying if you read the last chapter (codependent & counterdependent behaviors), "you said at the end of your last article, that both the codependent and counterdependent types of behavior were reactions to fear of abandonment."

That is true. The codependent type of behavior is an attempt to overcome the core belief that we are unworthy and unlovable by working real hard to earn love from another. The more a classic codependent feels they are being abandoned the harder they work. The counterdependent is someone who is so convinced of their core unworthiness that their defense is to not open themselves up enough to admit they need another because they are sure they will be abandoned if anyone else sees who they really are (I used to feel if I ever truly opened up to someone, they would run away screaming in horror at my shameful being.) So, they abandon before they can be abandoned (this includes abandoning themselves by being attracted to people who are unavailable - saves them from taking the risk.)

Both types of behavior are dysfunctional and self defeating. Codependents are drawn to people who will abandon them (this abandonment does not have to be physical - it can be emotional so that the relationship continues but the codependent person has to settle for crumbs instead of truly getting their needs met.) Some counterdependents let down their guard once every 5 years or so and let in someone who will perfectly betray and abandon them in order to prove that they were right in the first place to not open up to people.

It is very boring and incredibly painful to keep repeating dysfunctional relationship patterns. The way to stop repeating those patterns is to start healing the wounds that we suffered in childhood. A big part of this process is awakening to the reality that it is not our fault that our relationships haven't worked out. We were set up to fail to get our needs met in relationships by the unhealthy environments we grew up in, by the dysfunctional and dishonest definitions and role modeling that we experienced. We were powerless to do things any differently than we did them until we started to examine our patterns and discover the ways in which our childhood experiences have been running our lives.

One of the most important steps in learning what Love really is - in starting to Love ourselves in healthy ways - is to start working on forgiving ourselves for being little kids who were wounded by being raised by people who were wounded when they were little kids.

Chapter 8 - Letting Go of Unavailable People
"stop seeing other person as the problem or the solution"

"In our disease defense system we build up huge walls to protect ourselves and then - as soon as we meet someone who will help us to repeat our patterns of abuse, abandonment, betrayal, and/or deprivation - we lower the drawbridge and invite them in. We, in our Codependence, have radar systems which cause us to be attracted to, and attract to us, the people, who for us personally, are exactly the most untrustworthy (or unavailable or smothering or abusive or whatever we need to repeat our patterns) individuals - exactly the ones who will "push our buttons."

This happens because those people feel familiar. Unfortunately in childhood the people whom we trusted the most - were the most familiar - hurt us the most. So the effect is that we keep repeating our patterns and being given the reminder that it is not safe to trust ourselves or other people .

Once we begin healing we can see that the Truth is that it is not safe to trust as long as we are reacting out of the emotional wounds and attitudes of our childhoods. Once we start Recovering, then we can begin to see that on a Spiritual level these repeating behavior patterns are opportunities to heal the childhood wounds." - Codependence: The Dance of Wounded Souls

Codependency is an incredibly insidious, treacherous dis-ease. It is a compulsively reactive condition in which our ego programming from childhood dictates how we live our lives today. As long as we are not in recovery from our codependency, we are powerless to make clear choices in discerning rather someone we are attracted to is a available for a healthy relationship - we are in fact, doomed to keep repeating patterns.

Emotionally we are drawn to people who feel familiar on an energetic level. That is, people who, on an emotional vibrational level, resonate with us as being familiar. It feels to us as if we have a strong connection to those people. In other words, we have an inner radar system that causes us to be attracted to people who resonate vibrationally in a way that is familiar on an emotionally intimate level. We are attracted to people whose inner emotional dynamic is similar to our most powerful and earliest experience of emotional intimacy and love - our parents.

No matter how much we are making an effort on a conscious level to not pick anyone like our parents, energetically we feel a strong attraction to people whose inner emotional dynamic is similar to our first experience of love. It was very important for me to get aware of the reality that if I met someone who felt like my soul mate, I had better watch out. Those are exactly the people who will fit my patterns - recreate my wounding.

It was very important for me to recognize the power of this type of attraction. And also to realize, that on a Spiritual level, these people were teachers who were in my life to help me get in touch with my childhood wounds. It was vital for me to start being aware that if I met someone who felt like my soul mate it did not mean we were going to live happily ever after. What it meant was that I was being given another potentially wonderful, and certainly painful, opportunity for growth.

Becoming conscious of these emotional energetic dynamics was a very important part of owning my power. My power to make choices, to accept consequences, to take responsibility for my choices and consequences - and to not buy into the belief that I was being victimized by the other person, or my own defectiveness.

Recognizing unavailability in the other person does not mean that I have to let go of the relationship - at least not immediately, it could be something I will decide to do eventually.

What is so important, is to **let go of focusing on that person as the cause of, or solution to, my problems**. We are in our codependency as long as we are focusing on the other person and buying into the illusion that if we just: work a little harder; lose some more weight; make some more money; do and/or say the right things; whatever; that person will change and be everything we want them to be.

Codependents focus on others to keep from looking at self. We need to let go of focusing on the other person and start focusing inside to understand what is happening. Our adult patterns, the people we have been in relationship with, are symptoms - effects of our childhood wounding. We cannot solve a problem without looking at the cause. Focusing on symptoms (which our society is famous for: war on drugs; war on poverty: etc.) will not heal the cause.

The reason that we get involved with people who are unavailable, is because we are unavailable. We are attracted to people who feel familiar because on some level we are still trying to prove our worth by earning the Love and respect of our unavailable parents. We think we are going to rescue the other person which will prove our worth - or that we need them to rescue us because of our lack of worth. The princess will kiss me and turn me from a frog into a prince, the prince will rescue me and take me to live in the castle, syndrome.

We need to own our own worth - our own "Prince or Princess" ness - before we can be available for a healthy relationship with some one who has owned their own worth.

It is not possible to love someone enough to get them to stop hating, and being unavailable, to them self. We need to let go of that delusion. We need to focus on healing our self - on understanding and healing the emotional wounds that have driven us to pick people who could not give us what we want emotionally. We need to develop some healthy emotional intimacy with ourselves before we are capable of being available for a healthy relationships with someone who is also available.

Part Two ~ Healthy Relationship Behavior

Partners in the Journey / Allies in Life

Chapter 9 - Interdependent, not codependent
Partners & Allies ~ Healthy Interdependence

"This dance of Codependence is a dance of dysfunctional relationships - of relationships that do not work to meet our needs. That does not mean just romantic relationships, or family relationships, or even human relationships in general.

The fact that dysfunction exists in our romantic, family, and human relationships is a symptom of the dysfunction that exists in our relationship with life - with being human. It is a symptom of the dysfunction which exists in our relationships with ourselves as human beings.

And the dysfunction that exists in our relationship with ourselves is a symptom of Spiritual dis-ease, of not being in balance and harmony with the universe, of feeling disconnected from our Spiritual source.

That is why it is so important to enlarge our perspective. To look beyond the romantic relationship in which we are having problems. To look beyond the dysfunction that exists in our relationships with other people.

The more we enlarge our perspective, the closer we get to the cause instead of just dealing with the symptoms. For example, the more we look at the dysfunction in our relationship with ourselves as human beings the more we can understand the dysfunction in our romantic relationships." - Codependence: The Dance of Wounded Souls

One of the first steps to opening up to the possibility of have a healthy relationship is to start changing the dysfunctional attitudes and beliefs we learned in childhood. Our attitudes, beliefs, and definitions set up our expectations and perspectives which in turn dictate our emotional relationships. In order to change our relationship patterns we need to change the attitudes and beliefs so that we will stop expecting the magic of fairy tales in our romantic relationships.

You are not going to live happily-ever-after once you find your prince or princess. There is no happily-ever-after on this plane of existence. You may find your prince or princess but they will have issues to deal with. Relationships are something that needs to be worked on - not some magic wand that makes everybody happy.

A healthy romantic relationship is based on interdependence. Codependence and interdependence are two very different dynamics.

Codependence is about giving away power over our self-esteem. Taking our self-definition and self-worth from outside or external sources is dysfunctional because it causes us to give power over how we feel about ourselves to people and forces which we cannot control.

If my self-esteem is based on people, places, and things; money, property, and prestige; accomplishments, popularity, relationships; looks, talent, intelligence; then I am set up to be a victim. People will not always do what I want them to; property can be destroyed by an earthquake or flood or fire; money can disappear in a stock market crash or bad investment; looks change as I get older. Everything changes. All outside or external conditions are potentially or ultimately temporary.

We got programmed to look outside to fill a hole within us. We need to start to learn how to be loving to ourselves in order to be able to start being able to be loving in a healthy way in our relationships.

> "In order to start being loving to ourselves we need to change our relationship with our self - and with all the wounded parts of our self. . . .
> . . . . The purpose of the work is to change our ego-programming - to change our relationship with ourselves by changing our emotional/behavioral defense system into something that works to open us up to receive love, instead of sabotaging ourselves because of our deep belief that we don't deserve love.
> (I need to make the point here that Codependence and recovery are both multi-leveled, multi-dimensional phenomena. What we are trying to achieve is integration and balance on different levels. In regard to our relationship with ourselves this involves two major dimensions: the horizontal and the vertical. In this context the horizontal is about being human and relating to other humans and our environment. The vertical is Spiritual, about our relationship to a Higher Power, to the Universal Source. If we cannot conceive of a God/Goddess Force that loves us then it makes it virtually impossible to be loving to ourselves. So a Spiritual Awakening is absolutely vital to the process in my opinion. Changing our relationship with ourselves on the horizontal level is both a necessary element in, and possible because we are working on, integrating Spiritual Truth into our inner process.) - Learning to Love our self - Inner Child Healing / Codependence Recovery

That is why it is so important to get in touch with our Spiritual connection. To start realizing that we have worth because we are children of God. That we are all part of the Eternal ONENESS that is the God Force/Goddess Energy/Great Spirit. We are Spiritual beings having a human experience - our worth as beings is not dependent upon any outer or external condition. We are Unconditionally Loved and we always have been.

The more we can start owning the Truth of who we really are and integrating it into our relationship with ourselves, the more we can enjoy this human experience that we are having. Then we can start learning how to be interdependent - how to give power away in conscious, healthy ways - because our self-worth is no longer dependent on outside sources. When we are not unconsciously using the other person to fill the hole inside and gain feelings of self-worth, then we are capable of being healthier in relationship. When our self-worth is not at risk in the relationship then another person can only add to us, they have no power to diminish us.

Interdependence is about making allies, forming partnerships. It is about forming connections with other beings. Interdependence means that we give someone else some power over our welfare and our feelings.

Anytime we care about somebody or something we give away some power over our feelings. It is impossible to Love without giving away some power. When we choose to Love someone (or thing - a pet, a car, anything) we are giving them the power to make us happy - we cannot do that without also giving them the power to hurt us or cause us to feel angry or scared.

In order to live we need to be interdependent. We cannot participate in life without giving away some power over our feelings and our welfare. I am not talking here just about people. If we put money in a bank we are giving some power over our feelings and welfare to that bank. If we have a car we have a dependence on it and will have feelings if it something happens to it. If we live in society we have to be interdependent to some extent and give some power away. The key is to be conscious in our choices and own responsibility for the consequences.

The way to healthy interdependence is to be able to see things clearly - to see people, situations, life dynamics and most of all ourselves clearly. If we are not working on healing our childhood wounds and changing our childhood programming then we cannot begin to see ourselves clearly let alone anything else in life.

The disease of Codependence causes us to keep repeating patterns that are familiar. So we pick untrustworthy people to trust, undependable people to depend on, unavailable people to love. By healing our emotional wounds and changing our intellectual programming we can start to practice discernment in our choices so that we can change our patterns and learn to trust ourselves.

As we develop healthy self-esteem based on knowing that the Force is with us and Loves us, then we can consciously take the risk of Loving, of being interdependent, without buying into the belief that the behavior of others determines our self-worth. We will have feelings - we will get hurt, we will be scared, we will get angry - because those feelings are an unavoidable part of life. Feelings are a part of the human experience that we came here to learn about - they cannot be avoided. And trying to avoid them only causes us to miss out on the Joy and Love and happiness that can also be a part of the human experience.

By changing our intellectual paradigm - our attitudes, beliefs, and definitions - we can stop expecting life - and romantic love - to be something it is not. We can stop expecting relationships to be magic just because falling in love feels magical. We can start having a realistic view of relationships which will allow us to be responsible enough to do the work it takes to work through issues, to keep communication happening, to form a healthy interdependent partnership with another human being. It is in taking responsibility and working through issues that the True magic of emotional intimacy can flower. The sacred magic that is Love is worth the effort.

Two people consciously working together can be a very beautiful experience.

Chapter 10 - Communication is Key
"What did you just hear me say?"

"If we are reacting out of what our emotional truth was when we were five or nine or fourteen, then we are not capable of responding appropriately to what is happening in the moment; we are not being in the now.

When we are reacting out of old tapes based on attitudes and beliefs that are false or distorted, then our feelings cannot be trusted.

When we are reacting out of our childhood emotional wounds, then what we are feeling may have very little to do with the situation we are in or with the people with whom we are dealing in the moment." - Codependence: The Dance of Wounded Souls

The single most important component in a healthy relationship is the ability to communicate. If two people have the capacity to communicate with each other, then any issue can be worked through to some kind of clarity.

For the purpose of this discussion I am going to divide communication into two levels: surface communication having to do with ideas, facts, details, concepts, etc. - and emotional communication. In reality, of course, all communication contains aspects of both levels - and in relationship, the emotional level is by far the most important and most difficult.

In terms of surface communication, it is very important to establish a common language. And I am not talking here about one person speaking English and one speaking French. I am talking about two people who speak the same language linguistically but have different interpretations of various words due to a variety of factors - i.e. raised in different geographic, religious, or cultural environments, different educational or economic levels, different life experiences, etc. Two people who are on Spiritual paths might speak a different language because one has been involved in Twelve Step Recovery while another has been pursuing a Shamanistic path or Buddhist or whatever.

It is very important, right from the beginning of the relationship to strive for clarity in communication. The single most useful tool is simply **to ask**. "How do you define that word?" or "What did you just hear me say?" Very often, you will find that what the other person heard was not what you were attempting to convey. Attempting to clarify and develop a common language lays a good foundation for further communication.

It is also vital to recognize that certain words are emotional trigger words.

"One of the greatest blocks to communication is that some words are emotionally charged. They are words that trigger an automatic emotional reaction within us. To use a trigger word in an argument - a word such as "controlling" or "manipulative" - can turn a discussion into a battle instantly. When someone flings a trigger word at us, or we at them, it is like we have just shot an arrow into them. It usually causes them to go on the defensive and start flinging some arrows back at us - or perhaps go into some other defensive mode, such as crying or walking out.

Using trigger words blocks communication. And we usually use them consciously (although we certainly may not be honest enough to admit it at the time - or even later, depending on the level of our recovery.) We use them in reaction - because we have been hurt or are scared, because we are trying manipulate and control the other person. (Using a word like "manipulate" or "control" to describe someone else's behavior to them, is almost always an attempt to control and manipulate the person we are accusing of that behavior.)

For the purposes of this discussion, what is important is to realize that trigger words fall into realm of cause and effect. We are born with a certain personality - we are not born with certain words programmed as emotional triggers. Emotional triggers fall entirely in the province of experience. We have an emotional charge attached to certain words because of our life experience. In other words, we have a relationship to that word that is a result of emotional experiences in our life." - Spirituality for Agnostics and Atheists

It is really important to identify what each person's emotional trigger words are in order to be able to communicate - in order to avoid automatic reactions based upon the past. Old wounds and old tapes cause us to have emotional trigger words and it is vitally important to get conscious of what our own personal ones are so that we can learn to be less reactive - and to get in touch with what our partner's trigger words are so that we can avoid them when possible. (i.e. In my early recovery I worked to stop calling myself "stupid" so much and changed it to "silly" because that felt gentler to me. For my wife however "silly" is a trigger word that feels worse to her than being called stupid.)

In terms of the emotional level of communication, there are many aspects to consider. I will touch on a symptomatic one here in this article and then expand on the challenges of emotional intimacy in the next article in this series.

The symptomatic one is something that may seem simple but is actually one that relatively few people in our dysfunctional culture have mastered - the ability to listen. In order to Truly listen it is necessary **to be present** - and the difficulty with being present is caused by unhealed emotional wounds. If we are not able to be emotionally honest with ourselves then it is impossible to be present and comfortable in our own skins in the moment. Obviously then, we are also incapable of being present with, and emotionally honest with, others.

Listening is far more than just the absence of talking or the appearance of paying attention. Listening involves more than just hearing the words that another person is saying. In order to Truly hear what another person is attempting to communicate, it is necessary to be tuned in to what is going on underneath the words. Communication is only partly about content - just as important in communication are things like body language, eye contact, underlying emotional currents.

When we are present in our bodies in the moment and paying attention it is easy to discern if the other person is really talking **to us** - as opposed to talking **at us**, or telling a story. In the beginning of any relationship, people tell each other stories about their past - it is part of getting to know each other. What is important is to be able to be present while telling the story. That involves not just listening to the other person but also listening to ourselves.

Being present starts with being conscious of ourselves - it involves listening and paying attention to ourselves and our end of the communication. If I am listening to myself while telling someone a story about my past, I can catch myself when I get to a part of the story that I have creatively embellished over the years. As we learn and grow, our perspective of our past changes and it is very important to be able to listen to ourselves so that we can catch ourselves in places where we have exaggerated or rationalized something from our past. One of the important parts of the healing process is telling our story - and if we just regurgitate an old tape by rote we are not being present and paying attention.

If we have the capacity to be present with ourselves while telling our story, that means we also have the capacity to be present with the other person. I can be in the middle of telling a story and see in the other person's eyes that they aren't listening - which gives me the space to stop and ask what is going on. If I am not present enough to see the other person isn't listening then I am just talking **at** that person. And conversely, if I am conscious I will be able to recognize when that person is talking **at** me.

Communication involves being able to talk to and listen to - the ability to be present in our bodies in the moment.

Chapter 11 - Emotional Honesty Necessary
"How old are you feeling?"

"If you are in a relationship, check it out the next time you have a fight: Maybe you are both coming out of your twelve-year-olds. If you are a parent, maybe the reason you have a problem sometimes is because you are reacting to your six-year-old child out of the six-year-old child within you. If you have a problem with romantic relationships maybe it is because your fifteen-year-old is picking your mates for you." - Codependence: The Dance of Wounded Souls

The single biggest problem with most relationships is that there are too many people involved. A romantic relationship is supposed to be two people in partnership sharing of who they are, sharing their hearts, minds, bodies, and souls with each other.

Anyone who has not done their emotional healing is bringing a plethora of people into any relationship they get involved in. Some of these people include: parents, siblings, relatives; ministers, teachers, the junior high school bully; everyone that they have ever had a romantic relationship with; the Prince and Princess of fairy tales, the lyrics of songs, and the characters from books and movies. Just to think of how many ghosts are in the room, when two unconscious people are interacting (inter-reacting), is mind boggling. Think back on how unconscious you were in past relationships - and how your past kept you from being present and seeing the other person with any clarity.

Anyone who is unconscious to how the people and events of their past have shaped who they are today, is incapable of being present in the now and having a healthy relationship. When we are reacting unconsciously to the emotional wounds and old tapes from our childhoods, we are being emotionally dishonest in the moment - we are mostly reacting to how we felt in a similar dynamic in the past, not clearly responding to what is happening in the present.

As I said in the last article in this series, the single most important component in a healthy relationship is the ability to communicate. We cannot communicate clearly when we are in reaction because we are not being emotionally honest with ourselves.

"When we have a strong reaction to outer stimuli - other people or life events - it is important to learn to separate the inner child's reaction from our adult reaction. I usually figure that about 80% of a strong reaction is about old unresolved issues and only 20 % about what is actually happening now. Until we start separating now from the past, we are incapable of responding to what is happening now in an age appropriate manner. It is impossible to be present in the now and respond honestly to what is happening if we are not conscious of how much inner child reaction is involved." - Inner Awareness - Internal Census

We all learned to see life and self from a dysfunctional perspective - from a perspective that taught us it was shameful to be bad or wrong. We learned to blame. Since the perspective of life which civilization is founded upon is black and white, right and wrong - we got the message that if we could not figure out how to blame someone else, then it must be our fault. Toxic shame is the feeling that I am somehow defective, that there is something wrong with who I am as a being. That feeling of being defective is so painful that we are willing to do almost anything to avoid sinking into the bottomless pit - which I call the abyss - of pain and shame within.

"Out of our codependent relationship with life, there are only two extremes: blame them, or blame me. Buy into the belief that they are to blame for what I am feeling - or I am to blame because I am a shameful unworthy being. The emotional pain of feeling unlovable to our parents - which is a reflection of unbearable anguish of feeling separated from The Source - can feel like a bottomless pit of agonizing suffering. At the core of our wounding is the unbearable emotional pain resulting from having internalized the message that God - our Source - does not Love us because we are personally defective and shameful.

Our addictions, compulsions, and obsessions; our continuing quest to reach the destination, to find the fix; our inability to be present in the now through worrying about the future or ruminating about the past; are all tools that we used to avoid the emotional pain. Our behavior patterns and dysfunctional relationships (of all kinds, with other people, with money, with our gender and sexuality) are symptoms. Codependence is a defense system that was adapted by our damaged egos to try to avoid falling into the abyss of shame and pain within.

We formed our core relationship with self, other people, and life based upon this feeling of toxic shame." - Chapter 2 of Attack on America - A Spiritual Healing Perspective

So we blame someone or something outside of ourselves to protect our self. A dysfunctional civilization which teaches us to look outside for our self worth, also teaches us to look outside for a villain. Codependence is an emotional defense system which tries to take ego credit for things that go the way we want them to, and blames someone else when they do not.

If a person has not been working on healing these emotional wounds, then any feedback will be felt as criticism - as being wrong or bad - and the persons defense system reacts by becoming defensive. The best defense is a good offense, as they say, so many times we go on the offensive pointing out where the other person is wrong or bad. When confronted we blame. We either blame the other or we blame ourselves - in which case we sink into depression and despair, into alcohol, drugs, and food, etc.

This is the reason that most relationships turn into power struggles about who is right and who is wrong. Who has more right to feel victimized by the other. We come up with whatever justification and rationalization we can to deflect the blame from ourselves - as a way of self preservation.

These behaviors are not bad or shameful. They are the inevitable dynamic set up when two people, who have not healed their emotional wounds and changed their dysfunctional programming, interact. We are powerless over the dynamic until we start becoming co-creators of our life by healing the past so that it is not dictating our life today.

It is impossible to Truly hear what another person is saying when we are busy loading up the big guns for our counter attack. We cannot be present in the moment if our emotional defenses are triggered by what is happening now. And these triggers can be a tone of voice, a gesture (pointing a finger), a word or phrase, almost anything. When old wounds are gouged we are pulled out of the now into our feelings from the past.

Once we start learning how to recognize when we are reacting and being defensive, then we can start getting more emotionally honest - with our self and with others. When we learn how to intervene in our own process so that we are not living life in reaction to old wounds then we start being capable of having healthy emotional intimacy. When two people are both working on their healing there is a possibility of communication and emotional honesty.

The more we heal the past, the fewer people are intruding on our relationship in the moment. Those people - our parents or past romantic partners - will still be in our psyche but we will be conscious enough to recognize them when they start invading the now. Then we can communicate what we are learning about our self from our reactions to our partner and share our pain and fear and anger and sadness with her/him - that is True emotional intimacy.

Chapter 12 - Partners in the Journey
"My issues are my responsibility"

"It is through healing our inner child, our inner children, by grieving the wounds that we suffered, that we can change our behavior pattern

That does not mean that the wounds will ever be completely healed. There will always be a tender spot, a painful place within us due to the experiences that we have had. What it does mean is that we can take the power away from those wounds. By bringing them out of the darkness into the Light, by releasing the energy, we can heal them enough so that they do not have the power to dictate how we live our lives today. We can heal them enough to change the quality of our lives dramatically. We can heal

them enough to Truly be happy, Joyous and free in the moment most of the time." -
Codependence: The Dance of Wounded Souls

A healthy romantic relationship is about two whole, independent people choosing to become partners in the life journey for as long as that works for both of them. This is, of course, a theoretical concept. Because of the cultural dysfunction and emotional trauma all of us have experienced due to the human condition, we are never, in this lifetime, going to be a completely healthy person with no emotional wounds - and we are never going to meet someone else that has no emotional wounds.

The goal is to be in the process of healing and to choose a partner who is also in the process of healing. Then we have the opportunity to achieve some True emotional intimacy and to have some companionship on our journey. The person who can support us in our journey is also going to be the teacher we need to push our buttons so that we can bring to Light the emotional wounds that need to be healed and the subconscious programming that needs to be changed.

If we expect a romantic relationship to "fix" us so that we can live happily-ever-after then we are setting ourselves up to be victims. If we define a successful relationship as one that lasts forever and meets all of our needs then we will end up blaming ourselves or the other person when that insane expectation is not met. (That a relationship could last for the rest of our lives is not an insane expectation - that someone else can meet all of our needs, all of the time, is - but if we believe that longevity is the only way a relationship can be successful we are setting ourselves up to sabotage the relationship and not appreciate the gifts we are receiving in the now.)

It is vitally important to make healing and Spiritual growth our number one priority so that we can look to the other person for help and support - not expect them to rescue us and give us self worth. Healing is an inside job. My issues are my responsibility to work through, it is not the other persons job to compromise her self to accommodate my fears and insecurities. If I am choosing wisely when I enter into a relationship then I will choose someone who will be compassionate, patient, and supportive of me while I work through my issues.

And no matter how wisely I choose, or how much healing and recovery the other person has had, she will still be a human being with her own issues to work through so she will not always be able to be compassionate, patient, and supportive. For one person to expect another to always be there for them, to always have the space and time to be available to us, is an insane expectation.

We do want to choose someone who is willing to work through issues. When another person is willing to do the work with us, a relationship can be an incredibly nurturing, magical space to explore what True Love means - some of the time. It can not be that all of the time. There might be periods of time - days, weeks, even months - where things are going beautifully and it feels like we may have reached happily-ever-after. But then things will change and get different. That is how the life process works - it will not be someone's fault. It will be a new opportunity for growth for both people.

Two people who are working through their issues and are willing to do the grief work, can turn an argument about some stupid, mundane life event into some mutual deep grieving. That is True emotional intimacy.

When we are willing to own our power to be the neutral observer who can see our responsibility in whatever is happening without shame and judgment, and can also have the courage and willingness to hold the other person responsible for their behavior without shame and judgment - then the magic can really happen.

Two people who have negotiated some guidelines to help them in times when they are vulnerable and reactive - can transform an argument about some symptom into an opportunity to heal some core wounding.

The way that can look is: an argument/disagreement starts about some behavior that is upsetting (someone is late, or forgets something that is important to the other, or says something in an insensitive way, etc.); at some point one of the individuals says "Time out. I think I might be reacting to some old stuff."; The other person backs off the argument enough to say "How old are you feeling?"; etc. Two people who have created the space to do this can then get down to the cause underneath the reaction, which might be something like: one person is reacting out of the child inside who never felt important, respected, or heard - while the other person is reacting out of the inner child who was always being criticized and given the message that there was something wrong with them. At that point, they are dealing with the core cause of the reaction not the symptomatic behavior. They can achieve a place of True emotional honesty and intimacy where they can get in touch with their individual wounds and grieve together. That is the kind of emotional intimacy which can form a very deep bond and be Joyously healing for both people.

To be willing to be conscious and emotionally honest with ourselves is a courageous act of faith that will allow us to progressively increase the number of moments in each day that we have the ability and freedom to be happy and Joyous in the now. To find another being who is willing to join us in this adventure, and to explore True emotional intimacy with us, is a priceless gift to be cherished and treasured.

Chapter 13 - Healthy Joyous Sexuality
"You are not the source of each other's Love."

"The gift of touch is an incredibly wonderful gift. One of the reasons we are here is to touch each other physically as well as Spiritually, emotionally, and mentally. Touch is not bad or shameful. Our creator did not give us sensual and sexual sensations that feel so wonderful just to set us up to fail some perverted, sadistic life test. Any concept of god that includes the belief that the flesh and the Spirit cannot be integrated, that we will be punished for honoring our powerful human desires and needs, is - in my belief - a sadly twisted, distorted, and false concept that is reversed to the Truth of a Loving God-Force.

We need to strive for balance and integration in our relationships. We need to touch in healthy, appropriate, emotionally honest ways - so that we can honor our human bodies and the gift that is physical touch.

Making Love is a celebration and a way of honoring the Masculine and Feminine Energy of the Universe (and the masculine and feminine energy within no matter what genders are involved), a way of honoring its perfect interaction and harmony. It is a blessed way of honoring the Creative Source." - Codependence: The Dance of Wounded Souls

Often in my writing I state that romantic relationships are the greatest arena for Spiritual and emotional growth available to us. I believe that this is the Truth because it is the area that is most important to us. Recently I saw a communication from the Dalai Lama in which he stated a very simple Truth: we all want to the same thing, to be happy and feel Loved. I would simplify that even further to say: feeling Loved makes us happy - so ultimately we all want the same thing, to feel Loved.

Romantic relationships are not the only type of relationships that we can feel Loved in, of course, but they are the only relationships in which we can completely connect with another being with all the levels of our being: physical, emotional, mental, and Spiritual.

There is absolutely nothing wrong with wanting to connect with another being on a physical level. A Loving God/Goddess/Great Spirit would not give us sensual and sexual sensations that feel so wonderful unless we were meant to enJoy them. Making Love - becoming one with another being in the moment - is so powerful because it is symbolic of the Highest Truth, that we are all ONE.

Being sexual with another being without connection on the other levels however, is ultimately pretty empty and shallow - but a shadow of how glorious the uniting can be when there is True Spiritual union, mental connection, and emotional intimacy.

Of these levels of connection, the one that is hardest to achieve because of the dysfunction we were raised in, is the level of emotional intimacy.

When both people in a romantic relationship are in recovery from their emotional wounds and dysfunctional intellectual programming there is the potential for a partnership that touches the Divine - that has moments when the connection is nothing short of Sacred. The greatest gift of romantic relationships is that they can help us to remember how much we Truly are Loved - that who we are on the Highest level is LOVE. Here is a quote from A Wedding Prayer/Meditation on Romantic Commitment that I wrote for two friends at the beginning of 1999 (and that I will be including as the last chapter in this Part 2.)

> "You are together because you resonate on the same wave lengths, you fit together vibrationally, in such a way that together you form a powerful energy field that helps both of you access the Higher Vibrational Energy of Love, Joy, Light, and Truth - in a way that would be very difficult for either one of you to do by yourself. You are coming together to touch the face of God. You are uniting your energies to help you access the Love of the Holy Mother Source Energy.
>
> You are not the source of each other's Love. You are helping each other to access the LOVE that is the Source." Chapter 20 Meditation on Romantic Commitment

The purpose of romantic relationships is Spiritual - and the more that we remember that who we Truly are is Spiritual Beings having a human experience, the more we can enjoy the human part of the interaction including the sexual coming together.

That does not mean that it is bad or wrong if you are presently in a relationship that does not include connection on all levels. One of the tricky things about romantic relationships is that the only way to really learn to do a romantic relationship in a healthy way is to be in one. We all need time alone between relationships to process our feelings, do our grieving, and heal our relationship with self - but ultimately, it is only in a relationship that the buttons to our deepest wounds and greatest fears are pushed. That is why romantic relationships are such a great arena for Spiritual growth - because they are so personal that they bring us face to face with our deepest wounds.

As I say repeatedly in my book and on my web site, we need to take the shame and judgment out of our internal process and realize that we are in boarding school being guided from lesson to lesson on our journey home to Love - to the Divine Source of which we are all perfect parts. Do not judge yourself for the relationship you are in - or for not being in a relationship. Maybe the Divine Plan is for you to be in five more relationships before you get into one that will last. Maybe being alone in this lifetime is healing the Karma we need to heal to be with our Twin Soul in the next lifetime. We do not, and cannot, know what the Divine Plan is - what we can do is align ourselves with Truth so that we can own the power to Love ourselves more, which gives us the capacity to open up to receiving more Love from others.

The more that we awaken to the Truth that the whole purpose of life is Spiritual - that everything and everyone in our life is a perfect part of our Spiritual growth process - the easier it becomes to allow ourselves to overcome our fears and take the risk (rather that means getting involved in a relationship or leaving one that is not working) that Truly there is a God-Force that has a Loving plan for us that is unfolding perfectly, with no accidents, coincidences, or mistakes.

The more that we have faith in the power of LOVE, the more we are able to take the risk of opening ourselves to Love, the more opportunities we will have to Truly start integrating Spiritual Truth into our human experience. Then we can have the opportunity to enJoy more fully all of the gifts of this beautiful playground that is the illusion of human life on Earth - including the incredible gift of being able to Touch with Love.

Chapter 14 - Romantic Love as a Concept
"expecting love to be something which it is not"

"We learned about life as children and it is necessary to change the way we intellectually view life in order to stop being the victim of the old tapes. By looking at, becoming conscious of, our attitudes, definitions, and perspectives, we can start discerning what works for us and what does not work. We can then start making choices about whether our intellectual view of life is serving us - or if it is setting us up to be victims because we are expecting life to be something which it is not." - Codependence: The Dance of Wounded Souls

Consciousness raising is a process of enlarging the intellectual paradigm which we base our relationship with life upon. As I have stated previously in this series, our beliefs, attitudes, and definitions determine our expectations and perspectives - which in turn dictate our emotional relationships to everything and everyone in our environment.

And when I say everything, I am not just talking about objects. Everything includes ideas, concepts, opinions, etc.

In order to have healthier romantic relationships it is very important to examine our concept of romantic love. If we do not have a healthy concept - realistic definitions and beliefs about - romantic love, then we do not have much chance of having a healthy relationship. If our concept of romance is based on the fairy tales and books, songs and movies, from our childhoods, then we are set up to be disappointed in our romantic relationships.

Read the quotation above and substitute 'love' everywhere it says 'life' and you might better understand why you have felt like a victim in romantic relationships. We were set up to be victims in romance because we were taught that it is a magical paradise where we will have all of our needs met - and live Happily-ever-after. We were taught that getting the romance was the goal and that after that everything was smooth sailing.

Obviously that is not how it works in reality.

It is part of the dysfunctional nature of society that we are set up to believe that love, and life, are something other than what we are led to expect them to be. It is also part of the dysfunctional nature of society - and of civilization as we have inherited it - that we react to not having our expectations met by blaming. We blame the other person, or we blame ourselves. And even underneath the blame we are pointing toward the other person, is the feeling deep inside of us that it is all our fault. That there is something unworthy and unlovable, something defective about who we are at our core. Usually, the louder and more emphatically we blame the other is a measure of how much shame we feel about ourselves deep within.

As long as we are blaming we are buying into the belief that we are victims - either of them, or of our self. It is very important to move out of the victim place into a place of empowerment.

Love as we have been programmed to understand the concept, is one of the great victimizers in our culture - and one of the biggest excuses for unhealthy behavior.

Whenever someone I have been working with answers the question "Why do you stay?" - in a relationship that is abusive or with someone who is unavailable - with the line "because I love him/her" my response is "No, what is the real reason." Because the "love" is never the bottom line. The bottom line is always fear. Fear of being alone, of not being able to support self, of never having another relationship, of getting in a worse relationship, etc.

If we are living life in reaction to fear, we are being victims - and there is no chance of us being healthy in a relationship if we are making our choices in reaction to fear.

That is why it is so important to have a Spiritual Awakening - to raise our consciousness. By being in recovery, on a healing path, we are realigning our intellectual paradigm away from one that is driven by fear to one that is based on Love. In awakening to the possibility that perhaps there is a Higher Power that Loves us, we can start seeing life as a growth process rather than a test we can fail. Then the events and people in our life become opportunities for growth rather than instruments of punishment.

Life then becomes an adventure. One that can be painful and scary, can feel like a stupid game sometimes, but one that can also be Joyous and wondrous and full of miracles at times. By changing our concept of romantic love, we can also make romance a great adventure to be explored rather than some test we can fail.

As long as we are here in this big amusement park that is life in human body, it is better not to allow fear and shame to keep us from experiencing the most exciting rides.

"This is a playground, this is a wonderful summer camp. It is full of beautiful colors and wondrous sights, animals and birds and plants, mountains and oceans and meadows, whales and butterflies. It is full of tastes and smells and sounds and sensations."

Romantic relationships are the greatest arena for Spiritual and emotional growth available to us. They are the most exciting ride. It is well worth the risk to take a chance on love if we are viewing it as a learning experience that is a perfect part of our life adventure rather than the goal in, and of, itself. Romance is part of the journey, part of the experience - not the destination.

There is nothing wrong with wanting the prince or princess to come into our lives. What is important is to know that they will have issues to work through - and they will push the buttons of our issues so that we are forced to face them. Romantic relationships are hard work because of the dysfunctional programming and emotional wounding we experienced in childhood. It is necessary to keep working on them to give them a chance to be healthy.

Being in love is a wonderful, magical feeling. It fills us with energy and lightens our spirit so that we feel we are soaring on the wings of Love. It is wonderful to feel that energy. What is dysfunctional is expecting it to last forever. It is important to know that the feeling of being in love is not going to last forever, or be there all of the time. Two people who are working on emotional intimacy - who are communicating and working through issues - can recapture that feeling again and again for years and years, but it is not going to always be the reality of your relationship.

The more we heal our childhood emotional wounds and change the dysfunctional intellectual programming the clearer we can see reality. The more we learn to have boundaries, to ask for what we need, to be direct and honest in our communication, the healthier we become in our relationships. Healthy enough to get out of them quickly if we see too many warning signs.

Romantic relationships can be a great adventure if our perspective and expectations of them are realistic and healthy.

Chapter 15 - Falling in love as a choice
taking responsibility for our feelings

"Learning discernment is vital - not just in terms of the choices we make about who to trust, but also in terms of our perspective, our attitudes. We learned about life as children and it is necessary to change the way we intellectually view life in order to stop being the victim of the old tapes."

"I spent most of my life being the victim of my own thoughts, my own emotions, my own behaviors. I was consistently picking untrustworthy people to trust and unavailable people to love." - Codependence: The Dance of Wounded Souls

One of the biggest areas in this culture that we are trained to relate to from a victim perspective is in relationship to romance. As I stated in the last chapter, paraphrase the quote from my book above, "it is necessary to change the way we intellectually view romance in order to stop being the victim of the old tapes."

Another way it is important to change our perspective of love is to own that falling in love is a choice. We learned that romance was magical - that finding our prince or princess was a destination to reach where we would live happily ever after. We learn about "falling in love" as if it were a camouflaged hole in the sidewalk that we just happened to fall into. This is something that I mentioned in the last chapter.

> "Love as we have been programmed to understand the concept, is one of the great victimizers in our culture - and one of the biggest excuses for unhealthy behavior." - Chapter 14 Romantic Love as a Concept

As I talked about in that article, it is vital for us to change our perspective of romantic love into one that is realistic. The attitudes, definitions, and beliefs that we hold on a subconscious and conscious level are what determine our perspectives and expectations - which in turn dictate our emotional reactions and our relationships.

It was vital for me in my codependency recovery to start learning how to take responsibility for my own emotions - and to realize that I had some power over them because I had the power to change the beliefs that were setting me up to have the unrealistic expectations that were causing me to see myself as a victim.

> "I expected life to be different than it is. I thought if I was good and did it "right" then I would reach 'happily ever after.' I believed that if I was nice to people they would be nice to me. Because I grew up in a society where people were taught that other people could control their feelings, and vise versa, I had spent most of my life trying to control the feelings of others and blaming them for my feelings.
>
> By having expectations I was giving power away. In order to become empowered I had to own that I had choices about how I viewed life, about my expectations. I realized that no one can make me feel hurt or angry - that it is my expectations that cause me to generate feelings of hurt or anger. In other words, the reason I feel hurt or anger is because other people, life, or God are not doing what I want them, expect them, to do.
>
> I had to learn to be honest with myself about my expectations - so I could let go of the ones that were insane (like, everyone is going to drive the way I want them to), and own my choices - so I could take responsibility for how I was setting myself up to be a victim in order to change my patterns. Accept the things I cannot change - change the things I can." - Serenity and Expectations - intimately interrelated

In order to start taking responsibility for my own emotions, it was necessary for me to start learning to have internal discernment so I could set an inner boundary between the emotional and mental components of my being. I needed to start recognizing that though I will sometimes feel like a victim in life, in romantic relationships, that did not mean I had to buy into the belief that I was a victim.

It is so empowering for us to start having a boundary between emotional and mental because of the way the internal dynamic of codependency works. The critical parent voice in our head beats up on us for our emotional wounds - for being defective and imperfect. The part of the dynamic that is so devastating to us is when we are feeling like a victim and our own mind is telling us it is all our fault. It comes in like a prosecuting attorney with tons of evidence to prove that it is our fault and tells us what losers and failures we are and how we screwed everything up. That is when we crash and burn and go into the abyss - go into despair and depression and just want to die. Or when we turn all of our energy into obsessively trying to blame the other person - maybe even stalking them literally or in cyber space - and rationalizing our behavior.

In recovery I learned how to be able to own, and have compassion for, my own emotional wounds - the times I felt like a victim - at the same time I was shutting up the critical parent's shame and judgment in my mind and choosing to look for the silver lining. I would tell myself that this was an opportunity for growth - a wake up call - and that the other person was a teacher who had come into my life to help me get in touch with wounds I needed to heal. I would ask myself how old I was feeling and recognize that the great majority of my emotional reaction was coming from old wounds that had been triggered.

As I mentioned in the first chapter of Part 2 it is vital to take our self worth out of the equation in romantic relationships (in all our relationship to the external for that matter.) As we learn to take our self worth out of the romantic interaction dynamic, then we can also start taking responsibility for the feelings we are having. Another person does not have power over our feelings unless we give them that power. It is vital to become conscious enough to start recognizing how we are giving away power over our feelings by having unrealistic expectations and perspectives.

As children we were taught a toxic perspective of love and romance that caused us to see the other person as the savior who would fill the hole we feel inside of our self. I grew up feeling unlovable and believing that if I found my princess, she could help me feel like a prince instead of like an unlovable frog.

When I "fell in love" with a woman, it was not a conscious adult choice - it was an unconscious reaction to the wounding and dysfunctional programming of my childhood. It is dysfunctional to allow the wounded parts of us to choose our mates.

"If you have a problem with romantic relationships maybe it is because your fifteen-year-old is picking your mates for you."

As the quote above from my book references, my fifteen year old was not capable of making discerning choices when it came to romance. Reacting unconsciously to old wounds, caused me to feel like a victim - either of my own unworthiness, or of the woman's inability to make me feel like a prince permanently. Falling in love feels magical, so it was possible for a woman to make me feel like a prince temporarily - but eventually she proves herself to be human and not a magical princess, and then I would feel like a victim because of my unconscious expectations.

It was vital for me to start owning that falling in love was a choice I was making - not some lightening strike that I was powerless over. As long as I was reacting unconsciously - not owning that I had some power over the beliefs I was empowering and therefore the feelings I was set up to experience because of the perspectives and expectations those beliefs created - then I was in my codependency and powerless to make choices. I was then doomed to end up blaming her for not being a magical princess and/or blaming myself for being such an ugly frog.

Here is story from my recovery about an opportunity to become clear about taking responsibility for my feelings when it comes to "falling in love."

"In the Premier edition of my Joy2MeU Journal, I shared in the Newsletter about an experience I had on April 1st 1990. I refer to it as my **April Fools Day Lesson about falling in love**. . . . I think that April Fools Day story is amusing and instructive so I include it here.

"Now about April 1st. April fools day here in the states - I am not sure if that is just an American thing or if it is more Universal. I also don't have any idea where it came from - just that it is a day when people play practical jokes and say "April Fools" - kind of stupid really.

On April 1st 1990 I met a woman that felt like my soul mate. And I knew that the fact that it was April Fools Day was no accident. It was my Higher Power saying - now pay attention.

This was shortly after I had moved to Cambria California - which is the only area that I have ever lived or visited that really felt like "home" energetically. I was living in a wonderful place - mostly it was wonderful because I had a hot tub. The place itself was a very small studio apartment that was furnished with way too many things for the limited space. But the hot tub was divine. I could sit in the hot tub naked in the middle of the night gazing at the stars and listening to the seals barking. It was a very short walk to a small forest that contained a meadow with what to me felt like a sacred mound. . . . . I could then walk up a forested ridge to the top of a hill - and there was the ocean. Often when I got to the top I would see whales. Often in the forest I encountered deer. I Loved it.

Well, on April the first of 1990 I was walking to this mound meadow when out of this house down the street from me appeared a beautiful woman heading out for a walk herself. We felt this immediate connection and ended up talking in the meadow on the mound for hours. It felt wonderful and I knew that I could fall madly in love with this woman.

Now, I was aware that it was April Fools Day, so that evening when I got home I did some writing and meditating. . . . I had gotten very clear by that time in my recovery that a bottom line for me in staying clear with myself and on my path was to stop buying into the illusion of victimization.

And before I go on with this April Fools story, I want to make clear what I mean by the illusion of victimization. . . . . . What is dysfunctional for me is when I am feeling like a victim out of an inner child wound and listening to the Critical Parent tell me that I am a failure, loser, unlovable, etc. That is when I start spiraling downward real fast, that is when I crash and burn. When I am allowing that to happen (which is the natural and normal dynamics of the disease and not something to feel ashamed of - the disease gets us to trash ourselves and then turns around and tells us to beat our self up for trashing ourselves - Truly insidious and powerful.) When I am caught in this disease dynamic (being my own perpetrator and victim) is when I create negative emotional states that I can get caught in for periods of time. Depression, despair, self pity, resentment, etc. are not emotions but emotional states that are created by negative attitudes that I am buying into. In each of those emotional states I am buying into the belief that I am the victim. In order not to create negative emotional states I have to catch myself anytime I am buying into the belief that I am the victim (of myself for being flawed or defective - or others - including the Divine Plan) - and again not beat myself up for it.

When I am buying into the belief in victimization I am lying to myself (letting the disease's lies have power.) Anytime I catch myself coming from a victim perspective I am not telling myself my Highest Truth.

Learning how to take my power back from the disease by not buying into victim illusions was probably the single most important facet of my recovery. A big milestone in that process occurred on April 1st 1990.

And you thought I was off on a tangent again didn't you. :-)

One of the biggest areas in this culture where we are trained to come from a victim perspective is in relationship to romance. We are taught about "falling in love" as if it were a camouflaged hole in the sidewalk that we were powerless over falling into. Falling in love is a choice - which is what I got to get real clear on starting on that April Fools Day in 1990.

Falling in love is a state of mind which is very different from Loving someone. Love is a vibrational frequency that we can tune into. What we learned growing up was love that was an addiction - with the other person as our drug of choice, our Higher Power. Love is not something that someone else gives to us - it is something that another being can help us to remember and access.

I understood much of this only theoretically - and not that much - that afternoon in the meadow by the sea. What I had gotten real clear on by that time is that buying into being a victim was disempowering and dysfunctional for me. So that evening I got real clear with myself. It went something like this:

"OK. Let's look at this. Here is a beautiful woman who feels like she might be my soul mate. Having that powerful an emotional, energetic reaction to her could mean that she is my soul mate but it is much more likely to mean that she is unavailable in a way that is perfect for my patterns. I have choices here. (Empowerment is all about owning that we always have choices.) I can run away in fear that she is a repeat of old patterns but if I do that I won't learn anything. I can choose to explore what this connection with her is - in which case I will probably get hurt.

Since getting hurt is an inevitable part of life and I definitely need to learn some lessons about romance and emotional intimacy - I think that I will explore what our connection is - but do it differently than I ever have before. I will make a commitment to myself (our first commitment needs always to be to our self) to learn whatever lessons I need to learn from this woman and will remain alert so that I do not buy into any victim beliefs. I am choosing to go into the emotional place that she will lead me to learn lessons about my self. I will not buy into the belief that she is victimizing me. When I am hurting because: she is not doing what I want her to; when she is not opening up to the potential of how wonderful we could be together; when she is reacting to her fears and wounds; I will always remember that I choose to venture down the path this way and that any feelings that result will be my responsibility - they will be the consequences of my choice. They will not be her fault. She does not have the power to hurt me unless I give it to her - and I am choosing to give her some power over my feelings.

I also know that I do not have to give her any power over my self esteem. How she reacts to me will not be because there is something wrong with me, or because I have done something wrong. My self worth is not dependent on any outside source - including, and especially, someone that I am choosing to fall in love with.

I commit to myself not to beat myself up for my choices but rather to strive to have compassion for any wounds that are uncovered or new wounds that are suffered. I will stay conscious and stay alert to the lessons that are there to be learned - and I will also have a lot of fun playing around with the energy of being in love. I haven't let the romantic in me out to play for quite awhile and it will feel really good to dance with that wonderful vibrational high that comes from being in love. I will keep firm boundaries with that wonderful romantic part of me in order to not build up expectations that will cause more pain than is necessary.

So, yes I choose to go where this beautiful teacher can take me and learn what I need to learn - and also to allow myself to grieve when wounds are uncovered or gauged anew. Let's go for it! Full speed ahead on a romantic adventure! As a responsible adult on a Spiritual Path that is being guided home to Love."

Okay, Okay - so the above is a little advanced for where I was at that time on my path. It is probably a more accurate depiction of where I was back in December in my latest romantic adventure. But it is, in essence, what happened back then. I didn't have all the words and levels of understanding that I do now - but I was clear that I needed to make a commitment to myself to not buy into the belief in victimization. That whatever feelings resulted were my responsibility. It was the clearest, most mature and responsible place from which I had ever embarked on a relationship adventure - and a very important milestone in my process.

That is why April 1st is an important day in my personal 'important dates' cosmology.

Okay, Okay, yes I will tell you the outcome. She ended up marrying an old boy friend who was not capable of even saying "I love you" to her. I commiserated with her for many hours about how unavailable he was to her and how painful that was. And in the end she married him (for a year or so - I don't know where she is now. I would love to get in touch with her again.) She was a perfect actress to cast in an emotional learning experience that helped me see my pattern about being attracted to unavailable women on a new level. I stayed true to my commitment on a level that was remarkable for where I was at in my process at the time. It was a wonderful - and very painful - opportunity for growth that I am very grateful I experienced. I send her blessings and Love wherever she is - and Thanks.

It was a perfect chapter in the unfolding of my life story.

So that is the story of April 1st . . . " - April 2nd 1999 Newsletter in Preview issue of Joy2MeU Journal

Learning to take responsibility for our emotions as we are learning to be emotionally honest with ourselves is a vital part of codependency recovery." - excerpted in Joy2MeU Update Newsletter April 2009

It was wonderfully empowering for me to start telling myself - and integrating into my perspective of romance - that I had a choice when it came to falling in love. Once I owned that I had that choice, I was able to stop "falling in love" with women who were completely unavailable to me. I was able to start taking responsibility for my feelings instead of feeling like a victim of what "she had done to me" because she had not lived up to my expectations.

The reality is that I have choices in life, and I need to take responsibility for the consequences of those choices. If I choose to get involved with someone romantically, the responsibility for any emotional reactions are mine - not the other persons. I may feel like the victim of her behavior, but I can tell myself the Truth - which is that I am responsible for the feelings because I was the one who choose to give her some power over my feelings.

We are, of course, drawn to certain people. We are drawn to people who feel familiar energetically. They might feel familiar because you have known them in past lives - maybe they are your twin soul or soul mate. That doesn't mean they will not have issues to deal with. In fact, there will probably be more issues because of the Karma involved.

More likely, they feel familiar because they fit your patterns. That is, they are the type of unavailable or abusive or addictive person that you have always been drawn to because of your childhood wounds. As I have noted, I realized at a certain point in my recovery that if someone felt like my soul mate I had better beware / be aware.

Sometimes, it is both kinds of familiarity. The point is to pay attention and make a conscious choice. You do not get involved with someone because you are forced to - on some level you choose to get involved. Even if it feels like a soul compulsion it is still vital to view it as a choice in order to not buy into feeling like a victim.

Personal empowerment comes through owning that we have choices. Realizing that "falling in love" can be a conscious, discerning choice is a key to learning how to stop seeing ourselves as victims in romantic relationships.

Chapter 16 - A Valentine's Day Prayer
"have compassion for your wounded self"

"I needed to learn how to set boundaries within, both emotionally and mentally by integrating Spiritual Truth into my process. Because "I feel feel like a failure" does not mean that is the Truth. The Spiritual Truth is that "failure" is an opportunity for growth. I can set a boundary with my emotions by not buying into the illusion that what I am feeling is who I am. I can set a boundary intellectually by telling that part of my mind that is judging and shaming me to shut up, because that is my disease lying to me. I can feel and release the emotional pain energy at the same time I am telling myself the Truth by not buying into the shame and judgment." - Codependence: The Dance of Wounded Souls

When I wrote the original version of this article to be published in February 2000, I wanted to help people take some of the emotional charge out of Valentines. I had realized in my recovery that Holidays - as well as times like birthdays and anniversaries were times that can really be emotional triggers for us. (In fact it was my pattern of setting myself up to be abandoned on important days - specifically my birthday in July 1987 - that was what finally caused me to surrender to the need for me to do the emotional work that I was so scared of doing.)

"After I had been in recovery a few years - in the course of trying to figure out how I set myself up to be a victim with my expectations - I had a very important insight about holidays. I realized that holidays - not just Christmas and New Years Eve but Thanksgiving, Valentines Day, etc. - along with days like anniversaries and my birthday were the times which I judged myself the most. My expectations of what a holiday "should" be, of where I "should" be at a certain age, of how my life "should" look at this particular time, were causing me to unmercifully beat myself up. I was buying into the disease voice which was telling me that I was a loser and a failure (or going to the other extreme and blaming someone else for my feelings.) I was giving power to the toxic shame that told me that I was unworthy and unlovable.

I realized that I was judging myself against standards that weren't real, against expectations that were a fantasy, a fairy tale. The fairy tale that everyone should be happy and cheerful during the Christmas holidays is ridiculous just like the myth of happily-ever-after is a false belief that doesn't apply to this level of existence. The holidays are just like every other day of the year only magnified. That means there will be moments of happiness and Joy but there will also be moments of sadness and hurt." - Holidays, Anniversaries, and Birthdays

So, this is what I wrote for what I came to call a Valentine's Day prayer.

Valentines Day. The high holy Codependency feast Day. That is, a day when, for most of us, the disease treats us to a feast of self recrimination and self flagellation.

For a small minority of us, a true holiday of love. A time to celebrate the love we are feeling for a significant other in our life. A time to be grateful for the gift of romance, and to honor the partner who is enriching our life.

For a significant number of us - who are alone **in** a relationship - a time to pretend, or blame. To focus on what is good about the relationship we are in, in an attempt to convince ourselves that the payoff we are receiving is worth the price we are paying. A time to put on a happy face to cover up for a sad heart. A reminder that our hopes, and the dream of what the relationship would become, are sadly under fulfilled and that we have settled for less than we deserve. Often that internal conflict is deflected outward in blaming the other.

For another significant portion of us - who are alone - a painful reminder, usually accompanied by self judgment and shame, bitterness and cynicism. Unless our level of denial is great enough for us to truly convince ourselves that it is just another day and does not bring up any feelings - a day of sadness.

If you are one of the lucky few, enJoy it to the fullest. Glory in the magic of love. Let your Spirit soar on the wings of love. Let yourself feel the Love and Joy in the moment as if you have never been hurt, and as if this love will never go away. Grab the moment with gusto and let yourself cherish the fairy-tale-come-true feelings.

If you are part of the majority - either in a relationship that isn't working to meet your needs, or not in a relationship - focus on being kind to your self. Use this Valentine's Day as an exercise in Loving you.

Allow yourself to feel the sadness without buying into the messages of judgment and shame from the critical parent voice in your head. It is not your fault that you are alone - or that you have settled for crumbs in a relationship when you deserve the whole cake. It is not because you are unlovable or unworthy. It is not because you have made "stupid" "mistakes," or because you are a "loser" or a "failure."

And if you find yourself wallowing in resentment and blame, realize that underneath your need to point the finger at another is a place within you that needs to be forgiven by you.

It is extremely difficult to have a healthy relationship in a society that is founded on dysfunctional beliefs about the nature and purpose of being human. In a society that is not only emotionally repressive and dishonest, Spiritually hostile (based upon belief in separation instead of connection,) and shame based - but one that promotes, and programs us for, dysfunctional codependent relationships and toxic love.

We were set up to have unrealistic expectations of our self and of romance. We were set up: to make choices that would cause us to repeat dysfunctional patterns in relationships; to choose exactly the people who would repeat the emotional dynamics of abandonment, deprivation, unavailability, verbal abuse, etc.; to choose to open our hearts to people who would ignore, or stomp on, them. Often then, we learned to shut down our hearts in order to survive the emotional pain.

It is very sad. It is very sad that we have had our hearts broken. It is very sad that we have let go of getting our needs met. It is very sad that it is so hard to connect with another being in a healthy, Loving way. It is very sad that so many of us have had to shut down our hearts and locked the romantic part of us away in a deep dark place within us.

It is very sad - but it is truly tragic that we blame ourselves. We have been victimized by societies dysfunctional programming and we beat up on the victim of those forces that we were powerless over.

We do deserve Love in our lives. We deserve companionship and support and friendship. We deserve touch and affection and sexual fulfillment.

We all do!

That is the good news. The bad news is that we may not get to have that experience in this lifetime.

We do not have to like that reality - but we do need to accept it. Because accepting it is the key to stopping the self judgment and blame. Accepting that you can be happy and whole without a relationship, is the key to being able to let go of expectations and judgment so that you are be free to be happy, peaceful, and Joyous in some of the moments of today.

We have all lived multiple lifetimes in this hostile environment. That environment is now being changed. This new age we are in, is the time when - by healing our wounded souls and learning to manifest Love into our relationship with our self - we will bring about a critical mass that will shift the whole planet's relationship with Love.

Everything without is a reflection of within. As long as individual human beings are hating and resenting them self, feeling unworthy and unlovable - the world will remain an angry, violent, love retarded, hostile environment. By learning to overcome our programming to have a hostile environment within us - in our relationship with our self - we will change the world, transform it into a healthier more Loving place for the Magnificent Spiritual Beings who we Truly are to come into body and experience.

Make this Valentine's Day a True celebration of Love by choosing to Love and have compassion for your wounded self (own the emotional pain) at the same time you are allowing your Spiritual Self to nurture (tell yourself Spiritual Truth) and protect you (tell the critical parent voice to shut up.)

Chapter 17 - Pay Attention and Communicate
Start being the one doing the auditioning

"The process of Recovery teaches us how to take down the walls and protect ourselves in healthy ways - by learning what healthy boundaries are, how to set them, and how to defend them. It teaches us to be discerning in our choices, to ask for what we need, and to be assertive and Loving in meeting our own needs." - Codependence: The Dance of Wounded Souls

When I started writing this article I thought it was going to be the last in this series on Healthy relationships - it turns out that it is not. Some points that I wanted to make that haven't fit into other articles inserted themselves here. So this article is going to be about paying attention and some more aspects of communication.

1. Pay attention - to your own reactions and to the other person. People tell us who they are within a very short time of meeting them. Pay attention to what they are telling you. Watch and listen - this is part of being present that was spoken of in an earlier article. Do not let your desire for a relationship - you loneliness, horniness, starvation for nurturing and touch - blind you to the red flags the other person is waving before you. We are never going to meet someone who doesn't have issues, who doesn't wave some red flags - the point is to pay attention and see what this person's relationship to their own issues tells you about their ability to be healthy in a relationship.

Pay attention to your comfort level with them - to the emotional reactions you have when dealing with or thinking about the other person. Listen to your Spirit and heart more than you listen to your loins or the needy inner child places within you, and you will be able to see the other person more clearly for who they are - rather than trying to cast them in the role of who you want them to be for you.

One of the reasons that many of us didn't know how to pay attention is that we were so focused on giving a good impression so the other person would like us. A client of mine had a big "aha" recently when she realized that for all of her dating history she had related to men as if she were auditioning for them. Out of her low self esteem, she was always trying to get them to like her - rather than wondering if they were worthy of her attention.

As you learn to Love and respect self more, then you can start being the one doing the auditioning. The reason for spending some time getting to know someone else is to audition them to see if they are a person you want to have play a very important role in your life. By knowing that you are worthy and Lovable you are empowered to make choices about who you are going to invest time and energy in, instead of looking for someone to tell you that you are worthy.

2. Communicate - speak up. Be direct and honest - do not assume, interpret, or mind read - ask if you are not clear what the other person is saying, or what some behavior means to them. The foundation of a healthy relationship is built on communication.

It is very important to be emotionally honest. If you are afraid (they will get angry, leave you, etc.) say so - out loud. "I am afraid that if I tell you what I am feeling you will get angry." Just stating the fear can take some power away from it. If you are hurt or angry or scared, it is important to bring the feelings out into the open. And in very important to remember that the reason we are doing this is to share our inner self and to help ourselves take the power away from the feelings by owning them - the point is not to control and manipulate the other person. The purpose of saying "I am afraid you will get angry" is not to prevent the other person from getting angry, it is to help the other person understand you (in-to-me-see).

We need to own the feelings for our self - and in sharing them with the other we are developing emotional intimacy. If the other person invalidates our feelings or tries to fix us - that is something to pay attention to because it indicates that they may not be a safe person to share with emotionally.

Being able to communicate is the only way to develop a healthy relationship. Being direct and honest in our communication is the way to develop healthy boundaries so that a relationship has a chance to grow. Boundaries in relationships are about 95% negotiation. Most Boundaries aren't rigid (some are, like it is not ok to hit me or call me certain names or cheat on me, etc.) - mostly boundaries are a matter of negotiation, which of course involves direct, honest communication.

It also involves some compromise. We don't want to compromise our being, our essential self, in any relationship - but it is important to be able to compromise in the day to day details of life. Things like household chores, choices of activities or music or how time is spent, etc. It is vital to have a balance - a give and take - in terms of the compromise necessary in a relationship, not to have one person to do the majority of the compromising.

Another important point I want to make about honest communication, is that this does not mean that you have to tell the other person every thought and feeling that you experience. We need to practice discernment in what we share. As human beings we have untold number of thoughts during the course of a day. Some of those thoughts will inevitably be about past loves, or negative thoughts in relationship to our significant other. In fact, the disease often produces those kinds of thought specifically for the purpose of sabotaging the relationship. So, we do not have to share everything. It is possible to use honesty as a defense: i.e. when someone gets too close or Loving we tell them something that pushes them away.

The clearer we can see our self and understand our own issues, the easier it is to recognize when an impulse is coming from the disease - our wounds - so that we know that we do not have to share it with our significant other. (It is helpful to have a recovery friend to share these types of things with if they are bothering us.)

This brings us back to paying attention to ourselves and our own process - and having clear communication with ourselves. Healthy relationship starts at home, in our relationship with ourselves. Unless we are in recovery, doing our emotional healing, there is no chance of having a healthy relationship with our self - which makes it impossible to have a healthy relationship with anyone else.

Chapter 18 - Foundation for Healthy Romantic Relationships
The Greatest Arena for Spiritual growth

"The way we change the dance of Codependence to the dance of Recovery, the way we tame the dragon inside, is through integration and balance. One of the ways we do that is by stopping the dysfunctional behavior of looking for the Prince or Princess who is going to fix us and make us whole.

The Prince and the Princess exist within. That Prince, the Masculine Energy of Manifestation and Action, and that Princess, the Feminine Energy of Creativity and Nurturing, exist within us in perfect balance and harmony. They always have - and they always will.

As has been stated, we are not broken - we do not need fixing. It is our relationship with ourselves which needs to be healed; it was our sense of self that was shattered and fractured and broken into pieces - not our True Self." - Codependence: The Dance of Wounded Souls

Romantic relationships are the greatest arena for Spiritual and emotional growth available to us. A romantic relationship is an adventure in growth, an joint expedition into intimacy. A relationship cannot "fix" us - is not the goal where happily ever after begins.

A relationship will be work. It will be challenging and exciting, frustrating and painful. It will help us to access Joy and get us in touch with grief. It will offer lots of opportunities for helping us learn about our self and our wounds.

In order to have the opportunity to become healthier in relationship to romance and intimacy, it is vital to start building a solid foundation within ourselves upon which it might be possible to have healthier relationship. Healthy relationship starts at home, in our relationship with ourselves. Unless we are in recovery, doing our emotional healing, there is no chance of having a healthy relationship.

I want to restate here, that recovery is not a black and white, 1 or 10 process. The goal is not to have a perfectly healthy relationship - the goal is to become gradually healthier in our relationship interactions. Progress not perfection is what is possible. There is no destination to reach, we make gradual progress in getting healthier and learning to love ourselves more - as I say in my book in this quote.

"When I say that you cannot Truly Love others unless you Love yourself - that does not mean that you have to completely Love yourself first before you can start to Love others. The way the process works is that every time we learn to Love and accept ourselves a little tiny bit more, we also gain the capacity to Love and accept others a little tiny bit more.

When I say that you cannot start to access intuitive Truth until you clear out your inner channel - I am not saying that you have to complete your healing process before you can start getting messages. You can start getting messages as soon as you are willing to start listening. The more you heal the clearer the messages become.

When I talk about ways that we use to go unconscious---like workaholism, or exercise, or food, or whatever - I am not saying that you should be ashamed if you are doing some of these things.

We cannot go from unconscious to conscious overnight! This healing is a long gradual process. We all still need to go unconscious sometimes. Recovery is a dance that celebrates progress, not one that achieves perfection."

If you are striving to learn to be healthier in relationship, it needs to start with learning how to Love self. If we are not respecting, honoring, and Loving our self - then it doesn't matter how much someone else Loves or respects us - it won't work to make us happy and at peace.

(I also want to note that there is nothing bad or shameful about being in a relationship that doesn't meet the criteria I have talked about in this series. Progress in recovery means learning to Love ourselves by gradually stopping the self judgment and shame. Each of us needs to decide what works for us on our path. No one has a right to tell someone else what their path is - or to judge someone else's path. You may be in a relationship that works for you on some level - financial security for instance - and you are the only one that can decide if the payoff you are getting is worth the price you are paying. It is your choice and you will be the one who lives with the consequences - so do whatever you need to do to be at peace with yourself. Living our life according to anyone else's values but our own is dysfunctional.)

Until we start learning how to be emotionally honest with ourselves, we do not have the capacity to be Truly honest with another. If we are reacting to old wounds and old tapes without learning how to process through those issues - then we will end up feeling like a victim. If we cannot see ourselves clearly then we will not be able to see the other person clearly.

It is also important to see romance clearly. It is vital to have clear and realistic expectations of romance - to have a perspective of romantic relationship that is empowering to both people

We need to put some energy into changing our definitions of what a romantic relationship is supposed to be so that the dysfunctional perspectives and expectations we learned in childhood will not set us up to react defensively and personalize the other persons behavior.

For each of us, our first commitment needs to be to Self. (Self as in True Self, Spiritual Self) We are each responsible for our own life. If we allow ourselves to give away power over our self esteem, we are being the victim of our codependency - and we will end up feeling like a victim of other people. Empowerment involves seeing reality as it is and making the best of the choices we have available to us. Each of us has the power to improve the quality of our own life by being committed to our self/Self.

If we decide to enter into an interdependent partnership, a relationship, with another person who is open to growing - then our commitment to self/Self will serve the relationship. As long as our commitment to be and become all we can be is served by a relationship then it is very important to be committed to working through the issues that arise. To sacrifice your higher good in the name of commitment to a relationship is codependent and an act of dishonesty to, and disrespect for, self/Self. Commitment to a relationship is important - but it comes second to the commitment to Self.

The other person is a teacher for us, as we are for them. Seeing a relationship as a joint adventure in growing and learning to Love is the key to creating healthy intimacy with another human being. It will not be easy, it will take some effort and energy, but it can be the most wonderful, incredible adventure of your life.

I am going to end this chapter by listing the characteristics of Love vs toxic love that I included in the first chapter of this book. The ones labeled toxic love could also be labeled codependent. Focusing on cultivating the ones labeled Love will lead to healthier, happier relationships with your self/Self, with others, and with life itself. It also will open you to the possibility of having a healthy, Loving romantic relationship.

1. **Love** - Development of self first priority.
Toxic love - Obsession with relationship.
2. **Love** - Room to grow, expand; desire for other to grow.

Toxic love - Security, comfort in sameness; intensity of need seen as proof of love (may really be fear, insecurity, loneliness)

3. **Love** - Separate interests; other friends; maintain other meaningful relationships.
Toxic love - Total involvement; limited social life; neglect old friends, interests.

4. **Love** - Encouragement of each other's expanding; secure in own worth.
Toxic love - Preoccupation with other's behavior; fear of other changing.

5. **Love** - Appropriate Trust (i.e. trusting partner to behave according to fundamental nature.)
Toxic love - Jealousy; possessiveness; fear of competition; protects "supply."

6. **Love** - Compromise, negotiation or taking turns at leading. Problem solving together.
Toxic love - Power plays for control; blaming; passive or aggressive manipulation.

7. **Love** - Embracing of each other's individuality.
Toxic love - Trying to change other to own image.

8. **Love** - Relationship deals with all aspects of reality.
Toxic love - Relationship is based on delusion and avoidance of the unpleasant.

9. **Love** - Self-care by both partners; emotional state not dependent on other's mood.
Toxic love - Expectation that one partner will fix and rescue the other.

10. **Love** - Loving detachment (healthy concern about partner, while letting go.)
Toxic love - Fusion (being obsessed with each other's problems and feelings.)

11. **Love** - Sex is free choice growing out of caring & friendship.
 Toxic love - Pressure around sex due to insecurity, fear & need for immediate gratification.

12. **Love** - Ability to enjoy being alone.
Toxic love - Unable to endure separation; clinging.

13. **Love** - Cycle of comfort and contentment.
Toxic love - Cycle of pain and despair.

(List compiled with the help of the work of Melody Beattie & Terence Gorski.)

Chapter 19 - Taking self worth out of the Romantic equation
"The Prince and the Princess and the Dragon are all within us"

"One of the false beliefs that it is important to let go of, is the belief that we need another person in our lives to make us whole. As long as we believe that someone else has the power to make us happy then we are setting ourselves up to be victims.

A white knight is not going to come charging up to rescue us from the dragon. A princess is not going to kiss us and turn us from a frog into a prince. The Prince and the Princess and the Dragon are all within us. It is not about someone outside of us rescuing us. It is also not about some dragon outside of us blocking our path. As long as we are looking outside to become whole we are setting ourselves up to be victims. As long as we are looking outside for the villain we are buying into the belief that we are the victim.

As little kids we were victims and we need to heal those wounds. But as adults we are volunteers - victims only of our disease. The people in our lives are actors and actresses whom we cast in the roles that would recreate the childhood dynamics of abuse and abandonment, betrayal and deprivation.

We are/have been just as much perpetrators in our adult relationships as victims. Every victim is a perpetrator - because when we are buying into being the victim, when we are giving power to our disease, we are perpetrating on the people around us and on ourselves.

We need to heal the wounds without blaming others. And we need to own the responsibility without blaming ourselves. As was stated earlier - there is no blame here, there are no bad guys. The only villain here is the disease and it is within us." - Codependence: The Dance of Wounded Souls

I state in my book that codependence is a lousy word to describe the phenomena it has come to be associated with. A more accurate term would be outer or external dependence. We are programmed to give power over our sense of self worth - over how we feel about our self - to external sources and outside conditions.

Nowhere is the result of this programming more disastrous on a personal level than in the area of romantic relationships. Our subconscious and emotional programming started with fairy tales that taught us that when we meet our prince or princess we will live happily-ever-after. Movies and books and songs reinforced the original programming that in order to be whole and happy we must be in a relationship.

The result of this programming is that we are set up to feel like failures in romantic relationships. When we give power over how we feel about our self to another person in a romantic relationship we are practicing toxic love - making the other person our drug of choice, our higher power.

A healthy romantic relationship is an interdependent relationship - not a codependent one. An interdependent relationship is one where two people who have a healthy sense of Self worth, choose to become partners, to form a union. Two whole individuals - or more accurately (since as I have stated, we are all wounded and learning to access a True sense of self/Self worth) two people who are in recovery from their codependency working on owning their inherent worth and wholeness as beings, working on learning to be emotionally healthy and honest - who form an alliance / partnership with each other, not two half people who come together to feel whole.

In a healthy interdependent relationship as I mentioned in Chapter 9, we give the other person some power over our feelings - not over our self worth. Giving another person some power over our feelings is a completely different thing than giving them power over our self worth.

When we choose to give power away over our feelings we give the other person the power to help us feel happy. That also means we are giving them the power to hurt us. Caring for anyone or anything means we have an emotional investment in our relationship with that person or thing. To emotionally invest in a relationship is to take the risk of getting hurt - of getting our hearts broken - if we lose that relationship.

But it is not having our heart broken - it is not pure grief / emotional pain - that can be so debilitating, paralyzing, and agonizing when a relationship ends. It is the loss of self worth that we feel - the level to which we have invested, are dependent upon, the relationship to feel good about ourselves - that causes us to feel like we are going to die, that can make us feel like we want to die. The blame and shame and judgment caused by our codependency creates artificial feelings of inadequacy, of trauma, of agony. The unresolved abandonment / rejection / betrayal issues from our childhood are triggered and throw us into a place where we feel the hopelessness and powerlessness that we felt as a child.

The critical parent disease voice - old tapes / subconscious and conscious intellectual ego programming - tells us what losers and failures we are. The wounded inner child places react out of pain and shame from our childhood - the places within us where we feel unlovable and defective. We blame ourselves for the relationship ending with codependent messages like: if only I had not said that; I should have done that; I will never have a good relationship; I will always be alone; etc. Or we go to the other extreme and try to blame it all on the other person. People stalk and murder ex lovers because of the blow they feel they have suffered to their self worth - because they feel they have lost the source / drug that was making life bearable.

Getting our hearts broken is a normal and natural part of life. Blaming our self or the other person is codependency. The emotional pain of a heart break is very painful, but it gets better over time. The blame and shame of codependency causes us to be bitter and resentful, causes us to avoid relationships or to pick another person who will recreate our wounds - another person to try to fill the hole we feel inside of our self.

"Loving and losing is better than never loving" when all we experience is a broken heart. It is the blame and shame of the disease that makes us feel like failures who are incapable of loving - like a victim of our own unworthiness.

At the end of 1998, when I had reached a place in my recovery where I was secure in my self/Self worth, the Universe presented me with an opportunity to experience a romantic relationship in which my worst fear of rejection seemed to manifest - and I did not blame her or me. It was an incredible experience - very painful, but also very liberating.

>"It Truly is a completely different experience to have a relationship where my self-worth is not at risk . . . . . if my self-worth is not at risk then another person can only add to me, they have no power to diminish me. What a gift." - An Adventure in Romance - Loving and Losing Successfully

As that relationship was ending, before it ended, I wrote what I think is one of the most beautiful pieces I have ever written which I mentioned in a previous chapter and will include as the next chapter. It is called: A Wedding Prayer /Meditation on Romantic Commitment.

"You are not the source of each other's Love. You are helping each other to access the LOVE that is the Source.

The Love that you see when you see your soul in the others eyes is a reflection of the LOVE that you are. Of the Unconditional Love that the Great Spirit feels for you.

It is very important to remember that the other person is helping you to access God's LOVE within you - not giving you something that you have never had before." - Chapter 20 A Wedding Prayer / Meditation on Romantic Commitment

Anytime we see another person as our source of love, we will feel a need to control and manipulate that person to be what we want them to be - to be there for us to feed off of emotionally so we can feel good about our self. There is nothing Loving about using another person emotionally because we do not know how to feed ourselves by accessing the True Source.

Love can feel magical and wonderful - can help us feel like we are soaring as the other person helps us to access the higher vibrational frequencies of Love and Joy. To have the opportunity to experience Love is one of the major reasons we have come into human body - but thinking a romantic relationship is what give us worth is codependent and dysfunctional. Romantic relationships can be wonderful opportunities for growth and Spiritual Awakening when we start seeing them realistically, when we stop allowing the perspective of the magical thinking romantic within us to dictate our relationship with romance.

"You are not going to live happily-ever-after once you find your prince or princess. There is no happily-ever-after on this plane of existence. You may find your prince or princess but they will have issues to deal with. Relationships are something that needs to be worked on - not some magic wand that makes everybody happy." - Chapter 9 Interdependent, not codependent

Chapter 20 - Meditation on Romantic Commitment
"Love in that moment as if you have never been hurt"

Early in the morning On January 1st, 1999 I wrote out the following to be read at the Commitment Ceromony of two friends that day. I am editing it for inclusion in this book - and I am thinking that I didn't really write this for them as much as I wrote it to be guideline for myself over 5 years later when I got into the relationship that I am still in now, in the summer of 2012 as I prepare to publish this book. I was writing theoretically and intuitively for the most part at 3 am on the morning, because my longest relationship up until that point in my life had been for 2 years - and I was not that conscious when I was in it. If I hadn't written this on that morning all those years ago, I don't think this relationship I am in now - which became a marriage in January 2011 - would have survived.

" . . . What I believe is that you two have been together many times before in other life times. You made a sacred pact to come together in this lifetime to help each other heal the wounds you need to heal - to serve as teachers and guides and support for each other as you go through this school of Spiritual evolution that we are all in.

It doesn't matter what you call that - twin souls, soul mates, whatever - what matters is that you honor the power of the connection that you feel. And that is why you are here today. To stand here in front of the people you care the most about, to stand here in front of God/The Goddess /The Great Spirit/The Universal Source - and make public Acknowledgment and Affirmation of the sacred commitment that already exists between you.

This is kind of your Soul's way of tricking yourself into agreeing to what your Souls already agreed to. In other words, you were powerless in this lifetime to do anything but end up at this moment.

And someplace along the way, I agreed to show up today to remind you, that this is not the ending where the music swells and the romantic couple rides off into the sunset to Live Happily Ever After. This is just the beginning.

Because Yes you are "gifts from heaven" to each other - but like all gifts in this multi-leveled paradoxical experience of life - there is good news and bad news. The good news is that you have found your soul mate and you are going to touch ecstasy together - you are on the path to learning about the True meaning of Love. That is great news because LOVE is all there Truly is and the only thing that is important.

The bad news is that you have a lot of stuff to work through. You have lifetimes of history. You have Loved each other intensely and wounded each other grievously. You each have specific wounds from your paths in this lifetime that are reflections of the ways in which you have been wounded in other lifetimes.

You each have emotional "buttons" that trigger old defensive reactions, fears and insecurities - and you are sitting next to the person who was specifically prepared and trained to be a specialist in pushing your buttons. The gift you will give each other by pushing those buttons will help each of you uncover the wounds that need to be healed.

You have come together to teach each other, to help each other heal, to support and encourage each other in your quest to find your True Self.

If you keep healing, working through your stuff - then you do not have to do the dysfunctional cultural dance of toxic romance here. This does not have to be "the 'I can't live without you, can't smile without you' addictive, make the other person your Higher Power, be the victim, lose yourself, power struggle, right and wrong, trapped, taken hostage, poor abused me, Two Step."

What you are doing today is making a conscious commitment in the Light, to support each other on your healing, Spiritual paths. That's paths plural. Your paths are going to run together - hopefully for the rest of your lives - but they are not going to become one path. You are individual, unique, Special, Magnificent, Powerful Beings who are choosing to become allies, to become partners in the journey to each of you being and becoming all you are meant to be.

You are together because you resonate on the same wave lengths, you fit together vibrationally, in such a way that together you form a powerful energy field that helps both of you access the Higher Vibrational Energy of Love, Joy, Light, and Truth - in a way that would be very difficult for either one of you to do by yourself. You are coming together to touch the face of God. You are uniting your energies to help you access the Love of the Holy Mother Source Energy.

You are not the source of each other's Love. You are helping each other to access the LOVE that is the Source.

The Love that you see when you see your soul in the others eyes is a reflection of the LOVE that you are. Of the Unconditional Love that the Great Spirit feels for you.

It is very important to remember that the other person is helping you to access God's LOVE within you - not giving you something that you have never had before.

It is important to remember that so you can remind yourself that the fear, lack and scarcity messages that will come up - the possessiveness, the jealousy, the clinging, the fear of abandonment and betrayal, the feeling smothered - are coming from the wounded parts of you that got trained and traumatized by this dysfunctional society to view life from fear, lack and scarcity. Those messages are lies - that is the illusion. The True Reality of The Universal Source is Joy, Love, and Abundance.

The Abundance of Love and Joy that you can help each other to feel by coming together - are vibrational levels that you then each will be able to access within yourself. You are helping each other to remember how to access that Love - helping each other to remember what it feels like and that "Yes!" you do deserve it.

It is very important to remember that so that you can Let Go. Let Go of believing that the other person has to be in your life, has to do things in a certain way, has to feel a certain way at a certain time. As long as you believe that the other person is the source of your happiness you will feel compelled to try to control them so that you can stay happy. You can not control them and be happy.

You will need to Let Go. And Let Go, and let go again. On a daily basis. Let go of believing that the other person has to be in a good mood or has to like the same things or wants to do things at the same time. Let go of expecting that they can be there for you in the way you want all of the time. They can't. They are human. No one can meet all of another person's needs. You each need to have resources / friends outside of your relationship. You each need to have parts of your life that aren't dependent upon the other.

You will hurt each other, scare each other, make each other angry. Which will then give you the gift of being able to work through those issues to a deeper level of emotional intimacy.

You have got some stuff to work through - that is both the bad news and the good news. Because as you reach those deeper levels of emotional intimacy your love will deepen and grow in ways in which you can't even imagine. You are boldly going where neither of you has ever been before. And you have a friend and a partner who is willing to make a sacred commitment here today to go on this adventure with you.

Celebrate that!! It is an incredible gift!

Grab each moment you can and be present with it.

By being willing to be present to feel the difficult feelings - hurt, sadness, anger, fear;

by being willing to walk through the terror of embracing life - the terror that this commitment to intimacy can bring up;

by being willing to take the risk of being abandoned and betrayed - to take the risk of completely exposing yourself to another being;

you are opening yourself to Joy and Love to depths and on dimensions that you have only had the slightest taste of so far.

BE each other's sanctuary. Be patient and kind and gentle whenever you can make that choice.

The more you do your healing and follow your Spiritual path the more moments of each day you will have the choice to Truly be present the moment.

And in the moment you can make a choice to embrace and feel the Joy fully and completely and with Gusto.

In any specific moment you will have the power to make a choice to feel the Love in **that** moment as if you have never been hurt and as if the Love will never go away.

Completely absolutely unconditionally with fearless abandon you can embrace the Love and Joy in the moment.

Glory in it!

Loving is the Grandest, most sublime adventure available to us.

Lets your hearts sings together.

Let your souls soar to unimagined heights.

Wallow in the sensual pleasure of each others bodies.

Roar with the Joy of being fully alive.

Go for it!!!!

Part Three ~ Deeper Within (emotionally) & Further Out (metaphysically)

From Fear of Intimacy to Twin Souls

Chapter 21 - Uncover, Discover, Recover
Consciousness / Awareness + Discernment can help us find balance

"Learning discernment is vital - not just in terms of the choices we make about who to trust, but also in terms of our perspective, our attitudes.

We learned about life as children and it is necessary to change the way we intellectually view life in order to stop being the victim of the old tapes. By looking at, becoming conscious of, our attitudes, definitions, and perspectives, we can start discerning what works for us and what does not work. We can then start making choices about whether our intellectual view of life is serving us - or if it is setting us up to be victims because we are expecting life to be something which it is not." - Codependence: The Dance of Wounded Souls

I spoke in the Author's Foreword to this book about how "We were set up to feel like failures in romantic relationships by the dysfunctional perspectives and expectations of love and romance we learned growing up." And as I mentioned while referring to the three blind men describing the elephant joke quote from my book at the beginning of the Author's Foreword, in order to change our relationship with anything we need to change our perspective of it. That means getting conscious of what perspectives we are reacting out of and starting to ask "Is my intellectual view of love and romance working for me?"

What is so important is to stop blaming your self - or the people you have been involved with - for the problems you have had in relationships. You were truly set up - as were the people you were involved with. It is not your fault! You were brainwashed and conditioned to have an intellectual perspective of love and romance that is dysfunctional, that doesn't work because it is based upon fairy tale thinking. And it is vital to realize that the programming from your childhood is still in your subconscious dictating how you are reacting to life even if you have consciously discarded that thinking as an adult.

It is not your fault!! That is a huge thing to realize. That is great news!! And you have the power to change it! More great news!!! You can change it by getting into codependency recovery / inner child healing, doing the the work I talk about on my website Joy2MeU.com and in my book: **Codependency Recovery: Wounded Souls Dancing in The Light** *Book 1 Empowerment, Freedom, and Inner Peace through Inner Child Healing.*

There is nothing wrong with who we are - it is our relationship with our self and romance that got messed up in childhood. We have the power to change that programming in order to change how we are relating to our self - this is really great news!

"Inner child work is in one way detective work. We have a mystery to solve. Why have I have I been attracted to the the type of people that I have been in relationship with in my life? Why do I react in certain ways in certain situations? Where did my behavior patterns come from? Why do I sometimes feel so: helpless; lonely; desperate; scared; angry; suicidal; etc.

Just starting to ask these types of questions, is the first step in the healing process. It is healthy to start wondering about the cause and effect dynamics in our life.

In our codependence, we reacted to life out of a black and white, right and wrong, belief paradigm that taught us that is was shameful and bad to be wrong, to make mistakes, to be imperfect - to be human. We formed our core relationship with our self and with life in early childhood based on the messages we got, the emotional trauma we suffered, and the role modeling of the adults around us. As we grew up, we built our relationship with self, other people, and life on the foundation we formed in early childhood.

When we were 5, we were already reacting to life out of the emotional trauma of earlier ages. We adapted defenses to try to protect ourselves and to get our survival needs met. The defenses adapted at 5 due to the trauma suffered at earlier ages led to further trauma when we were 7 that then caused us to adjust our defenses, that led to wounding at 9, etc., etc., etc.

Toxic shame is the belief that there is something inherently wrong with who we are, with our being. Guilt is "I made a mistake, I did something wrong." Toxic shame is: "I am a mistake. There is something wrong with me."

It is very important to start awakening to the Truth that there is nothing inherently wrong with our being - it is our relationship with our self and with life that is dysfunctional. And that relationship was formed in early childhood.

The way that one begins inner child healing is simply to become aware.

To become aware that the governing principle in life is cause and effect.
To become aware that our relationship with our self is dysfunctional.
To become aware that we have the power to change our relationship with our self.
To become aware that we were programmed with false beliefs about the purpose and nature of life in early childhood - and that we can change that programming.
To become aware that we have emotional wounds from childhood that it is possible to get in touch with and heal enough to stop them from dictating how we are living our life today.

That is the purpose of inner child healing - to stop letting our experiences of the past dictate how we respond to life today. It cannot be done without revisiting our childhood.

We need to become aware, to raise our consciousness. To create a new level of consciousness for ourselves that allows us to observe ourselves.

It is vitally important to start observing ourselves - our reactions, our feelings, our thoughts - from a detached witness place that is not shaming.

We all have an inner critic, a critical parent voice, that beats us up with shame, judgment, and fear. The critical parent voice developed to try to control our emotions and our behaviors because we got the message there was something wrong with us and that our survival would be threatened if we did, said, or felt the "wrong" things.

It is vital to start learning how to not give power to that critical shaming voice. We need to start observing ourselves with compassion. This is almost impossible at the beginning of the inner child healing process - having compassion for our self, being Loving to our self, is the hardest thing for us to do.

So, we need to start observing ourselves from at least a more neutral perspective. Become a scientific observer, a detective - the Sherlock Holmes of your own inner process as it were.

We need to start being that detective, observing ourselves and asking ourselves where that reaction / thought / feeling is coming from. Why am I feeling this way? What does this remind me of from my past? How old do I feel right now? How old did I act when that happened?" - Inner Child Healing - How to begin

Recognition, awareness, is the first step in healing. Becoming aware is the beginning of getting to know our self - so that we can start getting honest with ourselves. As long as we are reacting unconsciously out of old tapes and old wounds, we are not capable of seeing ourselves clearly - which means we can't see other people clearly either. As long as we are reacting to life out of toxic shame and the fear of being wrong - we are not capable of seeing our self with any compassion or objectivity.

Growing up in codependent cultures we learned that self worth was a competitive issue because we were taught to have ego strength through comparison - better grades than, prettier than, better athlete than, nicer person than, etc. We don't love our neighbor as our self because we did not get taught to love our self - and because we are comparing out self to our neighbor, trying to feel good about our self by feeling better than them.

We need to learn to stop buying into the dynamics of codependency - outer or external focus, competitive comparison, destination thinking, keeping up appearances, looking good (or at least not looking bad), worrying about what other people think of us, trying to avoid being wrong, trying to always be right. trying to overcome the shame of being an imperfect human being - in order to start understanding our self and why we have lived our life the way we have. It is necessary to start learning how to have compassion for our self - and learn to accept that we are lovable and worthy - in order to become available to be loved.

We need to become - as I said in the quote from my inner child healing article above - the Sherlock Holmes of our own inner process so that we can start changing the programming - stop having perspectives and expectations of romance and love that are dysfunctional. We need to start becoming more conscious and owning our power to change how we are relating to love and romance - change our relationship with our self, life, and other people into ones that work better to help us find some Joy and Love in life.

"The only way that we can be in recovery from codependency is to start changing the way we are looking at, and relating to, our self. We have to get more conscious of what is going on inside of us in order to change how we are relating to our self - so that we can change the way we relate to life and other people.

In other words, we need to start taking responsibility for our own lives. We need to start owning our power to change our relationship with self. We need to start learning how to make choices instead of just react. We can have the ability to respond - response ability - to life differently once we start becoming more conscious.

And the key to becoming more conscious is to start learning how to process what is going on in our lives in a way that will give us more clarity.

"The process of processing is a dynamic that in many ways is easier to demonstrate over time than it is to explain. Explaining it on an intellectual level is complicated and difficult because the process itself involves being able to look at multiple levels. The recovery process is spiritual, emotional, and mental. These levels are separate but intimately interrelated.

In learning how to achieve some emotional balance in our lives, it is necessary to be able to look at our self, our own inner process, and the life dynamic itself, from different perspectives. It is this looking at different levels that is the process of processing. Processing is a matter of looking at, filtering, discerning, getting clear about what is happening at any given moment in our relationship with life, with ourselves, with everything that is stimulating us." - The Recovery Process for inner child healing 1: Sharing my experience, strength, and hope

Consciousness involves being actively conscious of how different parts of us are reacting to whatever is happening in our lives at any particular moment. I learned that I needed to observe / keep scanning / paying attention to / taking inventory of, what was happening in my internal dynamic and in my external environment continually in order to be on guard so that I wasn't allowing the old tapes and wounds from the past to define and dictate my experience of life today.

"It is in relationship to learning how to set internal boundaries that the process of processing is so important. Processing involves observing our own internal dynamic. Observing our thoughts and feelings. It is very important to raise our consciousness, to become more conscious, of our own process.

When we start observing our internal process then we can start discerning between the different levels involved - we can start separating out the codependent, dysfunctional messages from the information that is useful and informative. Then we can start setting internal boundaries within the mental, between the mental and emotional, and within the emotional levels of our being." - The Recovery Process for inner child healing 4 - the process of processing - internal boundaries

Codependency is not an issue we deal with and then get on with our lives. Recovery is a way of life. It is necessary to move through our life with consciousness in order to stop the childhood programming from running our lives. The more we recover, the less power the old tapes and old wounds have - but they do not go away.

"It is through healing our inner child, our inner children, by grieving the wounds that we suffered, that we can change our behavior patterns and clear our emotional process. We can release the grief with its pent-up rage, shame, terror, and pain from those feeling places which exist within us.

That does not mean that the wound will ever be completely healed. There will always be a tender spot, a painful place within us due to the experiences that we have had. What it does mean is that we can take the power away from those wounds. By bringing them out of the darkness into the Light, by releasing the energy, we can heal them enough so that they do not have the power to dictate how we live our lives today. We can heal them enough to change the quality of our lives dramatically. We can heal them enough to Truly be happy, Joyous and free in the moment most of the time."

In recovery we are developing a sense of balance, a feeling for what balance feels like, so that we can catch ourselves when we are swinging out of balance. We are here to experience being human and to do this healing. If we are not in recovery, then we can not be consciously present in the moment to enjoy our journey. I did not title my book the "dance" of wounded souls just out of poetic whimsy - life is a dance.

"Emotional balance is not a destination. It is a constantly changing dance. In doing our reprogramming intellectually, and our emotional and Spiritual healing - we are changing the music of our dance. We are choosing to have the opportunity to dance with Love and Joy, to dance in Light and Truth - instead of in darkness and disharmony. In order to have the capacity to dance with Love and Joy, we must first be willing to dance with our anger and fear, with the pain and sadness. Through owning our wounded inner children, we get to uncover and release the spontaneous, playful, Joyous Spiritual child within that is the one who will lead us home to LOVE.

Balance in dancing is about having a feeling for equilibrium, moving in harmony, adjusting, balancing, rebalancing. Likewise our inner dance of finding balance is an ongoing process - ever changing, fluctuating, oscillating in tune with the vibrational rhythms. Once we learn to have a sense of balance, a feeling for emotional clarity, then we are able to adjust and rebalance more quickly when some external (life event, other people's behavior) or internal (wounded child reaction, old tape kicking in) stimuli throws us out of balance." - The Recovery Process for inner child healing 4 - the process of processing - internal boundaries

The more conscious we become, the more we can relax and enjoy the journey.

"The healthier we get, the more emotional healing we do, the less extreme our emotional reaction / response spectrum grows. The growth process works kind of like a pendulum swinging. The less we buy into the toxic shame and judgment, the less extreme the swings of the pendulum become. The arc of our emotional pendulum becomes gentler, and we can return to emotional balance much quicker and easier. But we don't get to stay in the balance position. Life is always rocking our boat - setting our emotional pendulum to swinging. By not taking life events and other peoples behavior so seriously and personally, by observing our process with some degree of detachment instead of getting so hooked into the trauma drama soap opera victimology that is a reaction to our childhood wounds, we learn to not give so much power over our emotions to outside influences and events.

I have choices today in regard to how I am relating to myself, to other people, to life. I am able to accept the things I cannot change much more quickly, and change the primary thing which I have the power to change - that is, my attitude toward the things I cannot change - so that I do not get caught up in a victim perspective. By not buying into the illusion that I am a victim - of myself, of other people, of life - my emotional swings stay on a much evener keel and I experience a much gentler emotional spectrum in my day to day relationship with life." - Discernment in relationship to emotional honesty and responsibility 1

In my recovery I realized that about 90% of the stress in my life before codependency recovery was caused by the attitudes and beliefs I was empowering. Once I got aware of how my perspectives and expectations (which were reactions to my childhood programming and emotional wounds and therefore something I was powerless over until I got conscious of them) were setting me up to be a victim, then I could start owning the power to change my emotional experience of life . Then I could start to take responsibility for my life and eliminate the stress that I was creating in reaction to dysfunctional programming." - Joy2MeU Update August 2002

As I have mentioned in the quote above, there are multiple levels and facets to the process of recovery.

"The individual human being is a fully contained system involving multiple interrelationships within multiple levels. This is easy to see, and understand, when looking at the physical level. The interrelationship of the organs to each other, to the blood, to the skin, to the nervous system, etc. - is a dance of grand, and compelling, complexity.

Just as grand, and compelling, is the complexity of the dance of interrelationship between the mental, emotional, and spiritual components/levels that dynamically interact to form the make up of the individual being - the persona, personality, consciousness, of the self. The more awareness is acquired about the different levels of the self, and the interrelationships between those

levels, the easier it becomes to diagnose the dysfunctional interaction dynamics."
- Codependency Recovery: Wounded Souls Dancing in The Light *Book 2: A Dysfunctional Relationship with Life* Author's Foreword

One of the levels of codependency recovery is intellectual - becoming aware of the conscious and subconscious intellectual programming so that we can start changing the programming that is not working for us. Another level is the emotional. We have a dysfunctional relationship with our own emotions because grew up in emotionally dishonest, dysfunctional cultures.

"We were trained to be dishonest. We also got taught to be emotionally dishonest. We got told not to feel our feelings with messages like, don't cry, don't be afraid - at the same time we saw how our parents lived life out of fear. We got messages that it was not okay to be too happy when our exuberance was embarrassing to our parents. Many of us grew up in environments where it was not okay to be curious, or adventurous, or playful. It was not okay to be a child.
In any society where:

> emotional dishonesty is not just the standard but the goal (keep up appearances, don't show vulnerability);

> as children we learned that we had power over other people's feelings (you make me angry, you hurt my feelings, etc.);

> being emotional is considered negative (falling apart, loosing it, coming unglued, etc.);

> gender stereotypes set twisted, unhealthy models for acceptable emotional behavior (real men don't cry or get scared, it is not ladylike to get angry);

> parents without healthy self esteem see their children as extensions of self that can be either assets or deficits in their own quest for self worth;

> families are isolated from any true reality of community or tribal support;

> shame, manipulation, verbal and emotional abuse are considered standard tools for behavior modification in a loving relationship;

> long embedded societal attitudes support the belief that it is shameful to be human (make mistakes, not be perfect, to be selfish, etc.);

> any human being is denigrated and held to be less worthy for any inherent characteristic (gender, race, looks, etc.);

results in a very emotionally unhealthy society.

We were set up to be codependent. We were trained and programmed in childhood to be dishonest with ourselves and others. We were taught false, dysfunctional concepts of success, romance, love, life. We could not have lived our lives differently because there was no one to teach us how to be healthy. We were doing the best we knew how with the tools, beliefs, and definitions we had - just as our parents were doing the best they knew how.

We have new tools now. We have information and knowledge that was not available until recently. We can change the way we live our lives. It is important to stop shaming ourselves for living life the way we were programmed to live, in order to start learning how to live in a way that is more functional - in a way that works to help us have some peace and happiness in our lives. The only way to be free of the past is to start seeing it more clearly - without shame and judgment - so that we can take advantage of this wonderful time of healing that has begun.

Codependency has been the human condition. We now have the knowledge and power to change our relationship with ourselves. That is how we can change the human condition." - The Condition of Codependency

One of the reasons communication is so hard between people is because we were never taught how to understand our own internal communication. We were taught to focus externally and to have a dysfunctional relationship with our own emotions.

"Emotions have two vitally important purposes for human beings. Emotions are a form of communication. Our feelings are one of the means by which we define ourselves. The interaction of our intellect and our emotions determines how we relate to ourselves.

Our emotional energy is also the fuel that propels us down the pathways of our life journey. E-motions are the orchestra that provide the music for our individual dances - that dictate the rhythmic flow and movement of our human dance. Our feelings help us to define ourselves and then provide the combustible fuel that dictates the speed and direction of our motion - rather we are flowing with it or damming it up within ourselves." - Discernment in relationship to emotional honesty and responsibility 2

All human beings feel the same basic emotions. All human beings have the same basic emotional dynamics - and the same fundamental internal dynamics in terms of the interrelationship of the mental and emotional components of our beings. Codependency can look very different on the outside - but the internal dynamics are the same. I sometimes compare codependency to Baskin & Robins (an ice cream franchise that advertised that they had 64 flavors) saying, there may be 64 flavors but it is all still ice cream. My codependence may look very different from yours on the outside, but the internal dynamics are basic and the same for all humans.

It is so important to learn to become more conscious of our own internal dynamics - and learn to intervene to set internal boundaries so that we don't let the old tapes / programming cause us to shame and judge ourselves for being imperfect human beings. If we don't start stopping the shame and judgment internally, we will not ever be available to be in a relationship that is loving.

"We need to take the shame and judgment out of the process on a personal level. It is vitally important to stop listening and giving power to that critical place within us that tells us that we are bad and wrong and shameful.

That "critical parent" voice in our head is the disease lying to us. Any shaming, judgmental voice inside of us is the disease talking to us - and it is always lying. This disease of Codependence is very adaptable, and it attacks us from all sides. The voices of the disease that are totally resistant to becoming involved in healing and Recovery are the same voices that turn right around and tell us, using Spiritual language, that we are not doing Recovery good enough, that we are not doing it right.

We need to become clear internally on what messages are coming from the disease, from the old tapes, and which ones are coming from the True Self - what some people call "the small quiet voice."

We need to turn down the volume on those loud, yammering voices that shame and judge us and turn up the volume on the quiet Loving voice. As long as we are judging and shaming ourselves we are feeding back into the disease, we are feeding the dragon within that is eating the life out of us. Codependence is a disease that feeds on itself - it is self-perpetuating.

This healing is a long gradual process - the goal is progress, not perfection. What we are learning about is unconditional Love. Unconditional Love means no judgment, no shame."

I had to become more aware of my own internal process to start recognizing when I was reacting to old tapes and old wounds. As long as I was not aware, then I was doomed to keep repeating my patterns of reacting to extremes - I was powerless. By becoming more aware I could start owning the power to make choices - to be discerning - about what I allow to run my life, what attitudes and feelings I am allowing to define my self and my life experience. Then I could start setting internal boundaries so that I could take power away from the old tapes and the old wounds.

"I needed to learn how to set boundaries within, both emotionally and mentally by integrating Spiritual Truth into my process. Because "I feel feel like a failure" does not mean that is the Truth. The Spiritual Truth is that "failure" is an opportunity for growth. I can set a boundary with my emotions by not buying into the illusion that what I am feeling is who I am. I can set a boundary intellectually by telling that part of my mind that is judging and shaming me to shut up, because that is my disease lying to me. I can feel and release the emotional pain energy at the same time I am telling myself the Truth by not buying into the shame and judgment.

If I am feeling like a "failure" and giving power to the "critical parent" voice within that is telling me that I am a failure - then I can get stuck in a very painful place where I am shaming myself for being me. In this dynamic I am being the victim of myself and also being my own perpetrator - and the next step is to rescue myself by using one of the old tools to go unconscious (food, alcohol, sex, etc.) Thus the disease has me running around in a squirrel cage of suffering and shame, a dance of pain, blame, and self-abuse.

By learning to set a boundary with and between our emotional truth, what we feel, and our mental perspective, what we believe - in alignment with the Spiritual Truth we have integrated into the process - we can honor and release the feelings without buying into the false beliefs.

The more we can learn intellectual discernment within, so that we are not giving power to false beliefs, the clearer we can become in seeing and accepting our own personal path. The more honest and balanced we become in our emotional process, the clearer we can become in following our own personal Truth."

What we are doing in recovery is learning to live life by the rules that life actually works by - in alignment with metaphysical law - instead of the rules we learned as children which do not work at all. Trying to do things "right" / perfect or find the "right" person to help us get to "happily-ever-after" doesn't work.

> "One of the reasons for the human dilemma, for the confusion that humans have felt about the meaning and purpose of life, is that more than one level of reality comes into play in the experience of being human. Trying to apply the Truth of one level to the experience of another has caused humans to become very confused and twisted in our perspective of the human experience. It is kind of like the difference between playing the one-dimensional chess that we are familiar with, and the three-dimensional chess played by the characters of Star Trek - they are two completely different games.
>
> That is the human dilemma - we have been playing the game with the wrong set of rules. With rules that do not work. With rules that are dysfunctional." - Author's Foreword from Codependence: The Dance of Wounded Souls

The rules we learned for romantic relationships are even more dysfunctional than the rules we learned for doing life in general. It is vital to get more awareness so that we can practice discernment and own our power to change our relationship with self, with life, with other people - especially with another person in a romantic relationship.

The articles in this section of the book will hopefully help you in your understanding: of how you were programmed and brainwashed with dysfunctional perspectives - and that you can change that programming; of how you were taught to have a dysfunctional relationship with your own emotions so that you don't know how to be emotionally honest and intimate with your self - let alone with another person; of how to have a perspective of metaphysics that is balanced enough to help you be healthier in your relationships with your self and life now. I will also be sharing how I was able to heal my fear of intimacy enough to go from having a relationship phobia to being in a successful relationship for many years now. I hope you find this information helpful.

Chapter 22 - Emotional Intimacy = in to me see
"need to be able to Love our self, to be available for a Loving relationship"

"Learning what healthy behavior is will allow us to be healthier in the relationships that do not mean much to us; intellectually knowing Spiritual Truth will allow us to be

more Loving some of the time; but in the relationships that mean the most to us, with the people we care the most about, when our "buttons are pushed" we will watch ourselves saying things we don't want to say and reacting in ways that we don't want to react - because we are powerless to change the behavior patterns without dealing with the emotional wounds.

We cannot integrate Spiritual Truth or intellectual knowledge of healthy behavior into our experience of life in a substantial way without honoring and respecting the emotions. We cannot consistently incorporate healthy behavior into day to day life without being emotionally honest with ourselves. We cannot get rid of our shame and overcome our fear of emotional intimacy without going through the feelings."

"It is necessary to own and honor the child who we were in order to Love the person we are. And the only way to do that is to own that child's experiences, honor that child's feelings, and release the emotional grief energy that we are still carrying around."
- Codependence: The Dance of Wounded Souls

One of the hardest things for any of us to do is to learn to have compassion for our self. In childhood we felt like it was our fault that our wounded parents treated us in the way they did. We felt that any abuse, deprivation, neglect, and/or abandonment (actual or emotional) was because there was something wrong with who we were - that we were defective or bad or evil or unlovable in some way.

As long as we have not done the work to heal our relationship with the child who we were - with the inner child wounded places that still exist within us - we are not available to Love our self. When we are not able to Love our self, then we are more comfortable in relationships with people who are emotionally unavailable. Being emotionally unavailable to our self makes us emotionally unavailable to others - and will cause us to sabotage any relationship where the other person is Loving us more than we feel we deserve to be Loved.

And I am not talking about consciously telling our selves we are Lovable. I am not talking about an intellectual - or even an intuitive - level of awareness where we know and believe we are Lovable. It does not matter how much we believe intellectually we are Lovable - although working on believing that by introducing Loving programming such as positive affirmations is a vital step in the process of healing - if we have not worked on changing the emotional programming.

When I use the term emotional programming, I am referring to both the emotional wounding / unresolved grief and the subconscious and conscious intellectual ego programming that resulted from the ways we were traumatized and how we interpreted the messages we got from the behavior, communication, and role modeling of our parents and any other significant older people in our lives in childhood. We have within us emotional wounds - inner child places - that are a result of arrested states of ego programming from different ages in our childhood.

It is impossible to become aware of all the subconscious programming without doing our grief work. It is necessary to go through what I refer to in my book as the black hole of our grief in order to bring the subconscious programming to Light. Anything that is in the dark within us has power. The emotional wounds and old tapes from our childhood have power as long as we have not done the grieving and the ego reprogramming work that is necessary to start opening our hearts to our self.

As long as we are disconnected / disassociated from ourselves emotionally, we cannot be emotionally honest or intimate with ourselves. As long as we have not been willing to go through the black hole of our grief so that we can own and reconnect emotionally with the child who we were - we can not be fully or clearly in touch with our own heart and soul.

Intimacy is "in to me see." We need to be able to see into our self - and be willing to take the action necessary - to stop allowing the emotional wounds and old tapes to run our lives and sabotage our relationships. We need to learn to open our hearts to our self, in order to be capable of Truly opening our hearts to another person. If we can't open our hearts to our self, then we will continue to choose emotionally unavailable people to get involved with in our romantic relationships. We are doomed to be in relationships that do not meet our needs - or to avoid relationships - until we start learning to have compassion for the child that we were.

I am going to end this column with a quote from an article in my series on The True Nature of Love (now Chapter 33 in this work) to give an example of how important it is to do this grief work so that we can change the old tapes that have been dictating how we relate to Love and romance.

"We cannot get clearly in touch with the subconscious programming without doing the grief work. The subconscious intellectual programming is tied to the emotional wounds we suffered and many years of suppressing those feelings has also buried the attitudes, definitions, and beliefs that are connected to those emotional wounds. It is possible to get intellectually aware of some of them through such tools as hypnosis, or having a therapist or psychic or energy healer tell us they are there - but we cannot really understand how much power they carry without feeling the emotional context - and cannot change them without reducing the emotional charge / releasing the emotional energy tied to them. Knowing they are there will not make them go away.

A good example of how this works is a man that I worked with some years ago. He came to me in emotional agony because his wife was leaving him. He was adamant that he did not want a divorce and kept saying how much he loved his wife and how he could not stand to lose his family (he had a daughter about 4.) I told him the first day he came in that the pain he was suffering did not really have that much to do with his wife and present situation - but was rooted in some attitude from his childhood. But that did not mean anything to him on a practical level, on a level of being able to let go of the attitude that was causing him so much pain. It was only while doing his childhood grief work that he got in touch with the pain of his parents divorce when he was 10 years old. In the midst of doing that grief work the memory of promising himself that he would never get a divorce, and cause his child the kind of pain he was experiencing, surfaced. Once he had gotten in touch with, and released, the emotional charge connected to the idea of divorce, he was able to look at his present situation more clearly. Then he could see that the marriage had never been a good one - that he had sacrificed himself and his own needs from the beginning to comply with his dream / concept of what a marriage should be. He could then see that staying in the marriage was not serving him or his daughter. Once he got past the promise he made to himself in childhood, he was able to let go of his wife and start building a solid relationship with his daughter based on the reality of today instead of the grief of the past." - Chapter 33 The True Nature of Love-part 4, Energetic Clarity

"When I say that you cannot Truly Love others unless you Love yourself - that does not mean that you have to completely Love yourself first before you can start to Love others. The way the process works is that every time we learn to Love and accept ourselves a little tiny bit more, we also gain the capacity to Love and accept others a little tiny bit more."

Chapter 23 - Men and Women are from the same planet
"Our parents were our emotional and relationship role models"

"In this society, in a general sense, the men have been traditionally taught to be primarily aggressive, the "John Wayne" syndrome, while women have been taught to be self-sacrificing and passive. But that is a generalization; it is entirely possible that you came from a home where your mother was John Wayne and your father was the self-sacrificing martyr."

"As a child, I learned from the role modeling of my father that the only emotion that a man felt was anger. From my mother, whose definition of love included the belief that you cannot be angry at someone you love, I learned that it was not okay to be angry at anyone I loved."

"The point that I am making is that our understanding of Codependence has evolved to realizing that this is not just about some dysfunctional families - our very role models, our prototypes, are dysfunctional.

Our traditional cultural concepts of what a man is, of what a woman is, are twisted, distorted, almost comically bloated stereotypes of what masculine and feminine really are. A vital part of this healing process is finding some balance in our relationship with the masculine and feminine energy within us, and achieving some balance in our relationships with the masculine and feminine energy all around us. We cannot do that if we have twisted, distorted beliefs about the nature of masculine and feminine.

When the role model of what a man is does not allow a man to cry or express fear; when the role model for what a woman is does not allow a woman to be angry or aggressive - that is emotional dishonesty. When the standards of a society deny the full range of the emotional spectrum and label certain emotions as negative - that is not only emotionally dishonest, it creates emotional disease.

If a culture is based on emotional dishonesty, with role models that are dishonest emotionally, then that culture is also emotionally dysfunctional, because the people of

that society are set up to be emotionally dishonest and dysfunctional in getting their emotional needs met." - Codependence: The Dance of Wounded Souls

Men and women are not from different planets. Anyone who is trying to explain male - female relationships without taking into account the impact that culturally programmed emotional dishonesty, generational shame about sexuality, and centuries of patriarchal supremacy have had on how human beings relate to their own gender and sexuality - let alone to romantic relationships - is focusing on symptoms. It is not possible to bring about fundamental change or true understanding by focusing on symptoms. Just as it is not possible to understand our romantic relationship patterns without starting to see how our childhood wounding and programming was causal in producing those patterns.

Men and women are different of course, but not nearly as different as the emotionally dishonest, comically bloated stereotypes of normal male and female behavior - that have been the prototypes for society - would have us believe.

As I have shared elsewhere, we are only a generation or two removed from cultural treatment of both women and children as property. It is only within the last 25 years or so, that such things as healthy parenting classes existed to acknowledge the reality that though we may have to get a license to have a dog or drive a car, there are no such requirements for becoming a parent.

We learn how to relate to our self, our own emotions, our gender, our sexuality, our bodies (all distinctly different relationships though intimately interrelated) in early childhood from the role modeling of our parents - and the messages we get both directly from them and society, and indirectly from how their behaviors wounded and affected us. It was our parents - who were wounded in their childhood - who role modeled for us how male and female emotional beings act, and how they relate to each other.

It is because romantic relationships trigger so many of our old wounds and old tapes that I believe that romantic relationships are the greatest arena for Spiritual and emotional growth available to us. It is in the relationships that involve opening our heart to another person that our codependent defenses are most elaborate and powerful. It is not possible to see our issues in romantic relationship with any clarity until we start seeing our own inner process with more clarity. And then it is necessary, not just to start to understand the dynamics of our wounding and codependent patterns, but to start intervening in our own inner process to set boundaries within.

To start being healthier, we need to learn to set internal boundaries - not only with the critical parent voice, but with the various emotional wounds / inner child places within us.

"It was vitally important for me to learn how to have internal boundaries so that I could lovingly parent (which, of course, includes setting boundaries for) my inner children, tell the critical parent/disease voice to shut up, and start accessing the emotional energy of Truth, Beauty, Joy, Light, and Love. It was by learning internal boundaries that I could begin to achieve some integration and balance in my life, and transform my experience of life into an adventure that is enjoyable and exciting most of the time."

In the articles in inner child healing section of my web site (which I incorporated into my book **Codependency Recovery: Wounded Souls Dancing in The Light** *Book 1 Empowerment, Freedom, and Inner Peace through Inner Child Healing aka A Formula for Spiritual Integration and Emotional Balance*) I discuss some examples of the inner child wounds and how to start relating to them in a more Loving way, including: how to set a Loving boundary with the magical thinking child within; and how I learned to set a boundary with the 7 year old within me that wanted to die.

"Sometimes the first words I hear in the morning are his voice within me saying "I just want to die".

The feeling of wanting to die, of not wanting to be here, is the most overwhelming, most familiar feeling in my emotional inner landscape. Until I started doing my inner child healing I believed that who I really was at the deepest, truest part of my being, was that person who wanted to die. I thought that was the true 'me'. Now I know that is just a small part of me. When that feeling comes over me now I can say to that seven year old, "I am really sorry you feel that way Robbie. You had very good reason to feel that way. But that was a long time ago and things are different now. I am here to protect you now and I Love you very much. We are happy to be alive now and we are going to feel Joy today, so you can relax and this adult will deal with life."

. . . The integration process involves consciously cultivating a healthy, Loving relationship with all of my inner children so that I can Love them, validate their feelings, and assure them that everything is different now and everything is going to be all right. When the feelings from the child come over me it feels like my whole being, like my absolute reality - it isn't, it is just a small part of me reacting out of the wounds from the past. I know that now because of my recovery, and I can lovingly parent and set boundaries for those inner children so they are not dictating how I live my life. By owning and honoring all of the parts of me I now have a chance to have some balance and union within." - Union Within - healing the inner child

In the final article in my series of articles on the Serenity Prayer, I talked about choosing between instant and delayed gratification - making that choice is setting a boundary within.

"Human beings, as I say in one article I wrote for my web site, are kind of like water - we seek the course of least resistance. There is a human part of us that is lazy and wants to take the easier, softer way to getting what we want. Part of learning to be an adult is realizing that sometimes we need to do things we do not want to do in the short run because that is the more effective, and sometimes only, way of getting what we want in the long run - delayed gratification.

It is human not to want to get up out of a warm, cozy bed in the morning to go to work. It is mature to understand that the law of cause and effect dictates that if we don't go to work enough times, we won't have a warm, cozy bed. So, we choose to get up and go to work because that is the best choice for our own well being.

However, as I mention in other articles, if we get up and go to work because we "have to" then we will feel like a victim and be resentful instead of owning that we are making an empowered, Loving choice for our self. When we own our power to make choices instead of doing things because we "have to" or "should" we change our relationship with life - we start to feel empowered instead of feeling like a victim." - Intellectual Discernment - Choices, not "shoulds"

As I mentioned there, we also have archetypal energies - like the rebel - that we react out of dysfunctionally because of our wounding and programming.

"Not only do we have wounded inner child places within us, out of which we react in ways that are self destructive, we also have certain archetypal energies that are vital parts of our psyche. One of those is the rebel. We all have a rebel within us. When we "should" on our self, the rebel in us rebels by going to the opposite extreme - "I'll show you for shaming me, I'll do just the opposite." We act out against the "shoulds" in ways that are harmful us." - Intellectual Discernment - Choices, not "shoulds"

"Because of our broken hearts, our emotional wounds, and our scrambled minds, our subconscious programming, what the disease of Codependence causes us to do is abandon ourselves. It causes the abandonment of self, the abandonment of our own inner child - and that inner child is the gateway to our channel to the Higher Self.
The one who betrayed us and abandoned and abused us the most was ourselves. That is how the emotional defense system that is Codependence works.
The battle cry of Codependence is "I'll show you - I'll get me."

One of those archetypal energies that has caused most of us a lot of grief over the years is the romantic. The romantic within is a part of me that I have worked for years in having some balance with.

"Idealistic, dreamer, lover, creative part of us that is a wonderful asset when kept in balance - can lead to disastrous consequences when allowed to be in control of choices. Not good on taking responsible action would rather day dream about fairy tales and fantasies than deal with reality/grow up.
We often swing between: ·

Letting the romantic be in control - in which case the romantic wants the fairy tale so badly that he/she inevitably ignores all the red flags and warning signals that tell us very clearly that this is not the "right" person to cast in the part of the prince or princess;

and

Shutting down completely to this part of us because of the broken hearts we have experienced - throwing the romantic within into a dark dungeon inside and locking the door for years at a time. This often causes to become cynical, lose are ability to dream, give so much power to the fear of making of a "mistake" that we can lose the ability to risk opening up to the Joy of being Alive in the moment.

It is very important to find some balance with this part of ourselves in order to have any chance of success in a Romantic Relationship. **The romantic is a wonderful part of us that can help our Spirits to dance and sing and soar**. If we do not trust ourselves to be able to set boundaries for the romantic part of ourselves we can often sabotage relationships by being controlling and/or running away out of our fear of being hurt." - The Inner Children that need Boundaries

In an article I wrote almost 5 years ago now, I summarized pretty well what my relationship to the romantic had been for most of my life.

"I got in touch (in a CoDA meeting I think) with the fact that I was totally shut down to the romantic in me. Like all of the inner child places and archetypes within me - I had spent most of my life reacting to the romantic within me by swinging to extremes. I would let my "endless, aching need" to find "her" lead me to casting the "wrong" person in the part of the princess in my romantic fairy tale - and then when I got really hurt by allowing the romantic to be in control - I would shut down to it completely. I would throw the romantic me into an inner dungeon and throw away the key - until some time years later when I would repeat the pattern by letting the romantic take over again.

It made me sad to realize that I had left the romantic locked away for quite awhile again. The romantic within me is one of my favorite parts of me. The idealist and dreamer - creative and spontaneous and very Loving. I decided that I would start opening up to letting the romantic out on parole to see if it was possible to be open to doing a relationship in balance." - An Adventure in Love - Loving and Losing Successfully

(The reason I had Loved and lost successfully - title of article just quoted - is because it was the first time in my life that my self worth had not been at risk in a romantic relationship.)

It is vital to start recognizing how reactions out of old wounds and old programming / tapes have been dictating how we relate to romantic relationships. We need to be working on clearing up and becoming healthier in our relationships with our own emotions, our own gender, our own bodies, our own sexuality, our own archetypes, etc., in order to have a chance to be healthier in romantic relationships.

Chapter 24 - The Maiden and the Horndog
"the great majority of men are emotionally immature"

"Actually the term "Codependence" is an inaccurate and somewhat misleading term for the phenomenon it has come to describe. A more accurate term would be something like outer-dependence, or external dependence."

"As long as we look outside of Self - with a capital S - to find out who we are, to define ourselves and give us self-worth, we are setting ourselves up to be victims.

We were taught to look outside of ourselves - to people, places, and things; to money, property, and prestige - for fulfillment and happiness. It does not work, it is dysfunctional. We cannot fill the hole within with anything outside of Self."

"Not only were we taught to be victims of people, places, and things, we were taught to be victims of ourselves, of our own humanity. We were taught to take our ego-strength, our self-definition from external manifestations of our being.

Our bodies are not who we are - they are a part of our being in this lifetime - but they are not who we Truly are.

Looks deteriorate, talent dissipates, intelligence erodes. If we define ourselves by these external manifestations, then we will be victimized by the power we give them. We will hate ourself for being human and aging.

Looks, talent, intelligence - external manifestations of our being are gifts to be celebrated. They are temporary gifts. They are not our total being. They do not define us or dictate if we have worth." - Codependence: The Dance of Wounded Souls

In my book, I explain the evolution of the term Codependence from a word coined to describe the significant others of alcoholics (co-alcoholic) to a term which I use to describe the dysfunction in the human condition as we have inherited it. A codependent defines him or her self - and takes their feelings of self worth - from outer or external conditions / circumstances / manifestations.

I believe that we all have inherent worth because we are Spiritual Beings having a human experience - we are children of God/Goddess, part of The Great Spirit, emanations of The Source Energy - not because of any temporary outer conditions or external manifestations. When we focus on external sources - as we were programmed to do in childhood - to determine our worth we are worshipping false gods (to use Western terminology), we are too attached to the Illusion (in Eastern terms.)

Traditionally in dysfunctional civilized society on this planet men were programmed to be codependent (define self and take their feelings of self worth) from their work, their ability to produce. Women were programmed to be codependent on their relationships with men.

The bloated stereotypes of masculine and feminine that the quote from my book at the start of the last chapter mentioned - like all stereotypes - started with a grain of Truth that got twisted and distorted by the planetary conditions that dictated human evolution on the planet.

Besides all of the ways we are set up to have unhealthy relationships with our self by the dysfunctional cultures and role models we grew up with - we are also set up by our genetic species programming. The genetic survival programming that may have been necessary in the days of the early Homo Sapiens cavemen is thousands of years out of date and now can provide a source of conflict and misunderstanding between the genders.

One of the seemingly baffling differences between men and women, is that men are at their sexual peak period in their late teens, while women reach their peak period of sexual desire in their thirties. It almost seems like some kind of cruel Cosmic joke.

In order to find any perspective where this can somehow make some sense, it is important to look at historical context - both recent and ancient. Just as it is helpful in understanding how vital the inner child healing process is, to realize that we are only a generation or two removed from treating children like property, so too it is important to realize that teenagers did not exist as a subculture in society until recently. Until only a few generations ago teenagers of 14, 15, and 16 were married and on their own as young adults. The addition of the teenage years to the period of childhood rather than adulthood is a very recent phenomena in society. These years of raging hormones (and resultant emotional volatility) with no acceptable outlet has added new emotional trauma to the process of growing up.

In terms of ancient times, in order for the human race to survive in a hostile environment where living past the age of 30 was considered quite old, it was necessary to propagate the race as quickly as possible - be fruitful and multiply. One of Mother Natures ways of ensuring that this would happen was to give teenage males of the species a very strong sex drive that was aroused by the female body - most any female body - rather than to primarily seek strong emotional attachment to one female. This was necessary because the high mortality rate - both through death in childbirth of females and death through various means of both men and women - created a need to take on new and/or additional mates very soon to insure survival. It was necessary that the men be willing to copulate with (and thus also agree to protect and provide for) whomever needed a mate.

Early homo sapiens were forced to live together in close knit communities - and conform to community standards to remain a part of those communities. Thus the cultural proscription that a man would provide for a woman he impregnated was broken only at risk of expulsion and severe risk to survival. The perspective of teenagers as children rather than adults in some ways absolves teenage males of responsibility for their sexual behavior.

It was necessary for women on the other hand, to have as many children as they could in their healthiest childbearing years, to insure survival of the species. Therefore, it was more important for teenage women to be driven by their instincts to give birth rather than by sexual desire itself. In order to try to ensure protection and sustenance for themselves and their children during the vulnerable times of pregnancy and after childbirth women were programmed to desire to bond with one man to produce children and then to protect and provide for her and her children. Women were capable of, and did, hunt and provide protection for the clan during the times that they were not physically vulnerable due to pregnancy, childbirth, and early child rearing - it was during those months of vulnerability in a harsh environment that women needed a protector and provider.

This genetic survival programming is the source of the Maiden archetype in women. The Maiden is the romantic teenager whose instincts are to settle on one man and start having children - which manifests as daydreams that "her Prince will come." This Maiden is one level of the romantic within.

This genetic human programming can set up a woman to keep a man around for the illusion of having a male protector and supporter. I have worked with many women who not only did not need to be protected and supported by a man, but they in fact were providing the bulk of the support for the man. In the inner work the "maiden within" is the part of themselves that women can set a boundary with so that they do not unconsciously buy into the set up of believing that they have to have a man in their life to be OK. That certainly doesn't mean that there is anything wrong with having a relationship with a man or that the Prince isn't going to show up (he will definitely have issues to work through however.) The point is to be conscious about our choices. If we are reacting unconsciously to subconscious or genetic programming then we are giving power away and not owning our choices.

Men in modern day society are trained to be emotionally dishonest - get the message that it is not "manly" to be emotionally vulnerable - and that their worth and definition comes from what they do. This sets men and women up to have completely different priorities in regard to relationships. In a dysfunctional society a man can be a lousy husband and father - can be a really unpleasant and nasty human being - and still be considered successful and worthy of admiration if he is a success in the realm of money, property and prestige.

An unfortunate consequence of life in an emotionally dishonest and dysfunctional society - that is based on beliefs that deny men the full range of their emotional being - is that the great majority of men are emotionally immature. This is especially true in their relationships to women. Most men - in terms of how they view and relate to females - are stuck in a horny teenager place that I call: the "Horndog" [an archetype that Jung overlooked. ;-)]

It is very important for men to start being able to set boundaries with the "Horndog", with the horny teenager inside them. In order to have a chance for healthy relationship and emotional intimacy it is vital to stop letting the horny teenager be in control of our choices in romantic relationships (this is just as true for same sex relationships as heterosexual ones) or influence how we relate with women in general. This horny teenager within is not bad or wrong or shameful - it is a normal, natural result of growing up in the dysfunctional societies we grew up in. What is dysfunctional, and can sometimes lead to behavior to be ashamed of, is to allow that immature version of male animal lust to run the show. In order to be a mature, adult - a Real Man - it is vital to be conscious and emotionally honest enough to not allow the attitudes we developed as horny teenagers to dictate how we treat women today.

Chapter 25 - Sexuality Abuse - the legacy of shame based culture
"sometimes a woman wants to be treated like a sexual object"

"We live in a society where sex is somehow shameful and should not be talked about - but we use sex to sell cars. That is backwards. Human sexuality is a blessed gift

to be honored and celebrated not twisted and distorted into something demeaning and shameful."

"Our creator did not give us sensual and sexual sensations that feel so wonderful just to set us up to fail some perverted, sadistic life test. Any concept of god that includes the belief that the flesh and the Spirit cannot be integrated, that we will be punished for honoring our powerful human desires and needs, is - in my belief - a sadly twisted, distorted, and false concept that is reversed to the Truth of a Loving God-Force." - Codependence: The Dance of Wounded Souls

Sexuality abuse is a term that I came up with in my own codependency recovery. I have never heard or read of anyone else using this term. It is very accurately descriptive however of something that I have been working on healing in my recovery - and a form of wounding that I believe many others have suffered.

Sexuality abuse for me refers to any messages I got, or emotional trauma I suffered, in childhood which damaged my relationship with my own sexuality. Those message were both direct - from sources which outright taught me that sexuality was shameful and sinful - and indirect, from the role modeling of sexually repressed adults in my life. Those messages were compounded by the twisted, distorted relationship that American culture has with sexuality because of it's Puritan heritage.

The sinful, shameful direct messages came from the Catholic Church in it's general teachings, and specifically from nuns and priests that I encountered in 7 years of education in Catholic schools. I still have a distinct memory - one of those snapshots from the past that endure through the years because of the emotional content attached to them - of Sister Alberta when I was in the eighth grade. She told our class, that if we kissed for longer than 60 seconds, or if our bodies touched at all while kissing, it was mortally sinful. Mortal sins were the big ones, the death penalty felony of sins - the ones that, if one mortal sin stained your soul at death, you were consigned straight to hell to burn in everlasting damnation.

Any religion that teaches children that God loves them but may send them to burn in hell forever is Spiritually and emotionally abusive in my belief. And as the quote above from my book states, I believe that any concept of god that teaches that the Spirit and the flesh cannot be integrated is abusive and shaming - and does have an impact on anyone raised in such a religion in terms of their relationship with their own bodies and sexuality.

The Catholic Church in my experience is the champion of sexuality abuse however, because it was not necessary to actually **do** anything to commit a mortal sin - thinking about sex was enough to condemn one to hell. For a teenage boy to never think about sex is impossible - but I was so brainwashed that I did not even masturbate as a teenager. Now that is unnatural and abnormal. It was very sad to me to realize in recovery how much impact the words of codependents as emotionally crippled, sexually repressed, and shame based as Sister Alberta had on me growing up - and it makes me angry that those issues have contributed to the fear of intimacy that has affected my ability to have a healthy romantic relationship in my adult life.

The article this chapter is based upon was actually written in 2003 and I decided to add it to this book at the last minute while getting the final draft ready in late August 2012. I had thought about adding it earlier but couldn't really find a place for it - and knew this book was getting pretty long already. What made me decide to add it was that on one of my final reviews I was struck by the last chapter in which I talk about the Horndog.

"This horny teenager within is not bad or wrong or shameful - it is a normal, natural result of growing up in the dysfunctional societies we grew up in. What is dysfunctional, and can sometimes lead to behavior to be ashamed of, is to allow that immature version of male animal lust to run the show." - Chapter 24 The Maiden and the Horndog

Because of the sexuality abuse I described just above, I had greatly suppressed and felt ashamed of the Horndog within me. Drinking and drugging gave me permission to express my sexuality a lot in the years before I got sober. But it was mostly in one night stands or intermittent encounters with women I connected with occasionally but would ultimately be unavailable to because I would feel ashamed of the encounters. That was even more true after I got sober because I was actually feeling the fear instead of just denying it and rationalizing away my behavior. I always felt some shame about expressing my sexuality and had to fight against that shame - which would result in long periods of no sexual expression followed by episodes where I felt like I was using the person I had a sexual encounter with.

The relationship I am in now is the first time that I have been in a relationship (an actual relationship as opposed to a one night stand or occasional partner) with a woman to whom it was important to express her sexuality. In this relationship I realized that I needed to open up to embracing and expressing my Horndog because I had been out of balance in not owning my sexuality. It was important for me in this relationship to realize that sometimes a woman wants to be looked at and treated like a sexual object. (It was also important for me to not feel ashamed of using viagra or cialis because of the reality of what happens to men when they get older - and the fact that I was 56 when I got involved with a woman 14 years younger than me.;-)

So, the Catholic Church had a major impact on me personally but the whole puritan thing was also involved. That the puritan heritage of the United States has had such an impact on our society is kind of mind boggling. Attitudes towards sexuality in most of Western Civilization are much less shamed based than American attitudes. Even as sexually repressed as English culture still seems to be in many ways, it seems to have more freedom from it's Puritan past than the US. On a visit to England in the mid-seventies, I was pleasantly shocked to see nudity on television - but very little violence. American culture has glorified violence while maintaining a very conflicted and twisted relationship to sex - using it blatantly to sell cars (and almost everything else we market) as I say in my book, but still maintaining a Puritanical sense of shame in relationship to sexuality. Many of the politicians and ministers who strive to uphold the Puritan ethic in public are often caught acting a very different way in private - a great example of the hypocrisy and dishonesty inherent in a codependent society.

I grew up with parents who were sexually repressed and shame based in a society where Dick Van Dyke and Mary Tyler Moore were a married couple that were not allowed to sleep in the same bed on television. My parents gave me a book to explain the birds and bees - and said if I needed to talk about it to feel free to ask, at the same time their attitude and behavior very directly communicated that they were terrified of me asking. I had to look up a lot of the words from the book in the dictionary, and still would have been clueless had not my older cousin filled me in with a graphic description of what sex involved. I was horrified and started making plans to become a priest.

The role modeling of sexually repressed parents had an impact on most of the people of my generation. Many of us as a result swung to the other extreme in the sex, drugs, and rock and roll days of the sixties and seventies. Many of the children who grew up in the generations following us "baby boomers" had role models who expressed their sexuality in ways that were unhealthy and out of balance to the other extreme. Many of today's children are being subjected to knowledge of, and images of, sexuality that is out of balance to the other extreme - and I believe can also be classified as sexuality abuse.

I want to include in this month article - because I am on the topic of cultural role models and beliefs that can contribute to sexuality abuse - something I wrote in an article some years ago. It is an article about fathers, and how being raised by fathers who were emotionally crippled by dysfunctional societal beliefs has impacted us all. In that article, I wrote about a way that I believe many women in society have been wounded in a manner that I would describe as being - at least in part - sexuality abuse. I say at least in part because it also could be considered gender abuse - one of the ways in which women got the message that being a woman made them "less than." A form of wounding that I have never seen addressed anywhere else. I am going to conclude this Chapter with an excerpt from the Fathers article in which I talk about this particular type of wounding.

"There is an additional way in which women are wounded by their fathers that I have never heard, or read, anyone talk about. It is a devastating blow that many daughters suffer on a subconscious level. It comes at a very vulnerable time and contributes more evidence to the message that there is something wrong/less than about being a woman that most girls have already received in ample supply from society and the role modeling of their mothers.

This happens when girls start developing a female body. Their fathers, being males of the species, are naturally attracted to the awakening feminine sexuality of their daughters. Some fathers of course, act this out in incestuous ways. The majority of fathers however react to this attraction (which in shame-based western civilization is not acknowledged as normal but rather is so shameful that it is seldom even brought to a conscious level of awareness) by withdrawing from their daughters, emotionally and physically. The unspoken, subconscious message that the girl/woman gets is "when I turned into a woman Dad stopped loving me." Daddy's little princess is suddenly given the cold shoulder, and often is the recipient of angry (sometimes jealous) behavior from her father - who up until that time, often, has been much more emotionally available for his daughter than for his wife or sons.

In a healthy environment an emotionally honest father could recognize that his reaction was human - not something to be ashamed of - and also, not something to act out. He could then communicate with, and have healthy boundaries with, his daughter so that she would know she wasn't being abandoned by her Dad." - Wounded Parents - the tragic legacy of dysfunctional families

Chapter 26 - Old tapes / traditional gender roles for men and women
traditional family values in this society = patriarchal supremacy

"The act of suppressing emotions was always dysfunctional in its effect on the emotional, mental, and Spiritual health of the individual being. It was only functional in terms of physical survival of the species."

"Codependence is an emotional and behavioral defense system which was adopted by our egos in order to meet our need to survive as a child. Because we had no tools for reprogramming our egos and healing our emotional wounds (culturally approved grieving, training and initiation rites, healthy role models, etc.), the effect is that as an adult we keep reacting to the programming of our childhood and do not get our needs met - our emotional, mental, Spiritual, or physical needs. Codependence allows us to survive physically but causes us to feel empty and dead inside. Codependence is a defense system that causes us to wound ourselves."

"We live in a society where a few have billions while others are starving and homeless. We live in a society which believes that it is not only possible to own and hoard the resources and the land but one which can rationalize killing the planet we live on. These are symptoms of imbalance, of reversed thinking."- Codependence: The Dance of Wounded Souls

Yesterday one of my phone counseling clients was telling me about her brother's beliefs about the difference between men and women. He told her that women want to settle down with one man while men want to be with a lot of women - and that it went back to the days of cave men, so there was nothing to be done about it.

The very thing that I touched upon two chapters ago - except for the "nothing can be done about it" part. That was part of my point in the chapter about the Maiden and the horndog - we can do something about it. I was trying to point out how stereotypes arise from a grain of truth that has gotten twisted and distorted over the years - and that we don't have to be the victim of those stereotypes.

The very programming that helped the human race survive is now threatening to destroy the planet. We do not have to be the victim of genetic survival programming that is no longer necessary for survival - nor do we need to be the victim of our codependency.

Just as codependency is an emotional defense system that helped us survive childhood and results as adults in breaking our hearts, wounding our souls, and scrambling our minds - so too has the survival programming of our early days on the planet brought us to the brink of destroying the planet.

Human beings have the capacity to grow. Any time someone says anything to the effect: "That is just how it is." "That is just how I am." "I can't help myself." etc., they are making a victim statement.

We as human beings individually and collectively, not only have the capacity to grow and change, we will destroy the planet if we do not. That is one of the reasons that it is so important to be willing to question traditional values, roles, and beliefs - to be willing to change the old tapes.

As I point out so often in my writing, our attitudes, definitions and beliefs - the intellectual paradigm we are empowering (consciously or subconsciously) - determines our perspectives and expectations which in turn dictate our emotional reactions and relationships.

We do not have to be the victim of our childhood programming. In terms of the inner child healing process, we can learn to set boundaries with the Maiden and the horndog within so that we do not let the feelings arising from those parts of us dictate our attitudes and behaviors.

We also do not have to be the victim of tradition - of the programming from our days of living in caves, or any traditions that have developed since that time. The "traditional" context for viewing male and female roles (to say nothing of such areas as "family values" and marriage) in this society is patriarchal supremacy. As I say in the second article of my inner child healing series:

> "Modern civilizations - both Eastern and Western - are no more than a generation or two removed from the belief that children were property. This, of course, goes hand in hand with the belief that women were property." - Inner child healing - Why do it?

It is the underlying belief system that makes our perspective of men and women so dysfunctional - and has caused so much of the dysfunction in the human condition.

I spoke in a previous chapter about how traditionally in our society: "men were programmed to be codependent (define self and take their feelings of self worth) from their work, their ability to produce. Women were programmed to be codependent on their relationships with men."; and how in a dysfunctional society a man "can be a really unpleasant and nasty human being - and still be considered successful and worthy of admiration if he is a success in the realm of money, property and prestige."

Men are programmed to be emotionally dishonest - which causes them to be cut off from connection to their heart and soul. It is an emotionally dishonest patriarchy focused on material "success" in cultures whose value systems do not honor and respect individual dignity and worth, that can justify war - that has brought us to the brink of destroying the planet.

Women have a greater capacity for love - and more respect for individual human life - than men because that life grows in their bodies. This capacity for love and men's overwhelming attraction to the Feminine is part of the reason that men have feared, and attempted to subjugate, women in "civilized" cultures for thousands of years.

The Women's Movement caused many great and wonderful changes in society that have allowed women to start owning their individual worth and dignity - and has helped women to start seeing themselves as more than just extensions of men. Like any change that takes place however, there were both positive and negative affects. One of the negative affects of the Feminist Movement for many women is that they now feel that they are dependent on both relationship and career for their self worth. Many women feel that unless they are both successful in career, and in a romantic relationship, they are failures - because they are still looking externally for self worth.

The even more devastating negative affect of the Women's movement in my perspective, is that women who inherently are most heart connected because of their ability to give birth - have been given the right to compete with men who have never been heart connected in an economic system that does not honor the heart. In other words, women have won the dubious right to be more like men - in the emotionally dishonest, human doing prototype of traditional accepted male behavior.

A healthier trend that is also unfolding because of these changes, is that many men are becoming more like women in terms of owning their emotions and connecting to their hearts. When I say becoming more like women, what I really mean is that more men are connecting to their own feminine energy and owning their humanity - they are becoming healthier and more balanced as human beings. Women have been more in touch with their humanity in the history of the world than men who have been emotionally cut off from their heart and soul. Men who are blocked from accessing their own heart and souls are out of touch with their own humanity and thus able to act in ways that are inhumane.

For the men who are getting emotionally healthy and heart connected, acting out of the horndog within to have sex with many women with no emotional connection does not work. I believe that men who are learning to be emotionally healthier also tend to want to settle down with one person - like the Maiden archetype. This will lead us into the topic for the next chapter: monogamy.

Chapter 27 - Monogamy - A Spiritual Teachers Perspective
"I don't know any emotionally healthy people"

"We live in a society where sex is somehow shameful and should not be talked about - but we use sex to sell cars. That is backwards. Human sexuality is a blessed gift to be honored and celebrated not twisted and distorted into something demeaning and shameful."

"Trying to get our emotional needs met through sex does not work. It is dysfunctional. Human sexuality is a blessed gift when it is in balance with the emotional, mental and Spiritual. This is an emotionally dishonest society which knows very little about True, healthy emotional intimacy."

"The gift of touch is an incredibly wonderful gift. One of the reasons we are here is to touch each other physically as well as Spiritually, emotionally, and mentally. Touch is not bad or shameful. Our creator did not give us sensual and sexual sensations that feel so wonderful just to set us up to fail some perverted, sadistic life test. Any concept of god that includes the belief that the flesh and the Spirit cannot be integrated, that we will be punished for honoring our powerful human desires and needs, is - in my belief - a sadly twisted, distorted, and false concept that is reversed to the Truth of a Loving God-Force.

We need to strive for balance and integration in our relationships. We need to touch in healthy, appropriate, emotionally honest ways - so that we can honor our human bodies and the gift that is physical touch.

Making Love is a celebration and a way of honoring the Masculine and Feminine Energy of the Universe (and the masculine and feminine energy within no matter what genders are involved), a way of honoring its perfect interaction and harmony. It is a blessed way of honoring the Creative Source." - Codependence: The Dance of Wounded Souls

A friend sent me an e-mail a few months ago, asking me what I thought of polyamory. This is a belief system that holds it is possible to have emotionally and sexually intimate relationships with more than one person at a time. Or as I have seen it described: "responsible non-monogamy."

In my reply to her I stated that I had heard of it but did not really know a lot about it - and that I wondered how many people living that life style have ever done any healing of their childhood wounds. And then I shared with her an excerpt from my online journal which I am going to expand for this article.

Someone once said to me, that they thought monogamy was a screwed up concept that was a result of the shame around sexuality that has been so strong in Western Civilization. This person - who was a man (surprise) - thought that monogamy was unnatural.

There has certainly been a great deal of shame associated with sex in Western Civilization. This is especially true of America with it's Puritan heritage.

I told him that I had no idea what sex in a healthy society would be like. Perhaps in the fantasy land where everyone is Spiritually connected, everyone is emotionally healthy and in touch with their connection to everything - perhaps there, we Spiritual Beings could truly enjoy this experience of being in body by being sexual with anyone and everyone we felt like. I have no way of knowing what a healthy Spiritually evolved society would look like.

I then told him, that given the societies we grew up in, given the emotional dysfunction and wounding that we experienced, I did not think anything but monogamy had a chance of being healthy. That the only people I knew who could be sexual a lot with a lot of different partners, either were using drugs and alcohol, or were acting out addictively because of their emotional wounding. (And I was not just referring to sex addicts here, I also include love or relationship addicts who feel desperately incomplete alone and use their sexuality to try to get the love they are starved for - looking for love in all the wrong places and accepting sex when they really want love.)

The first challenge for us in recovery is to start learning how to be emotionally honest and intimate with our self - which means we also need to develop a healthy concept of, and relationship with, our self. This is a process that takes some time - as we learn to practice intellectual discernment in changing the dysfunctional programming from childhood, and emotional discernment that allows us to have internal boundaries so we can grieve our wounds and disarm the emotional mine field within us related to opening our hearts to another human being. To be able to do that with another person whom we are attracted to romantically / physically, who is also healing their relationship with self - is an incredible gift, and a rare opportunity. The more people that get into recovery on the level where they are healing their inner child wounds, the more chance that we can find someone who is doing this work.

Uncovering and healing all the different levels of dysfunctional programming and emotional wounds in regard to our own gender and sexuality - and changing how we relate to people that we are attracted to - is a process that takes time and energy. To think we could develop the needed level of emotional intimacy to engage in sexual activity in a healthy way with multiple partners is kind of insane in my opinion. To engage in sexual activity without developing healthy emotional intimacy is codependent and dysfunctional most of the time.

I specifically said "most of the time," because sometimes it can be the path to developing a healthy relationship. So many of us learned to jump right into the sexual relationship without knowing how to be emotionally intimate, and most of the time - because one (or both) of the partners are not willing to do the healing - that will end up leaving us feeling empty and beating ourselves up for another "mistake." If however, two people who are in recovery jump into a sexual relationship, it may be the stimulus that forces them to learn how to develop healthy intimacy. Sometimes two people who are not in recovery from their childhood issues will be led into recovery to heal their wounds because of a sexual encounter - if both people are willing to do the work.

Whatever the circumstances, healing ourselves and developing a healthy relationship with another person who is healing, takes an investment in time and energy that is huge - just to do it with one person. I have a hard time understanding how it could be done with multiple partners.

I just really don't know what healthy sexuality would look like for emotionally healthy people. I don't know any emotionally healthy people - just people who are in the process of learning to be emotionally healthy. What I do know, is that our childhood role modeling, emotional trauma, and intellectual programming causes codependency - which involves having a myriad of dysfunctional relationships inside of our self before we ever attempt to relate to another human being.

As I say towards the top of the home page of my web site Joy2MeU.com:

> "Codependency is about having a dysfunctional relationship with self! With our own bodies, minds, emotions, and spirits. With our own gender and sexuality. With being human. Because we have dysfunctional relationships internally, we have dysfunctional relationships externally.
>
> Codependency is an emotional and behavioral defense system which our egos adapted in early childhood to help us survive. We were raised in shame based, emotionally dishonest, Spiritually hostile environments by parents who were wounded in their childhood's by patriarchal, shame based civilization that treated children and women as property."

There are layers of wounding that need to be peeled off gradually as we do the healing and change the dysfunctional programming. We all have huge fear of intimacy issues because the first people we opened our hearts to - our parents - were wounded, and in turn they wounded us. In several places in my writing, I note that in my opinion romantic relationships are the greatest arena for Spiritual and emotional growth available to us - because being romantically, sexually involved with another person pushes all our buttons, triggers all of our deepest wounds and strongest defenses. For one person in codependency recovery to develop a romantic relationship with another recovering person, is a process that evolves over time and involves a lot of hard work - and a lot of emotions.

To find one recovering person who is willing to put in the time and effort, who is also someone we are attracted to emotionally, mentally, spiritually, and physically, is an incredible gift in my opinion. I really can't see it happening with several people at once.

I, personally, don't see how it would be possible for someone who was raised on this planet to have a healthy physically intimate, emotionally honest relationship with more than one person at a time.

Chapter 28 - Fear of Intimacy - the wounded heart of codependency
fear of intimacy = fear of abandonment, betrayal, and rejection

". . . if not healed, these early childhood emotional wounds, and the subconscious attitudes adopted because of them, would dictate the adult's reaction to, and path through, life. Thus we walk around looking like and trying to act like adults, while reacting to life out of the emotional wounds and attitudes of childhood. We keep repeating the patterns of abandonment, abuse, and deprivation that we experienced in childhood."

"We cannot allow ourselves to be Truly Intimate with ourselves or anyone else without owning our Grief." - Codependence: The Dance of Wounded Souls

Fear of intimacy is at the heart of codependency. We have a fear of intimacy because we have a fear of abandonment, betrayal, and rejection. We have a these fears because we were wounded in early childhood - we experienced feeling emotionally abandoned, rejected, and betrayed by our parents because they were wounded. They did not have healthy relationship with self - they were codependents who abandoned and betrayed themselves - and their behavior caused us to feel unworthy and unlovable.

"We exited the warm nurturing cocoon of our incubator into a cold, harsh world. A world run by Higher Powers (parents and any body else bigger than us - siblings, grandparents, hospital or orphanage personnel) who were wounded in their childhood. Gods who were not emotionally healthy, and did not know how to Love themselves. Our egos were traumatized - and adapted programming to try to protect us from the pain of emotional trauma that felt life threatening.

The people we Loved the most - our Higher Powers - hurt us the most. Our emotional intimacy issues were caused by, our fear of intimacy is a direct result of, our early childhood experiences. Our lives have been lived in reaction to the intellectual paradigms our egos adapted to deal with emotional trauma.

The part of a child's brain that is logical and rational, that understands abstract concepts (like time or death), that can have any kind of an objective perspective on self or life, does not develop until about the age of 7 (the age of reason.) As little children we were completely ego-centric and magical thinking. We did not have the capacity to understand that our Higher Powers were not perfect. We watched their role modeling, experienced their behavior as personal, and felt the emotional currents of our environments - worry, frustration, resentment, fear, anger, pain, shame, etc. - and were emotionally traumatized.

Our ego adapted itself to the environment it was experiencing. It developed emotional and behavioral defense systems in reaction to the emotional pain we experienced growing up with parents who were wounded codependents.

If you have ever wondered why it is so much easier to feel Spiritual in relationship to nature or animals, here is your answer. It was people who wounded us in childhood. It is people who our egos developed defense systems to protect us from.

I have told people for years, that the only reason to do inner child healing work is if we are going to interact with other people. If one is going to live in isolation on a mountain top meditating, it will be fairly easy to feel Spiritually connected. It is relating to other human beings that is messy." - Inner Child Healing - Reprogramming our dysfunctional ego defenses

Relating to animals or nature is safe because we will not be judged. Our pet will not abandon us because we are inherently defective. Nature will not reject us because we are personally shameful. People will - or at least it feels like that is what has happened in the past.

The Truth is that the ways that our parents treated us in childhood did not have anything to do with who we are - were not really personal. They were incapable of seeing themselves clearly. They certainly could not see us clearly - could not see our unique individuality from a perspective that allowed them to honor and respect us as beings separate from them. Their perspective of us was filtered through a prism of their own shame and woundedness. They projected their hopes and dreams, their fears and insecurities onto us. They saw us as the fix for their feelings of unworthiness, an extension of them that gave their life meaning - or perhaps they saw us as an inconvenience and a burden holding them back, preventing them from making their dreams come true. For some of us, a parent(s) was so caught up in their alcoholism or survival drama or career that most of the time they didn't see us at all.

And both our parents and society taught us very clearly - through direct messages and role modeling - to be dishonest. Our parents taught us that keeping up appearances, worrying about what the neighbors think, was more important than our feelings - because it was so important to them. Or, some of us experienced a parent who went to the other extreme, where they acted like they didn't care what anyone thought - which caused us to feel embarrassed and ashamed of their behavior because it was so out of balance, and caused us to worry about what the neighbors thought. They taught us to give power to other people by wearing masks and keeping secrets.

Even more importantly, our role models taught us to be emotionally dishonest. Because it wasn't safe to be emotionally honest we lost our self - did not know how to be emotionally intimate with our self, and instead constructed a false self image to survive. We learned to wear different masks for different people.

As children we were incapable of seeing ourselves as separate from our families - of knowing we had worth as individuals apart from our families. The reality we grew up in was the only reality that we knew. We thought our parents behavior reflected our worth - the same way that our codependent parents thought our behavior was a factor in rather they had worth.

"We live in a society where the emotional experience of "love" is conditional on behavior. Where fear, guilt, and shame are used to try to control children's behavior because parents believe that their children's behavior reflects their self-worth.

In other words, if little Johnny is a well-behaved, "good boy," then his parents are good people. If Johnny acts out, and misbehaves, then there is something wrong with his parents. ("He doesn't come from a good family.")

What the family dynamics research shows is that it is actually the good child - the family hero role - who is the most emotionally dishonest and out of touch with him/herself, while the acting-out child - the scapegoat - is the most emotionally honest child in the dysfunctional family. Backwards again.

In a Codependent society we are taught, in the name of "love," to try to control those we love, by manipulating and shaming them, to try to get them to do the right things - in order to protect our own ego-strength. Our emotional experience of love is of something controlling: "I love you if you do what I want you to do." Our emotional experience of love is of something that is shaming and manipulative and abusive.

Love that is shaming and abusive is an insane, ridiculous concept. Just as insane and ridiculous as the concept of murder and war in the name of God."

Rather our parents made us their reason for living - which is a form of toxic love in which the child is the drug of choice (causing a child to feel responsible for an adult's self worth is emotionally incestuous and abusive); or a burden to be carried, the scapegoat they blamed for ruining their lives; or treated us like we were an inconvenience in the moments when they even seemed aware of us; it wounded us. We felt betrayed - by our own unworthiness, because we were incapable of knowing they were not perfect. We felt abandoned and rejected by the gods in our lives.

It is vital for us in recovery to work on letting go of the myth that families are safe, loving, nurturing environments. They are not. Our family was where we were wounded - where we were programmed. Our cultural myth about families has set us up to not have a healthy relationship with our self - just as much as the fairy tales set us up to not know how to do romantic relationship in a healthy way.

> "It is vital to start seeing that normal is codependent. It is vital to start seeing clearly the dysfunction and emotional dishonesty in the families we grew up in, so that we can let go of our myth of family. Our dysfunctional families were an effect of the dysfunctional, emotionally dishonest, Spiritual hostile (belief in separation instead of connection), cultural environments in which they existed. It is not personal. It does not have anything to do with us. Just as the way our parents treated us in childhood wasn't personal. They were incapable of seeing who they really were, so they couldn't see us with any clarity. They were looking at us through the

filters of their fear and pain, they projected their shame and lack of self worth onto us. They tried to control our behavior with fear, guilt, and shame to protect their egos. They were dancing with their own wounds to the music of shame and fear - which made them incapable of meeting our needs, of demonstrating love for us in a healthy way. It was not their fault. It was not our fault. It was an effect of the families and culture they grew up in.

I believe that the concept of the nuclear family as a separate, isolated entity is dysfunctional in it's essence. I don't believe it is healthy to raise children in an environment separate from a sense of close knit community / clan / tribal identity. I don't believe that two parents as a cultural entity separate from community can possibly provide healthy, balanced parenting. Certainly one cannot. But children are wounded and traumatized by parents inability to separate their self worth from their emotional reactions to external forces rather there is one parent or two. Parents who were taught to take their ego strength from external comparison cannot avoid having an unhealthy emotional investment in children whom they - and society - see as an extension, a possession, that reflects their worth as individuals.

I have no idea what Hillary Clinton's book is about, but the concept that it "takes a village" to raise a child contains some fundamental Truth in my opinion. I do not believe that children are meant to be raised by two adults separate from community - and certainly not by a mother alone most of the time. The American Dream, a nuclear family living in isolation in the suburbs - with the father gone most of the day - is a dysfunctional ideal in my belief. Our normal societal model for what constitutes an ideal family is dysfunctional in its impact on the emotional, mental, and spiritual health of children raised in those families." - Codependency Recovery: Wounded Souls Dancing in the Light *Book 2: A Dysfunctional Relationship with Life* Chapter 10: Normal Families are Dysfunctional

We were wounded in our first relationships with other people. We were tiny, innocent, little beings who were completely dependent upon wounded people who did not Love themselves - and therefore were incapable of Loving us in a healthy way.

Feeling unlovable to the gods in our lives as tiny children was life threatening. It felt life threatening.

Our fear of intimacy is based upon painful, traumatic experience.

in to me see

The simplest and most understandable way I have ever heard intimacy described is by breaking the word down: **in to me see**. That is what intimacy is about - allowing another person to see into us, sharing who we are with another person.

Sharing who we are is a problem for codependents because at the core of our relationship with ourselves is the feeling that we are somehow defective, unlovable and unworthy - because of our childhood emotional trauma. Codependency is rooted in our ego programming from early childhood. That programming is a defense that the ego adapted to help us survive. It is based upon the feeling that we are shameful, that we are defective, unworthy, and unlovable. Our codependent defense system is an attempt to protect us from being rejected, betrayed, and abandoned because of our unworthy, shameful being.

We have a fear of intimacy because we were wounded, emotionally traumatized, in early childhood - felt rejected and abandoned - and then grew up in emotional dishonest societies that did not provide tools for healing, or healthy role models to teach us how to overcome that fear. Our wounding in early childhood caused us to feel that something was wrong with our being - toxic shame - and our societal and parental role models taught us to keep up appearances, to hide our shamefulness from others.

Toxic Shame - defective, unlovable

It is very important in recovery to start making a distinction - drawing a boundary - between being and behavior. Growing up in dysfunctional societies taught us to equate our worth - and judge the worth of others - based upon external appearances. We experienced love as conditional on behavior. Someone who behaves badly - i.e. not the way we want them to - is a bad person. Someone who behaves the way we want them to is a good person.

It is very important to stop judging our worth based upon the dysfunctional standards of societies that taught us it was shameful to be imperfect human beings.

"When I use the term "judge," I am talking about making judgments about our own or other people's beings based on behavior. In other words, I did something bad therefore I am a bad person; I made a mistake therefore I am a mistake. That is what toxic shame is all about: feeling that something is wrong with our being, that we are somehow defective because we have human drives, human weaknesses, human imperfections.

There may be behavior in which we have engaged that we feel ashamed of but that does not make us shameful beings We may need to make judgments about whether our behavior is healthy and appropriate but that does not mean that we have to judge our essential self, our being, because of the behavior. Our behavior has been dictated by our disease, by our childhood wounds; it does not mean that we are bad or defective as beings. It means that we are human, it means that we are wounded.

It is important to start setting a boundary between being and behavior. All humans have equal Divine value as beings - no matter what our behavior. Our behavior is learned (and/or reactive to physical or physiological conditions). Behavior, and the attitudes that dictate behavior, are adopted defenses designed to allow us to survive in the Spiritually hostile, emotionally repressive, dysfunctional environments into which we were born."

At the core of codependency is toxic shame - the feeling that we are somehow inherently defective, that something is wrong with our being.

[And I want to make note here, that anytime I talk about shame, rather I use the adjective toxic or not - I am talking about feeling toxic shame in relationship to "being," feeling personally defective. Some people in the field, notably John Bradshaw, make a distinction between toxic shame and healthy shame. I find it much simpler, and more useful, to use shame in reference to "being" and guilt in reference to behavior. I believe there is healthy and unhealthy guilt but any time I use the term shame I am talking about toxic shame. (The example that I have heard Bradshaw use of what he calls healthy shame, is that it is what keeps us from running down the street naked. I find that not only blatantly a judgment of behavior - but also based upon cultural standards that are not necessarily aligned with any kind of Spiritual Truth. Some of John's Jesuit background showing I think. ;-)]

The emotional trauma we suffered in early childhood created within us the feeling of toxic shame.

"We do not need fixing. We are not broken. Our sense of self, our self perception, was shattered and fractured and broken into pieces, not our True Self.

We think and feel like we are broken because we were programmed backwards.

We are not broken. That is what toxic shame is - thinking that we are broken, believing that we are somehow inherently defective.

Guilt is "I made a mistake, I did something wrong."

Shame is "I'm a mistake, something is wrong with me."

Again, the feelings of that little child inside who believes that he/she deserves to be punished."

At the foundation of our relationship with our self - and therefore with other people and life - is the feeling that we will die if we reveal ourselves to other people, because then they will see our shameful self. I felt deep within me (in those rare instances of breaking through my denial and blaming to a moment of honest clarity), that if I let anyone see who I really was, they would run away screaming in horror at the grotesque, deformed, shameful being that I was.

Our lives have been dictated by an emotional defense system that is designed to keep hidden the the false belief that we are defective. We use external things - success, looks, productivity, substances - to try to cover up, overcome, make up for, the personal defectiveness that we felt caused our hearts to be broken and our souls wounded in childhood. And that personal defectiveness is a lie. That feeling of toxic shame is a lie.

It was so painful that we had to lie to ourselves about it. We were forced to be emotionally and intellectually dishonest with ourselves by the codependent defenses we adapted. We had to learn how to live in denial of the pain and shame at the core of our relationship with ourselves. Codependency is a vicious form of Delayed Stress Syndrome, of Post Traumatic Stress Disorder. The emotional trauma caused us to disassociate - to not be present in our own skins in a conscious way - and to rationalize and deny our emotional experience of life. We built up a dishonest self image to try to convince ourselves that we had worth based upon some comparative external factors: looks, success, independence (the counterdependent rebel), popularity (people pleasers), righteousness (better than others, right to their wrong), or whatever. That false self image was not completely dishonest because it was formed in reaction to some basic aspects of who we Truly are - but it was a twisted, distorted, polarized perspective of our self adapted in response to toxic shame for the purpose of giving us some ego strength, some reason we could feel better than others.

That false self image, the masks we learned to wear, is something we invested a lot of energy into convincing ourselves was the truth. But deep inside, in our moments of insight and clarity, we knew we were hiding a shameful secret. Often we got that toxic shame about our being confused in our memories with some behavior in our childhood that felt shameful. It is very common for us to have a secret that involves a way in which we were abused - physically, sexually, etc. - that we go to great pains to avoid because we associate the feeling of toxic shame with that incident and think it was our fault.

We do not want other people to see in to us, because then they will learn our shameful secret. We have a fear of intimacy because of the false belief that our relationship with our self is based upon.

We have spent our lives trying to protect ourselves from a lie about who we are. We have spent incredible energy in our lives trying to keep the toxic shame hidden. The secret that is killing us and has made our lives miserable, the secret we have lived in reaction to - **is a lie**. We have been compulsively - because we were reacting to what felt like a threat to survival - living our lives in reaction to our need to keep secret who we feel we really are in the deepest part of our being.

> "Because as small children we did not have any perspective or discernment (prior to the age of reason, which occurs about 7 as our brains develop) we were incapable as viewing our parents as anything other than perfect Higher Powers. Our God and Goddess. Because our Higher Powers were wounded and did not know how to Love self, we were wounded and got the message that something must be wrong with us. Toxic Shame.

> *"That shame is toxic and is not ours - it never was! We did nothing to be ashamed of - we were just little kids. Just as our parents were little kids when they were wounded and shamed, and their parents before them, etc., etc. This is shame about being human that has been passed down from generation to generation.*
> *There is no blame here, there are no bad guys, only wounded souls and broken hearts and scrambled minds."*

Out of our codependent relationship with life, there are only two extremes: blame them, or blame me. Buy into the belief that they are to blame for what I am feeling - or I am to blame because I am a shameful unworthy being. The emotional pain of feeling unlovable to our parents - which is a reflection of unbearable anguish of feeling separated from The Source - can feel like a bottomless pit of agonizing suffering. At the core of our wounding is the unbearable emotional pain resulting from having internalized the message that God - our Source - does not Love us because we are personally defective and shameful.

Our addictions, compulsions, and obsessions; our continuing quest to reach the destination, to find the fix; our inability to be present in the now through worrying about the future or ruminating about the past; are all tools that we used to avoid the emotional pain. Our behavior patterns and dysfunctional relationships (of all kinds, with other people, with money, with our gender and sexuality) are symptoms. Codependence is a defense system that was adapted by our damaged egos to try to avoid falling into the abyss of shame and pain within.

We formed our core relationship with self, other people, and life based upon this feeling of toxic shame." - Chapter 2 of Attack on America - A Spiritual Healing Perspective

Because of the feeling that we were somehow shameful, were unworthy and unlovable, we adapted defenses to protect us. Those defenses caused us to keep recreating the emotional dynamics of our childhood.

Repeating Behavior Patterns - looking for love in all the wrong places

Codependence is doubly traumatic. We were traumatized as children - and the defenses we adapted to protect us caused us to traumatize ourselves as adults. We have experienced getting our hearts broken, our hopes and dreams shattered, again and again. We abandoned, betrayed, and set ourselves up to feel rejected over and over again. (Even those "family hero" types who achieve external "success" and financial abundance have to keep running from distraction to distraction and finding someone to blame so that they can deny the hole they feel within themselves. Achieving some material success makes it much easier to maintain the illusion of ego control and stay in denial of one's wounded soul. Being rich and famous can be a huge block to true emotional intimacy.)

As long as we are reacting unconsciously to our childhood emotional wounds and intellectual programming, we keep repeating the patterns. We keep getting involved with unavailable people. We keep setting ourselves up to be abandoned, betrayed and rejected. We keep looking for love in all the wrong places, in all the wrong faces. Is it any wonder we have a fear of intimacy?

"Codependence is an emotional and behavioral defense system which was adopted by our egos in order to meet our need to survive as a child. Because we had no tools for reprogramming our egos and healing our emotional wounds (culturally approved grieving, training and initiation rites, healthy role models, etc.), the effect is that as an adult we keep reacting to the programming of our childhood and do not get our needs met - our emotional, mental, Spiritual, or physical needs. Codependence allows us to survive physically but causes us to feel empty and dead inside. Codependence is a defense system that causes us to wound ourselves.

Some people, when they first get into Recovery, when they first start on a healing path, mistakenly believe that they are supposed to take down their defenses and learn to trust everyone. That is a very dysfunctional belief. It is necessary to take down the dysfunctional defense systems but we have to replace them with defenses that work. We have to have a defense system, we have to be able to protect ourselves. There is still a hostile environment out there full of wounded Adult Children whom it is not safe to trust.

In our disease defense system we build up huge walls to protect ourselves and then - as soon as we meet someone who will help us to repeat our patterns of abuse, abandonment, betrayal, and/or deprivation - we lower the drawbridge and invite them in. We, in our Codependence, have radar systems which cause us to be attracted to, and attract to us, the people, who for us personally, are exactly the most untrustworthy (or unavailable or smothering or abusive or whatever we need to repeat our patterns) individuals - exactly the ones who will "push our buttons."

This happens because those people feel familiar. Unfortunately in childhood the people whom we trusted the most - were the most familiar - hurt us the most. So the effect is that we keep repeating our patterns and being given the reminder that it is not safe to trust ourselves or other people

Once we begin healing we can see that the Truth is that it is not safe to trust as long as we are reacting out of the emotional wounds and attitudes of our childhoods. Once we start Recovering, then we can begin to see that on a Spiritual level these repeating behavior patterns are opportunities to heal the childhood wounds.

The process of Recovery teaches us how to take down the walls and protect ourselves in healthy ways - by learning what healthy boundaries are, how to set them, and how to defend them. It teaches us to be discerning in our choices, to ask for what we need, and to be assertive and Loving in meeting our own needs. (Of course many of us have to first get used to the revolutionary idea that it is all right for us to have needs.)"

As children we were victims - as adult we kept repeating the behaviors we learned as children - in one extreme or the other. The people in our lives were actors we unconsciously cast in roles that would recreate our childhood wounding so that we could try to heal it - try to get in right this time. We were energetically drawn to, and attracted to us, the people who would treat us in ways that felt familiar - because on some deep level we believed that is what we deserved. If our own parents could not love us, then we must not deserve to be loved.

In my Update Newsletter for October 2000, I talked about a mother and daughter that I had done some work with for a period of time. Then for a few years I had counseling sessions with one or both of them several times a year as issues came up. When I was originally writing this chapter I had a session with the mother. Her daughter had once again engaged in behavior that was dangerous and life threatening. She was very upset about an incident that her daughter had experienced - and was putting a lot of energy into blaming the daughter's boyfriend.

She kept saying how controlling, possessive, and abusive this boyfriend was and how she just couldn't understand it. She felt that her daughter had chosen the boyfriend over her own mother and out of the deep hurt she was feeling she was blaming. She mentioned several times how she had said to her daughter, "What is wrong with you!" Then she would swing to the other extreme and say, "Maybe I failed somehow as a parent." She was caught up in codependent polarized reaction to her fear, pain, and shame.

After letting her vent for a long period of time, I brought her back to focusing on her Spiritual belief system and applying the Serenity prayer to what was happening. I reminded her that the reason her daughter was in a relationship that was controlling, possessive, and abusive was because that was the only type of relationship the daughter was familiar with. I reminded her that she, in her concern and love for her daughter, out of her fear of her daughters self destructive behavior, had been controlling, possessive, and abusive. I pointed out that it was abusive to say something like, "what is wrong with you." - because it equates behavior with being. Doing something "wrong" does not mean there is something wrong with us. The daughter was in fact, just repeating her codependent patterns - and to me, her behavior was not only understandable, but very predictable. (And repeating the patterns was not a sign that she had not grown. This was a new opportunity for growth at a higher level of consciousness for her - a perfect part of her growth process, not some regression or slip into old behavior. We make progress gradually.)

Once I got her to stop reacting to her shame, fear, and hurt, and to stop viewing the situation from a polarized black and white, right and wrong, perspective - then she was able to get back to her recovery and start using the tools she has learned to help her let go of things she can't control and focus on her inner process which she can have some degree of control over in a Loving way.

The reality of codependence is that we get in relationship with people who feel familiar - people who will repeat our childhood emotional dynamics. We keep getting involved with people with whom we can recreate the emotional dynamics from our childhood in some way.

A large part of the tragedy of codependency - the insidiously dysfunctional nature of the disease - is that by repeating the patterns we keep setting ourselves up to be abandoned and rejected. To feel betrayed by our own unworthiness. To reinforce the lie that we are inherently, and personally, shameful and unlovable.

"I spent most of my life being the victim of my own thoughts, my own emotions, my own behaviors. I was consistently picking untrustworthy people to trust and unavailable people to love. I could not trust my own emotions because I was incapable of being honest with myself emotionally - which made me incapable of Truly being honest on any level."

We are attracted to people who are unable to meet our needs, who are unavailable on some level, as a protection from allowing ourselves to get close to someone who could be available to us - because then they would find out how shameful we are and reject us. Allowing someone to see into us, to see who we really are, feels to the disease like the last thing we want to do - and it generates incredible fear of allowing that kind of intimacy.

Codependency is an emotional and behavioral defense system that does not work. Our defense against pain and shame actually creates more pain - and causes us to keep repeating painful patterns in a way which reinforces the belief that we are somehow defective, that we have good reason to feel ashamed of ourselves.

Our fear of intimacy is reinforced by the evidence of how many "stupid" choices we have made in the past. Our experiences in childhood caused us to fear intimacy and feel that we were somehow unlovable - and our codependency caused us to keep creating new evidence of our inherent defectiveness.

Nasty stuff indeed!

We have a fear of intimacy for very good reasons. We have a lifetime of experiences that reinforce the original messages - that reinforces our feeling of being terrified of letting anyone get too close to us, see into us.

The only way to overcome our fear of intimacy is to get into recovery for our codependency - and do our inner child healing work so that we can learn to be emotionally honest and intimate with ourselves. Integrating a Loving Spiritual belief system into our relationship with self and life is an invaluable step in taking power away from the toxic shame so that we can start to Love ourselves and be open to being Loved by others.

"Learning what healthy behavior is will allow us to be healthier in the relationships that do not mean much to us; intellectually knowing Spiritual Truth will allow us to be more Loving some of the time; but in the relationships that mean the most to us, with the people we care the most about, when our "buttons are pushed" we will watch ourselves saying things we don't want to say and reacting in ways that we don't want to react - because we are powerless to chance the behavior patterns without dealing with the emotional wounds.

We cannot integrate Spiritual Truth or intellectual knowledge of healthy behavior into our experience of life in a substantial way without honoring and respecting the emotions. We cannot consistently incorporate healthy behavior into day to day life without being emotionally honest with ourselves. We cannot get rid of our shame and overcome our fear of emotional intimacy without going through the feelings."

"The key to healing our wounded souls is to get clear and honest in our emotional process. Until we can get clear and honest with our human emotional responses - until we change the twisted, distorted, negative perspectives and reactions to our human emotions that are a result of having been born into, and grown up in, a dysfunctional, emotionally repressive, Spiritually hostile environment - we cannot get clearly in touch with the level of emotional energy that is Truth. We cannot get clearly in touch with and reconnected to our Spiritual Self.

We, each and every one of us, has an inner channel to Truth, an inner channel to the Great Spirit. But that inner channel is blocked up with repressed emotional energy, and with twisted, distorted attitudes and false beliefs.

We can intellectually throw out false beliefs. We can intellectually remember and embrace the Truth of ONENESS and Light and Love. But we cannot integrate Spiritual Truths into our day-to-day human existence, in a way which allows us to substantially change the dysfunctional behavior patterns that we had to adopt to survive, until we deal with our emotional wounds. Until we deal with the subconscious emotional programming from our childhoods.

We cannot learn to Love without honoring our Rage!

We cannot allow ourselves to be Truly Intimate with ourselves or anyone else without owning our Grief.

We cannot clearly reconnect with the Light unless we are willing to own and honor our experience of the Darkness.

We cannot fully feel the Joy unless we are willing to feel the Sadness.

We need to do our emotional healing, to heal our wounded souls, in order to reconnect with our Souls on the highest vibrational levels. In order to reconnect with the God-Force that is Love and Light, Joy and Truth."

Chapter 29 - Grief, Love, & Fear of Intimacy
Grieving as part of forgiving my self

"It is necessary to own and honor the child who we were in order to Love the person we are. And the only way to do that is to own that child's experiences, honor that child's feelings, and release the emotional grief energy that we are still carrying around."
- Codependence: The Dance of Wounded Souls

I am not sure at exactly what point in my recovery that it took place - but it was probably around 2 and a half years. It was years later before I would understand its' huge significance in my life. At the time it was just a blessed relief.

I went to a meeting at my home group in Studio City. I was feeling a little crazy. Wound too tight and ready to explode. It was a familiar feeling. It was a feeling that I had drowned in alcohol or taken the edge off of with marijuana in the old days. But I couldn't do that anymore so I went to a meeting.

My friends name was Steve. He hadn't been my friend for very long although I had known him for years. He had been my agent years earlier and I had disliked him intensely. I was in the process of getting to know him, and like him, now that we were both in recovery.

He saw how up tight I was and asked me to go outside with him. He asked me one simple question: "How old do you feel?" "Eight," I said, and then I exploded. I cried in a way I didn't remember ever crying before - great heaving sobs wracked my body as I told him what happened when I was eight.

I had grown up on a farm in the Midwest. The summer that I turned eight I had my first 4-H calf. 4-H was to us rural kids kind of like boy scouts was to city kids - a club where farm kids had projects to learn things. I got a calf who weighed about 400 pounds and fed him all spring and summer until he weighed over a thousand pounds. I tamed him and taught him to allow me to lead him around on a halter so I could show him at the county fair. After the county fair there was another chance to show him at a town nearby and then sell him. Local business people would buy the calves for more than they were worth to give us kids incentive and teach us how to make money.

By the time I was eight, I was completely emotionally isolated and alone. I grew up in a pretty typical American family. My father had been trained to be John Wayne - anger was the only emotion he ever expressed - and my mother had been trained to be a self-sacrificing martyr. Since my mother could get no emotional support from my father - she had very low self-esteem and no boundaries - she used her children to validate and define her. She emotionally incested me by using me emotionally - causing me to feel responsible for her emotions, and feel ashamed that I couldn't protect her from my father's verbal and emotional abuse. The shame and pain of my father's seeming inability to love me coupled with my mother loving me too much at the same time that she allowed herself and me to be abused by fathers anger and perfectionism - caused me to shut down to my mothers love and close down emotionally.

And then into the life of this little boy who was in such pain, and so isolated, came a shorthorn calf which he named Shorty. Shorty was the closest thing to a personal pet that I have ever had. On the farm, there were always dogs and cats and other animals - but they weren't mine alone. I developed an emotionally intimate relationship with that calf. I loved Shorty. He was so tame that I could sit on his back or crawl under his belly. I spent uncounted hours with that calf. I really loved him.

I took him to the county fair and got a Blue Ribbon. Then a few weeks later it was time for the show and sale. I got another Blue Ribbon. When it came time to sell him, I had to lead him into the sale ring while the auctioneer sang his mysterious selling chant. It was over in a moment and I led Shorty out of the ring to a pen where all the sold calves were put. I took off his halter and let him go. Somehow I knew that my father expected me not to cry, and that my mother expected me to cry. By that time, I was very clear from the role-modeling of my father that a man did not cry - ever. And I had so much suppressed rage at my mother for not protecting me from my fathers raging that I was passive-aggressively doing things the opposite of what I thought she wanted. So, I slipped his halter off, patted him on the shoulder, and closed the gate - consigning my best friend to the pen of calves that was going to the packing house to be slaughtered. No tears for this eight year old, no sirree, I knew how to be a man.

That poor little boy. It wasn't until almost 30 years later, leaning up against the side of the meeting room, that I got the chance to cry for that little boy. With great heaving sobs, tears pouring down my cheeks, and snot running out my nose, I had my first experience with deep grief work. I did not know anything about the process at the time - I just knew that somehow that wounded little boy was still alive inside of me. I also did not know at the time that part of my life's work was going to be helping other people to reclaim the wounded little boys and girls inside of them.

Now I know that emotions are energy which if not released in a healthy grieving process gets stuck in the body. The only way for me to start healing my wounds is to go back to that little boy and cry the tears or own the rage that he had no permission to own back then.

I also know that there are layers of grief from the emotional trauma I experienced. There is not only trauma about what happened back then - there is also grief about the effect those experiences had on me later in life. I get to cry once again for that little boy as I write this. I have been sobbing for that little boy and the emotional trauma he experienced - but I am also sobbing for the man that I became.

I learned in childhood, and carried into adulthood, the belief that I am not lovable. It felt like I was not lovable to my mother and father. It felt like the God I was taught about didn't love me - because I was a sinful human. It felt like anyone who loved me would eventually be disappointed, would learn the truth of my shameful being. I spent most of my life alone because I felt less lonely alone. When I was around people I would feel my need to connect with them - and feel my incredible loneliness for human relationships - but I did not know how to connect in a healthy way. I have had a great terror of the pain of abandonment and betrayal - but even more than that, the feeling that I could not be trusted because I am not good enough to love and be loved. At the core of my being, at the foundation of my relationship with myself, I feel unworthy and unlovable.

And now I know that the little boy, that I was, felt like he betrayed and abandoned the calf that he loved. Proof of his unworthiness. And not only did he betray his best friend - he did it for money. Another piece of the puzzle of why money has been such a big issue in my life. In recovery I had learned that because of the power my father and society gave to money I had spent much of my life saying that money wasn't important to me at the same time that I was always focused on it because I never had enough. I have definitely had a dysfunctional relationship with money in my life and 8 year old Robby gave me a glimpse at another facet of that relationship.

Robby has also helped me to understand another piece of my fear of intimacy issues. I have been going through a transformation one more time in my recovery. Each time that I need to grow some more - need to surrender some more of who I thought I was in order to become who I am - I get to peel another layer of the onion. Each time this happens I get to reach a deeper level of honesty and see things clearer than I ever have before. Each time, I also get to release some of the emotional energy through crying and raging.

Through clearer eyes, and with deeper emotional honesty, I get to look at all of my major issues again to heal them some more. I used to think that I could deal with an issue and be done with it - but now I know that is not the way the healing process works. So recently I have gotten the opportunity to revisit my issues of abandonment and betrayal, of deprivation and discounting. My issues with my mother and father, with my gender and sexuality, with money and success. My issues with the God I was taught about and the God-Force that I choose to believe in. My patterns of self-abusive behavior that are driven by my emotional wounds - and the attempts that I make to forgive myself for behavior that I have been powerless over. And they all lead me back to the core issue. I am not worthy. I am not good enough. Something is wrong with me.

At the core of my relationship is the little boy who feels unworthy and unlovable. And my relationship with myself was built on that foundation. The original wounding caused me to adapt attitudes and behavior patterns which caused me to be further traumatized and wounded - which caused me to adapt different attitudes and behavior patterns which caused me to be further traumatized and wounded in different ways. Layer upon layer the wounds were laid - multifaceted, incredibly complex and convoluted is the disease of Codependence. Truly insidious, baffling and powerful.

Through revisiting the eight year old who I was I get to understand on a new level why I have always been attracted to unavailable people - because the pain of feeling abandoned and betrayed is the lesser of two evils. The worst possible thing, to my shame-based inner children, is to have revealed how unworthy and unlovable I am - so unworthy that I abandoned and betrayed my best friend, Shorty the shorthorn calf that I loved and who seemed to love me back. It is no wonder that at my core I am terrified of loving someone who is capable of loving me back.

By owning and honoring the feelings of the child who I was, I can do some more work on letting him know that it wasn't his fault and that he deserves forgiveness. That he deserves to be Loved.

So today, I am grieving once more for the eight year old who was trapped, and for the man he became. I am grieving because if I don't own that child and his feelings - then the man will never get past his terror of allowing himself to be loved. By owning and cherishing that child, I am healing the broken heart of both the child and the man - and giving that man the opportunity to one day trust himself enough to love someone as much as he loved Shorty.

To Steve G. - wherever you are - Thank You - I Love you

Chapter 30 - The True Nature of Love 1: what Love is not
"If someone loves you, it should <u>feel</u> like they love you."

"We live in a society where the emotional experience of "love" is conditional on behavior. Where fear, guilt, and shame are used to try to control children's behavior because parents believe that their children's behavior reflects their self-worth.

In other words, if little Johnny is a well-behaved, "good boy," then his parents are good people. If Johnny acts out, and misbehaves, then there is something wrong with his parents. ("He doesn't come from a good family.")

What the family dynamics research shows is that it is actually the good child - the family hero role - who is the most emotionally dishonest and out of touch with him/herself, while the acting-out child - the scapegoat - is the most emotionally honest child in the dysfunctional family. Backwards again.

In a Codependent society we are taught, in the name of "love," to try to control those we love, by manipulating and shaming them, to try to get them to do the 'right' things - in order to protect our own ego-strength. Our emotional experience of love is of something controlling: "I love you if you do what I want you to do." Our emotional experience of love is of something that is shaming and manipulative and abusive.

Love that is shaming and abusive is an insane, ridiculous concept. Just as insane and ridiculous as the concept of murder and war in the name of God." - Codependence: The Dance of Wounded Souls

One day several years into my recovery I had one of those insights, those moments of a light bulb going on in my head, that was the beginning of a major paradigm shift for me. It was one of those moments of clarity which caused me to start reevaluating the mental perspectives and definitions that were dictating my emotional reactions to life. My relationships with myself, with life, and with other people - and therefore my emotional reactions to life events and other people's behavior - are dictated by the intellectual framework/paradigm that is determining my perspective and expectations. So the intellectual attitudes, beliefs, and definitions that are determining my perspective and expectations dictate what emotional reactions I have to life - what my relationship to life feels like.

I am not sure if this particular insight came before or after I had started consciously working on recovery from my codependency issues. I count my codependency recovery as starting on June 3, 1986 - exactly 2 years and 5 months into my recovery in another twelve step program. It was on that day that I realized that my emotional relationship with life was being dictated by the subconscious programming from my childhood - not by the intellectual attitudes, beliefs, and definitions that I had consciously chosen as being what I believed as an adult. To my horror I could see clearly that my behavioral patterns in my adult life were based on the beliefs and definitions that were imposed on me in early childhood. And I could see that even though these subconscious beliefs were based partly on the messages I received, they were even more firmly grounded upon the assumptions that I made about myself and life because of the emotional trauma I had suffered and because of the role modeling of the adults that I had grown up around.

On that evening in 1986 I Truly was able to see and admit to myself that I had been powerless to make healthy choices in my life because the emotional wounds and subconscious programming from my childhood had been dictating my emotional reactions to life, my relationship with myself and life. The saying I had heard in recovery that 'if you keep doing what you are doing, you will keep getting what you are getting' suddenly became clear. On that day, a paradigm shift occurred that allowed me to see life from a different perspective - a perspective that caused me to become willing to start doing the work necessary to change that intellectual programming and heal those emotional wounds.

That is the way the recovery process has worked for me. I have an insight that allows me to see an issue from a different perspective. Once my perspective has started changing, the paradigm has started shifting, then I can see what needs to be changed in my intellectual programming in order to start changing my emotional reactions. I see where I have been powerless - trapped by old attitudes and definitions - and then I have the power to change my relationship to that issue, which will change my emotional experience of life in relationship to that issue.

(When I started writing this column, I was not planning on focusing so much on the process - oh well, I guess it was necessary, and hopefully will be helpful to my readers. Maybe, I just wanted to include the fact that my anniversary in codependence recovery is upon me. Whatever, I will get on with the column now.)

I don't remember how the particular insight that I am writing about here came about - whether I heard it, or read it, or just had the thought occur (which would mean, to me, that it was a message from my Higher Self/Higher Power - of course any of those methods would be a message from my Higher Power.) In any case, this particular insight struck me with great force. Like most great insights, it was amazingly simple and obvious. It was to me earth shattering/paradigm busting in it's impact. The insight was:

If someone loves you, it should <u>feel</u> like they love you.

What a concept! Obvious, logical, rational, elementary - like 'duh' of course it should.

I had never experienced feeling loved consistently in my closest relationships. Because my parents did not know how to Love themselves, their behavior towards me had caused me to experience love as critical, shaming, manipulative, controlling, and abusive. Because that was my experience of love as a child - that was the only type of relationship I was comfortable with as an adult. It was also, and most importantly, the relationship that I had with myself.

In order to start changing my relationship with myself, so that I could start changing the type of relationships I had with other people, I had to start focusing on trying to learn the True nature of Love.

This, I believe, is the Great Quest that we are on. Anyone in recovery, on a healing / Spiritual path, is ultimately trying to find their way home to LOVE - in my belief. LOVE is the Higher Power - the True nature of the God-Force/Goddess Energy/Great Spirit. LOVE is the fabric from which we are woven. LOVE is the answer.

And in order to start finding my way home to LOVE - I first had to start awakening to what Love is not. Here are a few things that I have learned, and believe, are not part of the True nature of Love.

Love is **not**:

Critical	**Shaming**	**Abusive**	**Controlling**	**Manipulative**
Demeaning	**Humiliating**	**Separating**	**Discounting**	
Diminishing	**Belittling**	**Negative**	**Traumatic**	
Painful most of the time		**etc.**		

Love is also not an addiction. It is not taking a hostage or being taken hostage. The type of romantic love that I learned about growing is a form of toxic love. The "I can't smile without out you," "Can't live without you." "You are my everything," "You are not whole until you find your prince/princess" messages that I learned in relationship to romantic love in childhood are not descriptions of Love - they are descriptions of drug of choice, of someone who is a higher power/false god.

Additionally, Love is not being a doormat. Love does not entail sacrificing your self on the altar of martyrdom - because one cannot consciously choose to sacrifice self if they have never Truly had a self that they felt was Lovable and worthy. If we do not know how to Love our self, how to show respect and honor for our self - then we have no self to sacrifice. We are then sacrificing in order to try to prove to ourselves that we are lovable and worthy - that is not giving from the heart, that is codependently manipulative, controlling, and dishonest.

Unconditional Love is not being a self-sacrificing doormat - Unconditional Love begins with Loving self enough to protect our self from the people we Love if that is necessary. Until we start Loving, honoring, and respecting our self, we are not Truly **giving** - we are attempting to **take** self worth from others by being compliant in our behavior towards them.

I also learned that Love is not about success, achievement, and recognition. If I do not Love my self - believe at the core of my being that I am worthy and Lovable - then any success, achievement, or recognition I get will only serve to distract me temporarily from the hole that I feel within, from the feeling of being defective that I internalized as a small child because the love that I received did not **feel** Loving.

I realized that this is what I had done for much of my life - tried to take self worth from being a 'nice guy' or from a princess or from becoming a 'success.' As I started awakening to what Love is not, I could then start exploring to discover the True Nature of Love. I started consciously realizing that this is what I had always been seeking - that my Great Quest in life is to return home to LOVE.

LOVE is the answer. Love is the key. The Great Quest in life is for the Holy Grail that is the True nature of Love.

Chapter 31 - The True Nature of Love 2: Love as Freedom
"traumatized by being Spiritually orphaned in an alien environment"

"The Universal Creative Force, as I understand it, is the energy field of ALL THAT IS vibrating at the frequency of Absolute Harmony. That vibrational frequency I call LOVE. (LOVE is the vibrational frequency of God; Love is an energy vibration within The Illusion which we can access; love is, in our Codependent culture, most often an addiction or an excuse for dysfunctional behavior.)

LOVE is the energy frequency of Absolute Harmony because it is the vibrational frequency where there is no separation.

Energy moves in wave-like patterns; what enables movement is the separation between the valley of the wave and its peak. The distance from peak to peak is called it's wavelength. It is a law of physics that as vibrational frequency rises, as it gets higher, the wavelength gets shorter. The frequency of LOVE is the vibrational frequency where wavelength disappears, where separation disappears.

It is a place of absolute Peace, motionless, timeless, completely at rest: The Eternal Now.

The Peace and Bliss of The Eternal Now is the True Absolute Reality of the God-Force." - Codependence: The Dance of Wounded Souls

What is Love? That is the question. I have been quite balled up the last week in attempting to write this column. No, that is not quite true - I have been unable to get into a space to even attempt to write this column. I need to get into a certain space - need to be feeling a special kind of creative energy - to write about a topic such as this. It was much easier to write last month's column about "what Love is not." Then I was writing about something much more concrete, much more black and white (the irony of this - since one of the characteristics of the disease is black and white thinking - is fodder for a completely different column.) The dynamics of the disease and the wounding process are very clear in my eyes. I have experienced the type of love that is shaming, abusive, manipulative, smothering, intrusive, addictive, etc., my whole life.

In fact, I learned a new word while writing this column. As I was composing the above paragraph, and taking note of how much easier it was to write last month's column, the word empirical came to mind.

So, I did what comes naturally when a word pops to mind - I looked it up.

empirical 1. Relating to or based on experience or observation. 2. Relying entirely or to excess upon direct, repeated, and uncritically accepted experience: opposed to metempirical.

Aha, a new word.

metempirical 1. Lying beyond the bounds of experience, as intuitive principles; not derived from experience; transcendental.

So, even though I just said that it was easier to write 'what Love is not' because of my experience - in Truth when I say that Love is not shaming and abusive, I am actually stating my intuitive Truth. If I were just relying on my experience, I would say "love is shaming and abusive and controlling," "love is being responsible for other people's feelings and well being," etc. - and that would be the Truth about love with a small l. When I say Love is not shaming, I am talking about the True Nature of Love as I intuitively understand it. Once I started to awaken to the reality that civilized society on this planet was based upon some false beliefs, then I started to be able to validate my intuitive feeling that something was dreadfully wrong here. I Knew deep inside, from a very young age, that this was not my home. I Knew that Love, if it was really such a wonderful thing, should not be so painful - just as I Knew it was ridiculous for both sides in a war to think that God was on their side and would help them kill the enemy.

Love that is Freedom

I could feel that Love must be something much greater than I had learned growing up. If Love is so wonderful, if Love is the answer - then Love should set us Free. That is what is coming up as I write this column - Love that is Freedom. Love that is Joy. Love that is the only Truth that has ever mattered.

Love that is Freedom - what does that mean? To me it means the Freedom to be OK with being me. The Freedom to relax and enJoy the moment. The Freedom to be - just be, without having to strive, to work for, to try to reach, to prove myself, to earn Love, to get "there."

It means: Freedom from shame. Freedom from judgment. Freedom from loneliness. Freedom from feeling separate, different, not a part of, not acceptable. Freedom from the endless, aching longing for something more. Freedom from the hole in my soul - from the bottomless abyss of pain and shame and sadness that I feel at the core of my being.

This place is not my home. When I yearn for Love, I am longing to go home.

> "I was 'transported with Joy', and my 'spirit was soaring', as I danced on the rock. And in my dancing and singing I Truly understood what those expressions meant. For in being 'transported' and 'soaring' I was merely tuning into the vibrational frequency that is Joy and Love and Truth. I could see clearly now how human beings throughout history had been trying to tune into Love. The primal urge that has caused humans to attempt to 'alter their consciousness', through drugs or religion or food or meditation or whatever, is no more than an attempt to raise one's vibrational frequency. All any soul in body has ever done is to try to return home to God - we were just doing it all backwards because of the reversity of the planets energy field." - The Dance of The Wounded Souls Trilogy Book 1 "In The Beginning . . . " Chapter 4

"Humans have always been looking for a way home. For a way to connect with our Higher Consciousness. For a way to reconnect with our creator. Throughout human history, human beings have used temporary artificial means to raise their vibrational level, to try to reconnect with Higher Consciousness.

Drugs and alcohol, meditation and exercise, sex and religion, starvation and overeating, the self-torture of the flagellant or the deprivation of the hermit - all are attempts to connect with higher consciousness. Attempts to reconnect with Spiritual Self. Attempts to go home."

Part of the reason that I have had trouble in writing this column is because of the intellectual context I was approaching it from. I was thinking that I had to know what I was talking about, had to be able to communicate to you the Truth about Love. That was pretty silly of me.* Love is what I am learning about. Love is what recovery and healing are all about. Love is the goal. Love is home.

*Actually, it was my disease at work - causing me to judge and shame myself for not feeling competent to write about the True Nature of Love. This disease of codependence is so incredibly insidious, treacherous, and powerful. It continually turns back in on itself. The disease doesn't want me to take the risk of Loving and trusting my self and then it turns around and causes me to judge myself because I don't Love my self. I don't Love myself because of the disease - the ego programming that is a result of being wounded and traumatized by being Spiritually orphaned in an alien environment. By being born into and raised in an emotionally dishonest and dysfunctional, Spiritually hostile, shame based, Love mutilated (mutilate - 1. To deprive of a limb or essential part. 2. To damage or injure by the removal of an important part.) civilization on a planet where civilized societies have evolved based on the belief in separation and fear-based hostility - separation between beings, separation between humans and their environment, and separation between the flesh and the Spirit. The civilization I was raised in is so sick and twisted that it took the teachings of the Master Teacher who came into body to teach us about Love and twisted those teachings into something shameful and hate-filled. Jesus Christ carried a message of Love - not shame and judgment.

"Due to the planetary conditions, the human ego developed a belief in separation - which is what made violence possible and caused the human condition as we inherited it. The reflection of that human condition on the individual level is the disease of Codependence. Codependence is caused by the ego being traumatized and programed in early childhood so that our relationship with ourselves and the God-Force is dysfunctional - that is, it does not work to help us access the Truth of ONENESS and Love. It is through healing our relationship with ourselves that we open our inner channel and start tuning into the Truth." - Jesus & Christ Consciousness

I have only a little experience with feeling Love that sets me Free - and that has come primarily since I have been in recovery. In those moments when I am able to connect with Love in it's True form, then I feel that all of the pain and suffering has been worth the experience. Then I get a taste of what home really feels like. Then I get to feel the Joy and Truth and Love that Truly does set me Free from the illusion of separation. In those moments, I can sometimes even feel grateful for that illusion. Because without the illusion of separation from The Source Energy, from Love - I would never have gotten the opportunity to experience Love.

I am going to end this column with a continuation of the quote from my book "The Dance of Wounded Souls" which I started it with. This quote is from the very end of my book. This is my intuitive Truth. This is an important part of the understanding which has led to the beginning of my liberation from the shame. This Truth has helped me to start Loving myself a little bit - to start Loving myself enough to be Free to start believing that maybe, just maybe I am Lovable and Loved.

"The Peace and Bliss of The Eternal Now is the True Absolute Reality of the God-Force.

The illusion of separation - the distance, the separation, between the peak and the valley - is what makes motion possible. Separation is necessary for energy to be in motion. The illusion of separation was necessary to create The Illusion.

As part of the ONENESS of ALL THAT IS, we are God and God is LOVE. We are part of the Truth of ONENESS vibrating at LOVE. As part of the ONENESS of LOVE we would never have been able to experience Love. It is kind of like, "If you are sugar then you never get to taste sugar."

In God we are LOVE. Without the illusion of separation we would never have had the opportunity to experience Love. Would never have been able to Love and be Loved.

Separation was necessary to allow us the incredible gift of experiencing Love, of Loving and being Loved.

The Illusion that caused all of the pain is also the vehicle for allowing us to feel and be Loved.

If you pursue your path of healing, I think that you will find as I have that it is very much worth it. It is worth it to be able to experience Love.

This is the Age of Healing and Joy. It is time to start remembering who you Truly are, to start feeling and tuning into the Truth which exists within you.

We are all butterflies.

We are all swans.

We are Spiritual Beings.

The Springtime of the Spirit has arrived: It is possible to learn to Love yourself.

It is possible to be happy, Joyous, and free - if you are willing to be scared and hurt, angry and sad.

You are Lovable.

You are Loved.

You are LOVE."

Chapter 32 - The True Nature of Love 3: Love as a Vibrational Frequency
"Emotions are energy. Energy has a vibrational frequency."

"Truth, in my understanding, is not an intellectual concept. I believe that Truth is an emotional-energy, vibrational communication to my consciousness, to my soul/spirit - my being, from my Soul. Truth is an emotion, something that I feel within.

It is that feeling within when someone says, or writes, or sings, something in just the right words so that I suddenly feel a deeper understanding. It is that "AHA" feeling. The feeling of a light bulb going on in my head. That "Oh, I get it!" feeling. The intuitive feeling when something just feels right . . . or wrong. It's that gut feeling, the feeling in my heart. It is the feeling of something resonating within me. The feeling of remembering something that I had forgotten - but do not remember ever knowing." - Codependence: The Dance of Wounded Souls

When I first got into recovery at the beginning of 1984, I was confronted with the Twelve Step concept of a Loving Higher Power. It was a strange and foreign concept to me at the time. The concept of God that I was taught about when I was growing up was not a Loving Higher Power. There is no Unconditional Love involved with a god who could send his children to burn in hell forever - even as a child I knew there was something very wrong with that belief.

So, I set out to try to figure out a concept of God that I could believe in as an Unconditionally Loving Higher Power. In retrospect I can see that what I was doing was a paradigm shift - a shift to a larger context - that would allow me to change my relationship with God, with The Universe, into one that would work for me to help me want to live instead of wanting to kill myself. At the time I didn't think in terms of relationship dynamics, I was just trying to find some reason to stay sober.

There were two memories that my initial search was based upon. One was the memory of how strongly I had resonated with the idea that "the Force is with you." There was something that felt very True in that statement to me. The other was a thought that had come to me in certain moments of clarity in the midst of my darkest hours. That thought was: either there is a Loving Force/God behind this human life experience that I was having or there wasn't. If there was, then everything had to be unfolding perfectly - with no accidents, coincidences, or mistakes. If there wasn't - if there was no God Force, or God was punishing and judgmental - then I did not want to play anymore.

My intentional codependence recovery started with the realization of how my relationship with life was being dictated by the concept of God I was taught about as a child - and still had programmed into my subconscious belief system - instead of what I was choosing to believe on a conscious, intellectual level. Focusing on changing that subconscious programming led me into healing the emotional wounds in which that programming was rooted. Healing the emotional wounds led me into doing deep grief work which I discovered involved releasing energy. The more I became clear that emotions were actual energy that needed to flow instead of being blocked, the easier it became for me to get in touch with my emotions and open up to healing them through energy release.

(Easier in terms of aligning with the way the process really works - not easier in terms of less painful. What I did learn, was that it was easier in the long run to feel and release the pain - and anger and fear - than to keep trying to stuff it.)

Thus, one piece of the puzzle fell into place. Emotions are energy. Energy has a vibrational frequency. Anger has a higher vibrational frequency than pain or fear - thus the human defense mechanism which allows us to turn pain or fear into anger because it is has more energy mass and therefore feels empowering instead of vulnerable and weak. Much of world history becomes clearer just by understanding how humans - as part of trying to survive - have reacted to fear and pain by getting angry and acting out that anger.

Quantum Physics

Another piece of the puzzle started to fall into place when I started to read books about quantum physics.

"One of the fascinating things about the Age of Healing and Joy that has dawned in human consciousness is that the tools and knowledge that we need to raise our consciousness, to awaken to consciousness, have been unfolding in all areas of human endeavor over time, and at an accelerated rate in the last fifty to one hundred years.

One of the most fascinating things to me, and a key in my personal healing process, is in the area of physics.

Physicists have now proven through Einstein's Theory of Relativity and the study of quantum physics that everything we see is an illusion.

Einstein, in looking at a macroscopic perspective of the Universe, said in his Theory of Relativity that there are more than three dimensions. Human beings can only visualize in three dimensions. We can only see three dimensions so we have assumed that that is all there is.

Einstein also stated that time and space are not the absolute variables that science has traditionally believed them to be - that they are, in fact, a relative experience.

Quantum physics, the study of the microscopic, the subatomic world, has gone even further. Quantum physics has now proven that everything we see is an illusion, that the physical world is an illusion.

Everything is made up of interacting energy. Energy interacts on a subatomic level to form energy fields which physicists call subatomic particles. These subatomic energy fields interact to form atomic energy fields, atoms, which interact to form molecules. Everything in the physical world is made up of interacting atomic and molecular energy fields.

There is no such thing as separation in the physical world.

Energy is interacting to form a gigantic, dynamic pattern of rhythmically repeating energy interactions. In other words, a dance of energy. We are all part of a gigantic dance of energy.

This Universe is one gigantic pattern of dancing energy patterns."

The Universe is one giant dance of energy. This realization led to the title of my book: The Dance of Wounded Souls. We are all dancing energy made up of dancing energy. I realized that the reason the dance was painful and dysfunctional is that humans have been dancing to the wrong music (wrong as in not aligned with the Truth of a Loving Force.) The dance of life for humans has been grounded in shame and fear, empowered by belief in separation, lack, and scarcity. These are lower vibrational emotions and beliefs based on the three dimensional illusion that humans experience as reality. As long as the dance of humans harmonizes to music - vibrational emanations - that are rooted in shame, fear, and separation the only way to do the dance is destructively.

As I did my deep grief work and started to clear up my internal process so that I could more clearly differentiate between Truth that was a vibrational communication from my Soul and the emotional truth that was coming from my wounded soul, I was able to start trusting myself to be able to discern Truth.

"Feelings are real - they are emotional energy that is manifested in our body - but they are not necessarily fact. What we feel is our "emotional truth" and it does not necessarily have anything to do with either facts or the emotional energy that is Truth with a capital "T" - especially when we our reacting out of an age of our inner child."

"The key to healing our wounded souls is to get clear and honest in our emotional process. Until we can get clear and honest with our human emotional responses - until we change the twisted, distorted, negative perspectives and reactions to our human emotions that are a result of having been born into, and grown up in, a dysfunctional, emotionally repressive, Spiritually hostile environment - we cannot get clearly in touch with the level of emotional energy that is Truth. We cannot get clearly in touch with and reconnected to our Spiritual Self.

We, each and every one of us, has an inner channel to Truth, an inner channel to the Great Spirit. But that inner channel is blocked up with repressed emotional energy, and with twisted, distorted attitudes and false beliefs."

I was able to have a more trusting and Loving relationship with myself through getting more in touch with my Spiritual Self, my Higher Self, and through that Higher Self with God as I was coming to understand God. I was able to start having a personal, intimate relationship with my own concept of a Higher Power / God / Goddess / Great Spirit. I learned to trust the vibrational communications, the feeling of something resonating within. I was studying Quantum Physics, Molecular Biology, religion, theology, philosophy, mythology, esoteric metaphysics, science fiction - whatever was brought into my path to study. In those studies I was sorting out the wheat from the chaff - I was picking out the nuggets of Truth from the twisted, distorted beliefs they were embedded within.

I started writing a book based on what I was learning. This book was the first book of a Trilogy that was an adult fable about the history of the Universe. In that book I wrote about different vibrational levels of reality. I was writing a mystical, magical fairy tale based on a belief system that made it possible to view life as fair and Loving from a Cosmic Perspective. The Higher Power in this belief system is so powerful that everything is unfolding perfectly, with no accidents, coincidences, or mistakes. And this Higher Power is unconditionally Loving because we are part of this Higher Power - not separate from it. We have never been separate from the God Force. Every human is just a little piece of the energy of ALL THAT IS which exists in perfect ONENESS because it vibrates at the frequency of Absolute Harmony that is LOVE.

We are extensions of, manifestations of, this Higher Power temporarily in human form experiencing life in a lower vibrational illusion of three dimensional reality. We are Spiritual Beings having a human experience - not sinful, shameful humans who have to earn the Love of the Source. We are here to experience being human - to go through the school of Spiritual Evolution.

"Spiritual Evolution is the process whereby the energy of ALL THAT IS gets to experience every aspect of the illusion of existence at vibrational frequencies lower than the frequency of LOVE. Existence at the lower vibrational frequencies is experienced by energy fields of consciousness known as Souls. These Souls exist on the Spiritual Plane within the illusion. The Spiritual Plane is the highest vibrational plane, that is the vibrational plane which exists closest to the Reality of ONENESS at LOVE. It is on the Spiritual Plane that the highest vibrational frequency range naturally available to human experience is generated (by the Souls). This frequency range is the transcendent Emotional energy of Love. This Love frequency range also contains frequencies which are experienced as Truth, Joy, Beauty, and Light as well as sometimes being called; the God within, the Goddess within, the Christ within, The Holy Spirit, etc.

It is this Love frequency that is the Light that guides the energy of ALL THAT IS through the school of Spiritual Evolution. For the Soul on the Spiritual Plane projects/extends downward vibrationally to manifest the soul/Ego which exists on the Mental plane within the Temporal Plane. It is the soul/Ego which experiences the illusion of separate, unique, individual identity and projects forth (downward vibrationally) the energy field of the soul/spirit/ego which actually inhabits the human body vehicle." - The Dance of The Wounded Souls Trilogy Book 1 "In The Beginning . . . " (History I)

In this Trilogy, I found a belief system that allowed me to believe that maybe I wasn't shameful - that maybe I was Lovable. As I was writing this book, I was also doing individual therapy with people. I was teaching them how to do the grief work to change their relationship with themselves and life. I saw the Trilogy as separate from the nitty gritty inner work - until they came together. The belief system I was writing about from a Cosmic Perspective of the Human Experience suddenly meshed perfectly with the inner child work that I was teaching people and learning myself. It was perfect. It all fit together. From that coalescing of the human emotional process with the Cosmic Perspective of life came my book The Dance of Wounded Souls.

Codependence is a reflection on the individual level of the original wound of humankind - feeling abandoned by God. Feeling unlovable and unworthy and somehow shameful because of feeling separate from The Source. We are not separate from the Source - it just feels like it.

"Once upon a time, in a place where there is no time, in a place where there is no place, God was alone.

God is a great sea of living energy that has always been, and always will be. This energy field, the great sea of living energy, is ALL THAT IS in Reality. Nothing has ever existed, or ever will exist, outside of, or separate from, the energy field of ALL THAT IS.

There is no substance, no movement, no change, no time or space, in the Reality of ALL THAT IS.

There is no time because God exists in the ETERNAL NOW. For this reason God is also known as I AM.

There is no substance or space because the Masculine Energy of Manifestation does not exist in the Reality of ALL THAT IS. This energy field that is God, I AM, is composed entirely of energy which can most familiarly be referred to as Feminine Energy and can, in this the Age of Healing and Joy, properly be called The Holy Mother Source Energy.

There is no energy in motion, that is Emotional energy, within the Reality of ALL THAT IS. The Holy Mother Source Energy exists in perfect peace, stillness, and tranquility, with no movement or change because the energy of ALL THAT IS is composed entirely of what can be called Mental Energy which vibrates at the frequency of Absolute Harmony. This frequency of Absolute Harmony is called LOVE.

God is The Holy Mother Source Energy, ALL THAT IS, vibrating at the frequency of LOVE.

God is LOVE.

The Reality of existence for God, I AM, The Holy Mother Source Energy, is the ONENESS of ALL THAT IS in the Absolute Harmony of LOVE. This existence in ONENESS is experienced by the ONE consciousness of ALL THAT IS as the state of mental harmony which is Infinite Bliss. For the Truth of God is that only ONE consciousness exists in the energy of ALL THAT IS.

God is, was, and ever will be, ALL-ONE.

And God was alone.

Now it came to pass that God, being the Mental energy of living intelligence and therefore ALL-Knowing, had a brilliant idea.

This idea is so brilliant that it has allowed God to remain ALL-ONE without being alone. In other words, this ingenious concept has allowed the Eternal I AM to share consciousness of the blessing of Infinite Bliss in ONENESS without changing the Reality of ALL THAT IS. Through this idea The Holy Mother Source Energy has created children composed of the energy of ALL THAT IS for the purpose of sharing LOVE.

(This God is one smart cookie.)

For God's idea was to dream of creating a reality different from the Reality of All THAT IS. Such a dream is properly called a Creation Dream. The story you are about to read is about the Creation Dream which you are experiencing at this moment.

For you are one of the children of God." - The Dance of The Wounded Souls Trilogy Book 1 "In The Beginning . . . " (History of the Universe ~ Prologue)

Love is a vibrational frequency. It is our direct channel to The Source. When we can tune into that higher energy vibration we are closer to our True Selves. In The Goddess we are LOVE. LOVE is home. Humans have never felt comfortable in this lower vibrational illusion - we know from a very early age that something is wrong with this place. So we try to alter our consciousness - to raise our vibrational frequency.

It is not bad or wrong that you are an alcoholic or drug addict or workaholic or love addict or food addict or whatever - it is just an attempt to go home. We have felt lost and alone and not a part of - and we did whatever we could to try to transform that painful level of consciousness into a higher level. The problem was that those outside means of altering our consciousness are temporary, artificial, and self-destructive. When we look to outer or external sources that interfere with consciousness to alter our consciousness, to make us feel better, we are worshipping false gods, we are giving power to the illusion - we are not owning our True Self and our own inner channel to God.

Now that does not mean there is anything wrong with outer stimulation helping us to access Love. What is dysfunctional is focusing on the outer or external as the **source** of the Joy. We can combine our energy with a place or a person or a group of people or an animal to form a more powerful energy field which makes it easier to access the higher vibrational Source energy. What outer or external sources can do is reflect back to us the Beauty of who we really are - that is a most powerful way of accessing the Love within ourselves.

We all can do it at times. The easiest place for many of us to access this Love energy is in nature. Watching a beautiful sunset or looking out over a magnificent landscape can make it easy to access the vibrational frequency of Love, Light, Truth, Beauty, and Joy. Small children can help many of us to tune into the Love within us. Music, or other vibrational emanations such as chanting or meditation or movement, can also facilitate this connection. Perhaps in your relationship to your dog or cat or horse, you can find the space to tune into the Love within.

What all of these things - from babies to whales to dancing - have in common is that they help us to **be** in the moment. It is in the moment that we can access the Love vibrational frequency within us.

It can be relatively easy to access Love and Joy in relationship with nature. It is in our relationships with other people that it gets messy. That is because we learned how to relate to other people in childhood from wounded people who learned how to relate to other people in their childhood. In our core relationship with ourselves we don't feel Lovable. That can make it very difficult to connect with other people in a clean and energetically clear way that helps us to access Love from the Source instead of viewing the other person as the source. We are so defended, because of the pain we have experienced, that we are not open to connecting with others. If we haven't done the grief work from the past we are not open to feeling our feelings in the moment. As long as we are blocking the pain and anger and fear, we are also blocking the Love and Joy. The more we heal our emotional wounds and change our intellectual programming the more capacity we have to be in the moment and tune into the Love within.

Try whenever you think of it to be in the moment. Take a deep breath and feel the air in your lungs - get consciously present in your body in the moment. Let go of tomorrow and yesterday, and see if you can't find something in your environment that will help you to tune into the Love energy within you. This is a new age - The Age of Healing & Joy - and we have greater access to the transcendent emotional energy than ever before in recorded human history. It Truly is a time for Joy. A time to change the dance from one of suffering and endurance into one that celebrates the gift of life.

"What is so wonderful, what is so Joyous and exciting, is that we now have clearer access to our Spiritual Higher Consciousness than ever before in recorded human history. And through that Higher Self to the Universal Creative God-Force.

Each and every one of us has an inner channel. We now have the capability to atone - which means tune into - to atone, to tune into the Higher Consciousness. To tune into the Higher vibrational emotional energies that are Joy, Light, Truth, Beauty, and Love.

We can tune into the Truth of "at ONE ness." Atone = at ONE. Atonement = at ONE ment, in a condition of ONENESS.

We now have access to the highest vibrational frequencies - we can tune into the Truth of ONENESS. By aligning with Truth we are tuning into the higher energy vibrations that reconnect us with the Truth of ONENESS.

This is the age of atonement, but it does not have anything to do with judgment and punishment. It has to do with tuning our inner channel into the right frequencies.

But our inner channel is blocked and cluttered with repressed emotional energy and dysfunctional attitudes. The more we clear our inner channel through aligning with Truth attitudinally, and releasing the repressed emotional energy through the grief process, the clearer we can tune into the music of Love and Joy, Light and Truth."

Chapter 33 - The True Nature of Love 4: Energetic Clarity
"We cannot heal our fear of intimacy without feeling the feelings"

"The key to healing our wounded souls is to get clear and honest in our emotional process. Until we can get clear and honest with our human emotional responses - until we change the twisted, distorted, negative perspectives and reactions to our human emotions that are a result of having been born into, and grown up in, a dysfunctional, emotionally repressive, Spiritually hostile environment - we cannot get clearly in touch with the level of emotional energy that is Truth. We cannot get clearly in touch with and reconnected to our Spiritual Self.

We, each and every one of us, has an inner channel to Truth, an inner channel to the Great Spirit. But that inner channel is blocked up with repressed emotional energy, and with twisted, distorted attitudes and false beliefs." - Codependence: The Dance of Wounded Souls

As I say in the last chapter, relating to nature is easy - relating to other people is messy. That is because we did not learn how to have a healthy relationship with ourselves in early childhood. We have to clear up our relationship with our self in order to see our self clearly before we can start to see our relationship to other humans clearly.

And I want to make a point right at the beginning of this article (as I did in Chapter 21) that this is a gradual process of finding a **sense of balance** - not an absolute destination. The language I have to use to describe this multi-leveled, multi-faceted growth process is very limiting.

"Unfortunately, in sharing this information I am forced to use language that is polarized - that is black and white.

When I say that you cannot Truly Love others unless you Love yourself - that does not mean that you have to completely Love yourself first before you can start to Love others. The way the process works is that every time we learn to Love and accept ourselves a little tiny bit more, we also gain the capacity to Love and accept others a little tiny bit more.

When I say that you cannot start to access intuitive Truth until you clear out your inner channel - I am not saying that you have to complete your healing process before you can start getting messages. You can start getting messages as soon as you are willing to start listening. The more you heal the clearer the messages become."

So, with that qualification about the limitations of language, I am now going to try to communicate as clearly as possible how clearing our relationship with ourselves can help us to be energetically clear in our relationship with other people and with life.

Giving power away

Many of the expressions that are in common usage in the language of human interrelationship are incredibly accurate on multiple levels. One such expression is 'giving your power away.' If we are not clear in our relationship with self, if we are reacting to the definitions of self that we learned in childhood, then we are giving power away both literally and figuratively on multiple levels.

The level that most people are not aware of, and that is important for the focus of this column, is energetically. When we give power away to other people because our relationship with self is dysfunctional, we actually allow cords of energy to tie us to those people. These cords (ribbons, cables, tethers, threads, strands) of energy exist on the Etheric plane - which is where the Life Force energy runs through the chakra system.

We can literally be drained of our Life Force by these dysfunctional connections to other people. All of us learned to allow ourselves to both be drained of Life Force by others as well as to steal Life Force energy from others to survive.

We need to steal Life Force energy from others because we are blocked from clearly accessing our own Life Force energy by our dysfunctional relationship with self. Because our inner channel is not clear. In clearing up our inner channel to tune into the higher vibrational emotional energy of Light, Love, Joy, and Truth, we are also accessing our own Life Force energy. (The Life Force energy and the vibrational range of Light, Love, Joy, Truth, and Beauty are not the same thing but they are intimately interrelated.)

So, when I talk about giving our power away on an energetic level, it is an actual drain of energy, of power. Our codependence/ego defense system is set up to help us survive by trying to keep us from being drained of power at the same time it tries to steal energy from outside sources. Since we cannot clearly access the Source energy we have available to us to within, we look externally for sources of power and energy.

"If a vampire came up to you and told you that he would die if you didn't allow him to drink your blood, most likely you wouldn't have any problem telling him no. In our codependency however, when we do not know how to say no to other people, how to have healthy boundaries, we are set up to react to - and swing between - the extremes of the black and white, 1 or 10 spectrum of codependent behavior. Those extremes are: to build huge walls against connecting with other people - which sets us up to be emotional anorexics; or to offer ourselves up as sacrificial lambs to the type of codependents that are overt emotional vampires.

I say overt because all codependents are emotional vampires to one degree or another because of our emotional wounds - our emotional anorexia. And we are set up to be emotional vampires as long as we are looking outside of ourselves for self definition and self worth." - Codependency Recovery: Wounded Souls Dancing in the Light *Book 2: A Dysfunctional Relationship with Life* Chapter 8: Codependents as Emotional Vampires

Codependency is outer or external dependence. We are dependent on outer or external sources to feed us the energy we need to survive. We make people, places, and things and/or money, property and prestige the Higher Power that we look to as the source of our energy, our power.

We are attached to those things literally on an energetic level by the cords of energy that are created on the Etheric plane due to the relationship between the bodies of our being that exist on that plane - which includes our mental and emotional bodies.

(In this chapter I am going to use several quotes from my Joy2MeU Journal where much of my metaphysical writing is available. It is not necessary to understand the metaphysical in order to do the inner child healing. In fact, many people focus on the metaphysical aspects as a way of avoiding doing the emotional healing - so sometimes it is best not to get too caught up in the metaphysical.)

"The holographic illusion which is the Physical plane is composed of multiple levels of illusions. The most basic illusion within the Physical plane is that substance and separation exist. They do not. Everything in the physical universe is composed of energy. This energy interacts to form energy fields. These energy fields interact according to energy patterns to form other energy fields, which in turn interact according to energy patterns to form other energy fields, which in turn interact....etc., etc. The interaction of the One energy produces energy fields on the sub-subatomic level. These energy fields interact to produce subatomic energy fields, which in turn combine/interact to produce the energy field that we call the atom. (Remember energy fields are formed by energy vortex interaction, and atoms are are little bundles of swirling energy.) These atoms interact/combine to form the energy field that is the molecule. Molecular energy fields interact to form every type of substance/matter which humans perceive.

All energy fields are temporary effects of energy vortex interaction. (Temporary is a relative term. Physicists measure the lifetime of some subatomic particles/energy fields in quintillionths of a seconds, while the planet Earth has existed for billions of years - both are temporary.) The energy patterns which govern these interactions are also energy fields in and of themselves. For example - the individual human mind is an energy field, but it is also an energy pattern that governs the flow of communications between a humans' Spiritual being and physical being, and within the seven bodies which make up the humans' being. (The seven bodies and the mind will be discussed later. Note that attitudes in the mind can block the flow of communication from the Soul because the mind is an energy pattern.)

Each energy field vibrates at certain frequencies, and is interrelated and interdependent with all other energy fields. Each letter in this sentence is an energy field composed of energy fields vibrating at certain frequencies, each combination of letters that forms a word, each combination of words that forms a sentence, etc., etc., etc. (Millions of atoms can go into making up a single letter - aren't you glad you asked.) Each word, each concept, each idea, is an energy field interacting according to energy patterns that are energy fields.

(Get the point? The bottom line is that nothing is what it appears to be. You are made up of the same subatomic, atomic, and molecular energy as the chair you are sitting in and the air you are breathing. Just bring to consciousness for a moment the fact that your physical body vehicle is composed of an uncountable number of energy fields interacting according to energy patterns. Just to imagine the number of energy fields interacting within your physical body at this moment is overwhelming. Now think of the number of energy fields and energy patterns that come into play when dealing with something outside of yourself, and then of course there is your emotional body and your mental body, etc. - and you wonder why relationships are so hard.) - The Dance of the Wounded Souls Trilogy Book 1 - "In The Beginning . . ." History of the Universe Part V

The fact that the mind is an energy field that is also an energy pattern of interaction is very important to realize. Communication from within (both internally between different parts of our being and from our spirit/Soul/Higher Power) and without - stimulation from our environment and everything/everyone in it - flows through the energy field that is the mind to our being.

Our experiential reality is determined by the interpretations of our mind - by the intellectual paradigm which we are using to define / determine / translate / explain our reality. The attitudes, definitions, and belief systems which we hold mentally dictate our emotional reactions. Attitudes, definitions, and beliefs determine perspective and expectation - which in turn dictates our relationships. Our relationships to our self, to life, to other people, to The God-Force / Goddess Energy / Great Spirit. Our relationships to our own emotions, bodies, gender, etc., are dictated by the attitudes, definitions, and beliefs that we are holding mentally / intellectually. And we acquired those mental constructs / ideas / concepts in early childhood from the emotional experiences, intellectual teachings, and role modeling of the beings around us. If we have not done our emotional healing so that we can get in touch with our subconscious intellectual programming then we are still reacting to that early childhood programming / intellectual paradigm even though we may not be aware of it consciously.

"The Truth is that the intellectual value systems, the attitudes, that we use in deciding what's right and wrong were not ours in the first place. We accepted on a subconscious and emotional level the values that were imposed on us as children. Even if

we throw out those attitudes and beliefs intellectually as adults, they still dictate our emotional reactions. Even if, especially if, we live our lives rebelling against them. By going to either extreme - accepting them without question or rejecting them without consideration - we are giving power away."

"It was impossible to start Loving myself and trusting myself, impossible to start finding some peace within, until I started to change my perspective of, and my definitions of, who I was and what emotions it was okay for me to feel.

Enlarging my perspective means changing my definitions, the definitions that were imposed on me as a child about who I am and how to do this life business. In Recovery it has been necessary to change my definitions of, and my perspective of, almost everything. That was the only way that it was possible to start learning how to Love myself.

I spent most of my life feeling like I was being punished because I was taught that God was punishing and that I was unworthy and deserved to be punished. I had thrown out those beliefs about God and life on a conscious, intellectual level in my late teens - but in Recovery I was horrified to discover that I was still reacting to life emotionally based on those beliefs.

I realized that my perspective of life was being determined by beliefs that I had been taught as a child even though they were not what I believed as an adult."

"I went home to do some writing and was pretty amazed at what it revealed. I realized that I was still reacting to life out of the religious programming of my childhood - even though I had thrown out that belief system on a conscious, intellectual level in my late teens and early twenties. The writing that I did that night helped me to recognize that my emotional programming was dictating my relationship with life even though it was not what I consciously believed.

I realized that the belief that "life was about sin and punishment and I was a sinner who deserved to be punished" was running my life. When I felt "bad" or "bad" things happened to me - I tried to blame it on others to keep from realizing how much I was hating myself for being flawed and defective, a sinner. When I felt good or good things happened I was holding my breath because I knew it would be taken away because I didn't deserve it. Often when things got too good I would sabotage it because I couldn't stand the suspense of waiting for god to take it away - which "he" would because I didn't deserve it.

I could suddenly see that I had been playing a game, with that punishing god I learned about in childhood, for all of my adult life. I tried not to show that I enjoyed or valued anything too much so that maybe god wouldn't notice and take it away. In other words, I could never relax and be in the moment in Joy or peace because the moment I showed that I was enjoying life god would step in to punish me." - Joy2MeU Journal Premier issue The Story of "Joy to You & Me"

We cannot get clearly in touch with the subconscious programming without doing the grief work. The subconscious intellectual programming is tied to the emotional wounds we suffered and many years of suppressing those feelings has also buried the attitudes, definitions, and beliefs that are connected to those emotional wounds. It is possible to get intellectually aware of some of them through such tools as hypnosis, or having a therapist or psychic or energy healer tell us they are there - but we cannot really understand how much power they carry without feeling the emotional context - and cannot change them without reducing the emotional charge / releasing the emotional energy tied to them. Knowing they are there will not make them go away.

A good example of how this works is a man that I worked with some years ago. He came to me in emotional agony because his wife was leaving him. He was adamant that he did not want a divorce and kept saying how much he loved his wife and how he could not stand to lose his family (he had a daughter about 4.) I told him the first day he came in that the pain he was suffering did not really have that much to do with his wife and present situation - but was rooted in some attitude from his childhood. But that did not mean anything to him on a practical level, on a level of being able to let go of the attitude that was causing him so much pain. It was only while doing his childhood grief work that he got in touch with the pain of his parents divorce when he was 10 years old. In the midst of doing that grief work the memory of promising himself that he would never get a divorce, and cause his child the kind of pain he was experiencing, surfaced. Once he had gotten in touch with, and released, the emotional charge connected to the idea of divorce, he was able to look at his present situation more clearly. Then he could see that the marriage had never been a good one - that he had sacrificed himself and his own needs from the beginning to comply with his dream / concept of what a marriage should be. He could then see that staying in the marriage was not serving him or his daughter. Once he got past the promise he made to himself in childhood, he was able to let go of his wife and start building a solid relationship with his daughter based on the reality of today instead of the grief of the past.

It was the idea / concept of his wife, of marriage, that he had been unable to let go of - not the actual person. By changing his intellectual concept / belief, he was able to get clear on what the reality of the situation was and sever the emotional energy chains / cords that bound him to the situation and to his wife. He was then able to let go of giving away power over his self-esteem (part of his self-esteem was based on keeping his promise to himself) to a situation / person that he could not control. He gained the wisdom / clarity to discern the difference between what he had some power to change and what he needed to accept. He could not change his wife's determination to get a divorce but he could change his attitude toward that divorce - once he changed the subconscious emotional programming connected to the concept.

Falling in love with a dream

It is letting go of the dream, the idea / concept, of the relationship that causes the most grief in every relationship break up that I have ever worked with. We give power and energy to the mental construct of what we want the relationship to be and cannot even begin to see the situation and the other person clearly.

Far too often - because of the concept of toxic / addictive love we are taught in this society - it is the idea of the other person that we fall in love with, not the actual person. It is so important to us to cast someone in the role of Prince or Princess that we focus on who we want them to be - not on who they really are. In our relationship with our self, we attach so much importance to getting the relationship that we are dishonest with ourselves

- and with the other person - in order to manifest the dream / concept of relationship that will fix us / make our life worthwhile. Then we end up feeling like a victim when the other person does not turn out to be the person we wanted.

"A white knight is not going to come charging up to rescue us from the dragon. A princess is not going to kiss us and turn us from a frog into a prince. The Prince and the Princess and the Dragon are all within us. It is not about someone outside of us rescuing us. It is also not about some dragon outside of us blocking our path. As long as we are looking outside to become whole we are setting ourselves up to be victims. As long as we are looking outside for the villain we are buying into the belief that we are the victim.

As little kids we were victims and we need to heal those wounds. But as adults we are volunteers - victims only of our disease. The people in our lives are actors and actresses whom we cast in the roles that would recreate the childhood dynamics of abuse and abandonment, betrayal and deprivation."

The attitude / dream / concept that has all the power is internal - it is not really about the other person. All of our emotional responses to life are based upon an internal relationship with our own intellectual paradigm / belief system / definitions. Other people are actually actors that we cast in the roles of the movie that we are projecting from our own mind. The foundation for what kind of movie we are making was laid in childhood due to our emotional wounds. If we want to change the quality of the movie, we need to get to the subconscious attitudes by grieving / clearing the emotional energy. Then we can change the music we are dancing to in our relationship with life and with other people.

Now, you have probably noticed that I have shifted from the metaphysical level back down to the practical level here - I am sorry if this is confusing. It can be difficult to speak about multiple levels simultaneously, but I find it necessary because it is so important to actually do the healing and not just get caught up in the intellectual gymnastics of trying to figure it all out.

The real point that I am trying to make here is that the healing process is an inside job. No one outside of you can drain you of energy, or exert power over you, unless it fits into the intellectual paradigm that your emotional wounds have set you up for. The cords / chains / threads of energy that connect us to other people connect us because of our beliefs. By changing the beliefs we can disconnect from the unhealthy linkage we have to other people. We can then learn how to connect energetically in ways that are healthy and Loving - We can learn the difference between healthy interdependence (which involves giving some power away over our feelings) and codependence.

"Codependence and interdependence are two very different dynamics.

Codependence is about giving away power over our self-esteem. . . .

Interdependence is about making allies, forming partnerships. It is about forming connections with other beings. Interdependence means that we give someone else some power over our welfare and our feelings.

Anytime we care about somebody or something we give away some power over our feelings. It is impossible to Love without giving away some power. When we choose to Love someone (or thing - a pet, a car, anything) we are giving them the power to make us happy - we cannot do that without also giving them the power to hurt us or cause us to feel angry or scared.

In order to live we need to be interdependent. We cannot participate in life without giving away some power over our feelings and our welfare. I am not talking here just about people. If we put money in a bank we are giving some power over our feelings and welfare to that bank. If we have a car we have a dependence on it and will have feelings if it something happens to it. If we live in society we have to be interdependent to some extent and give some power away. The key is to be conscious in our choices and own responsibility for the consequences.

The way to healthy interdependence is to be able to see things clearly - to see people, situations, life dynamics and most of all ourselves clearly. If we are not working on healing our childhood wounds and changing our childhood programming then we cannot begin to see ourselves clearly let alone anything else in life. "- Chapter 9 Interdependent, not codependent

We can have healthy ties / threads / cords of energy connecting us to other people but only by learning to see ourselves clearly. As long as our self definition is enmeshed with other people's attitudes and behaviors, we are incapable of making True choices about our own best interests. Until we start seeing ourselves clearly, we will continue to be energetically drawn to people who will recreate our childhood emotional wounds.

"3. Our emotions tell us who we are - our Soul communicates with us through emotional energy vibrations. Truth is an emotional energy vibrational communication from our Soul on the Spiritual Plane to our being/spirit/soul on this physical plane - it is something that we feel in our heart/our gut, something that resonates within us.

Our problem has been that because of our unhealed childhood wounds it has been very difficult to tell the difference between an intuitive emotional **Truth** and the **emotional truth** that comes from our childhood wounds. When one of our buttons is pushed and we react out of the insecure, scared little kid inside of us (or the angry/rage filled kid, or the powerless/helpless kid, etc.) then we are reacting to what our emotional truth was when we were 5 or 9 or 14 - not to what is happening now. Since we have been doing that all of our lives, we learned not to trust our emotional reactions (and got the message not to trust them in a variety of ways when we were kids.)

4. We are attracted to people that **feel familiar on an energetic level** - which means (until we start clearing our emotional process) people that emotionally / vibrationally feel like our parents did when we were very little kids. At a certain point in my process I realized that if I met a woman who **felt** like my soul mate, that the chances were pretty huge that she was one more unavailable woman that fit my pattern of being attracted to someone who would reinforce the message that I wasn't good enough, that I was unlovable. Until we start releasing the hurt, sadness, rage, shame, terror - the emotional grief energy - from our childhoods we will keep having dysfunctional relationships." - Feeling the Feelings

It does not make any difference what our conscious intellectual beliefs are as long as we are reacting energetically to old programming. That is why it is so vital to do the emotional healing. In order to clear our emotional body of the repressed emotional energy so that we can change the intellectual paradigm that is embedded in our mental body / mind, it is necessary to do the emotional healing. All of the intellectual knowledge of Spiritual Truth and healthy relationship behavior that we can acquire will not significantly transform the behavioral patterns that are being driven by the subconscious programming. We cannot heal our fear of intimacy so that we can open up to receiving Love without feeling the feelings.

"This grieving is not an intellectual process. Changing our false and dysfunctional attitudes is vital to the process; enlarging our intellectual perspective is absolutely necessary to the process, but doing these things does not release the energy - it does not heal the wounds.

Learning what healthy behavior is will allow us to be healthier in the relationships that do not mean much to us; intellectually knowing Spiritual Truth will allow us to be more Loving some of the time; but in the relationships that mean the most to us, with the people we care the most about, when our "buttons are pushed" we will watch ourselves saying things we don't want to say and reacting in ways that we don't want to react - because we are powerless to change the behavior patterns without dealing with the emotional wounds.

We cannot integrate Spiritual Truth or intellectual knowledge of healthy behavior into our experience of life in a substantial way without honoring and respecting the emotions. We cannot consistently incorporate healthy behavior into day to day life without being emotionally honest with ourselves. We cannot get rid of our shame and overcome our fear of emotional intimacy without going through the feelings.

Walking around saying "We are all one," and "God is Love," and "I forgive them all," does not release the energy. Using crystals, or white light, or being born again does not heal the wounds, and does not fundamentally alter the behaviors.

We are all ONE and God is LOVE; crystals do have power and white light is a very valuable tool, but we need to not confuse the intellectual with the emotional (forgiving someone intellectually does not make the energy of anger and pain disappear) - and to not kid ourselves that using the tools allows us to avoid the process.

There is no quick fix! Understanding the process does not replace going through it! There is no magic pill, there is no magic book, there is no guru or channeled entity that can make it possible to avoid the journey within, the journey through the feelings.

No one outside of Self (True, Spiritual Self) is going to magically heal us.

There is not going to be some alien E.T. landing in a spaceship singing, "Turn on your heart light," who is going to magically heal us all.

The only one who can turn on your heart light is you."

And, of course, the way we turn on our heart light is to tune into the energy, the power, of the Transcendent emotional energy of Love, Light, Joy, Truth, and Beauty. We need to open up to receiving Love - and we cannot do that without changing our relationship with the child who we were.

"It is necessary to own and honor the child who we were in order to Love the person we are. And the only way to do that is to own that child's experiences, honor that child's feelings, and release the emotional grief energy that we are still carrying around."

"A "state of Grace" is the condition of being Loved unconditionally by our Creator without having to earn that Love. We are Loved unconditionally by the Great Spirit. What we need to do is to learn to accept that state of Grace.

The way we do that is to change the attitudes and beliefs within us that tell us that we are not Lovable. And we cannot do that without going through the black hole. The black hole that we need to surrender to traveling through is the black hole of our grief. The journey within - through our feelings - is the journey to knowing that we are Loved, that we are Lovable."

The healing process is an inside job.

The relationship I need to heal is between me and me. Everything in my lesson plan / life experience is there for me to learn from so that I can heal my relationship with me. All the people who play a significant role in my life are teachers reflecting back to me some aspect of my relationship with my self - with my humanity, with my emotions, with my sexuality, with whatever - that needs healing. Through healing my relationship with me I am owning and honoring my connection to everything.

There is nothing wrong with who we are - it is our relationship to our self that is so messed up. We are all Spiritual Beings having a human experience. We all have Divine worth as children of The Source. We are all perfect parts of The Source. In our relationship with ourselves on this level we need to learn to open up to receiving the Love that is our True state of being - that is why we are here. To heal so that we can reconnect with Love.

It was impossible for me to start to get clear energetically in my relationships with others and life until I started to have boundaries that told me where I ended and other people began. As long as I believed that I was responsible for other people's feelings and behavior I could not start seeing myself clearly. As long as I was looking to other people for the juice / energy / power to feel OK about myself, I was set up to be a victim and recreate the old patterns.

This is The big paradigm shift. Shifting our intellectual paradigm - our attitudes, definitions, and beliefs - is necessary in order to raise our consciousness and open up to consciously accessing the Transcendent vibrational energy of Love, Light, Joy, and Truth. I had to stop looking outside for the answers and start accessing the Truth within. Only when I started to open up to the idea that perhaps, maybe, I was Lovable and worthy in a way that was not dependent on outside or external conditions, could I start to let go of defining myself in reaction to other people and other peoples belief systems.

In order to get clear on how to connect to others in a healthy way we must first realize and define how we are separate from others. On the level of our physical being, our ego-self, we are separate and need to own that before we can open up to consciously experiencing how we are connected to everyone and everything. We need to see our relationship with ourselves clearly in order to see our relationships to others clearly.

One of the things that I had to get clear on in order to start learning who I am was selfishness. I had been taught that it was bad to be selfish and that I should do things for others. I learned to steal energy from others through what I was telling myself were unselfish acts. I was just being a "nice guy" and did not expect anything in return - Bull. I always had expectations - I just was not being honest with myself about them - because I had been trained and conditioned in childhood to be dishonest with myself emotionally and intellectually.

I had to come to a realization that there is no such thing as an unselfish act. If I rescue a stranger from a burning car wreck, it does not have anything to do with the stranger - it has to do with my relationship with myself. I believe that every thing a human being does has a pay off - and it was a very important part of my growth process to start looking for those pay offs. I had to learn to get honest with myself and stop buying into the illusion that anything I did was for some one else. I had to stop looking outside for the energy boost I got from doing something nice so that I could own that the energy boost came internally.

The power / energy / juice that we need comes from within - not from outside. People, places, and things can sometimes help us to access the power that is within us - but they are not the source of that power. The source is within!

It has always come from within - we were just trained to look outside for it because of the reversity of the planets energy field of emotional consciousness has caused human beings to do human backwards. Codependence is a disease of reversed focus - looking externally for that which is available within us.

"Codependence is also a disease of reversed focus - it is about focusing outside of ourselves for self-definition and self-worth. That sets us up to be a victim. We have worth because we are Spiritual Beings not because of how much money or success we have - or how we look or how smart we are. When self-worth is dertermined by looking ourside it means we have to look down on someone else to feel good about ourselves - this is the cause of bigotry, racism, class structure, and Jerry Springer.

The goal is to focus on who we really are - get in touch with the Light and Love within us and then radiate that ourward. I think that is what Mother Theresa did - I can't know for sure because I never met her and it can be difficult to tell looking from the outside where a persons focus is - Mother Theresa could have been a raging codependent who was doing good on the outside in order to feel good about herself - or she could have been being True to her Self by accessing the Love and Light within and reflecting outward. Either way the effect was that she did some great things - the difference would have been how she felt about herself at the deepest levels of her being - because it does not make any real difference how much validation we get from ourside if we are not Loving ourselves. If I did not start working on knowing that I had worth as a Spiritual Being - that there is a Higher Power that Loves me - it would never have made any real difference how many people told me I was wonderful." - Question & Answer Page 2

The relationship I need to heal is between me and me. Everything in my lesson plan / life experience is there for me to learn from so that I can heal my relationship with me (which will heal the Karma I need to settle.) All the people who play a significant role in my life are teachers reflecting back to me some aspect of my relationship with my self - with my humanity, with my emotions, with my sexuality, with whatever - that needs healing. Through healing my relationship with me I am owning and honoring my connection to everything.

There is nothing wrong with who we are - it is our relationship to our self that is messed up. We are all Spiritual Beings having a human experience. We all have Divine worth as children of The Source. We are all perfect parts of The Source. In our relationship with ourselves on this level we need to learn to open up to receiving / accessing the Love that is our True state of being - that is why we are here. To heal so that we can reconnect with Love.

We can have healthy ties / threads / cords of energy connecting us to other people but only by learning to see ourselves clearly. As long as our self definition is enmeshed with other people's attitudes and behaviors, we are incapable of making True choices about our own best interests. Until we start seeing ourselves clearly, we will continue to be energetically drawn to people who will recreate our childhood emotional wounds.

"Both the classic codependent patterns and the classic counterdependent patterns are behavioral defenses, strategies, design to protect us from the devastating pain and debilitating shame of being abandoned because we are flawed, because we are not good enough, not worthy and lovable. One tries to protect against abandonment by avoiding confrontation and pleasing the other - while the second tries to avoid abandonment by pretending we don't need anyone else. Both are dysfunctional and dishonest." - Codependent & Counterdependent Behavior

On an energetic level, abandonment means feeling like we have been unplugged from our energy source. Abandonment feels life-threatening because the cords that bind us to other people, and feed us Life Force energy, gets unplugged and we do not know how to access that energy for ourselves. That is why it is so important to learn to plug in internally, access the Transcendent emotional energy of Love, Light, Joy, and Truth that is available to us within.

It is very important for us to learn to let go of our unhealthy attachments to other people and outside sources so that we can access the power from the Source that is available within. Learning how to define ourselves as separate, how to have boundaries that tell us who we are as individuals, is a vital step in starting to see ourselves with more clarity so that we can see others and life with more clarity.

And once again here, I want to make the point that clarity with our self is not an absolute destination. This healing is a gradual process of finding a sense of balance - a sense of what clarity feels like, so that we can look for and recognize when we have it and when we do not. In order to do that it is vital to learn how to be emotionally honest with ourselves so that we can be discerning in our relationship with our own mental and emotional process. Through that honesty we will achieve some energetic clarity as well.

Through that energetic clarity we will be able to access Love from the Source - and we will learn to Love and trust our Self to guide our self through this boarding school that is life as a human.

Chapter 34 - The True Nature of Love 5, Twin Souls, Souls Mates, and Kindred Spirits
"We are all more connected than we are different."

"Quantum physics has now proven that everything we see is an illusion, that the physical world is an illusion.

Everything is made up of interacting energy. Energy interacts on a subatomic level to form energy fields which physicists call subatomic particles. These subatomic energy fields interact to form atomic energy fields, atoms, which interact to form molecules. Everything in the physical world is made up of interacting atomic and molecular energy fields.

There is no such thing as separation in the physical world.

Energy is interacting to form a gigantic, dynamic pattern of rhythmically repeating energy interactions. In other words, a dance of energy. We are all part of a gigantic dance of energy.

This Universe is one gigantic pattern of dancing energy patterns." - Codependence: The Dance of Wounded Souls

"You are together because you resonate on the same wave lengths, you fit together vibrationally, in such a way that together you form a powerful energy field that helps both of you access the Higher Vibrational Energy of Love, Joy, Light, and Truth - in a way that would be very difficult for either one of you to do by yourself. You are coming together to touch the face of God. You are uniting your energies to help you access the Love of the Holy Mother Source Energy.

You are not the source of each other's Love. You are helping each other to access the LOVE that is the Source." - Chapter 20 Meditation on Romantic Commitment

As I have stated previously in this series, some of the expressions in our language are very accurate when applied to the energetic level of interaction. One of those expressions is about being on the "same wave length" with another person. Since the whole Universe and everything in it is a dance of energy interaction, it follows that there is such a thing as vibrational connection - such a thing as being more on the "same wave length" with some people than with others.

We are all more connected than we are different. As human beings, we share a basic emotional process that is the same for all of us. We share connections with other human beings that can allow us to feel on the same wave length with any human being in the right circumstances. We can watch a television show about someone who is completely different from us in terms of race, culture, language, etc. - and still resonate with them emotionally in a moment of tragedy, or triumph. Someone from our home town, who we might pass on the street without a second thought in the normal course of daily life, becomes a kindred spirit when we meet them in a foreign country.

Our relationship with a certain subject can cause us to feel a connection to someone else - because of their similar relationship with that concept or group or thing. Some examples: fishing or dogs or skiing or an athletic team or a specific cause or a certain philosophy, etc. Every human being on the planet is someone who we could feel connected to - feel on the same wave length with - in the right circumstances in relationship to some shared feeling, interest, and/or experience.

We are all kindred spirits in terms of our humanity - in terms of our relationship to the horizontal human experience. We are all kindred spirits with more connection than differences without even taking the vertical - the Spiritual relationship - into consideration.

"Codependence and recovery are both multi-leveled, multi-dimensional phenomena. . . . No facet of this topic is linear and one-dimensional, so there is no simple answer to any one question - rather there are a multitude of answers to the same question, all of which are True on some level. . . . . I am going to make a brief point about two dimensions of this phenomena in relationship to empowerment. These two dimensions are the horizontal and the vertical. In this context the horizontal is about being human and relating to other humans and our environment. The vertical is Spiritual - about our relationship to the God-Force." - Empowerment

(When talking about Spiritual relationships as vertical, I am referring to a dynamic up and down the vibrational scale - higher and lower vibrational frequencies. I am not talking about the higher vibrational frequencies as if they exist in some Heaven in the heavens, up in the sky somewhere. It would be just as accurate to refer to this dynamic as from within to without since each of us is an outward manifestation of the Source that is within us. All of the levels in the following discussion could also be referred to as coming from within outward. None of this exists outside of us - it exists within us.)

Metaphysical and Mystical

So, this brings us to the more Metaphysical and Mystical aspects of this article. I get uncomfortable in writing about my understanding of levels that are beyond human understanding for numerous reasons. The biggest one is that it is not really possible to explain the unexplainable. It is also not necessary to understand the metaphysical levels in order to do the healing. And as I have mentioned previously, some of us tend to focus on such areas as metaphysics, past lives, astrology, extrasensory or extraterrestrial phenomena as a way of avoiding doing the emotional healing - as a way of avoiding healing our internal relationship with self. Focusing on some of these areas can sometimes be almost as addictive as focusing on other people, or success, or any of the myriad of people, places and things that our disease would rather have us focus on than to deal with our own pain.

And my interpretation of these levels/phenomena/issues is just that - my interpretation. Anyone who is serving as a channel for information is limited by their own intellectual/experiential paradigm. Whether the person is psychic, or an astrologer, or channeling information from "beyond," whatever, it is always important to not give too much power to the details of what they say. Listen for any emotional messages that resonate - but be discerning about giving too much power to their interpretations in regard to details. What one person attributes to an angel another might attribute to an alien presence. Whether something is written in the stars or a theme from a past life doesn't really matter. What matters are questions like: How does this information apply to my healing process today?; How can this message help me see myself more clearly?; Can the information help me to forgive myself and be more Loving to myself?; Is the information and the way it is being presented about Love - does it support Love or is it empowering separation?

I didn't really start to investigate any of these areas until after I had been through treatment for codependence in the Spring of 1988. The day before I left the treatment center one of my counselors told me that I was a mystic. I had to look the word up in the dictionary.

> mystic - n. One who professes a knowledge of spiritual truth or a feeling of union with the divine, reached through contemplation or intuition. (New Illustrated Webster's Dictionary, 1993 printing.)

That person was an angel in my path because she stimulated me to create the space in my consciousness to be open to a different kind of inner communication. It was as if she had given me permission to own a gift that had become available to me because of the clearing of my inner channel that I had done/was doing - and shortly thereafter I started writing the first book of my Trilogy. I very seriously pursued learning about past lives and different planes of existence and all of the esoteric, metaphysical knowledge I could access. And that pursuit was important in helping me to enlarge my intellectual paradigm - but a few years later I realized that the whole purpose of the pursuit had been to bring about a shift in my relationship with myself, my concept of God/Goddess, and with life. The details that I had accessed about past lives and other dimensions of existence were not really important in terms of how I live my life today - but the shift in my paradigm, and therefore my relationships, was vital. At that point in time, I threw away all the notes I had taken about different past lives and such.

The whole purpose of my quest was to discover a belief system that could allow me to start believing that I am in fact Lovable and worthy. Figuring out how it all works isn't what is important - what is important is discovering the faith to believe that there is a Loving Force in control. That is what helped me start Loving myself more - to start relaxing and enjoying life a little bit more instead of always giving fear and shame all of the power.

So, anything in terms of details, that I share here are my interpretations. The interpretations that helped me to discover a belief system that served Love - that was functional in helping me to overcome the dysfunctional beliefs I was programmed with in childhood. That they may be different from someone else's interpretations does not mean that one is right and one is wrong. There are a plethora of ways to look at and interpret information which is beyond human understanding. Any explaining or defining of God is limiting - and the Goddess is unlimited.

The purpose of sharing this at all, is the hope it may help you to enlarge your intellectual paradigm - help you to build yourself a larger Spiritual container so that you can open up to accessing more Love in your life.

My quest to find some rational, logical way to explain how it is possible that there exists a Loving Higher Power when all around me I saw suffering and despair, unfairness and injustice, lead me to belief in reincarnation. I could see no way that life could be ultimately Loving if we only experienced one lifetime.

"We have all lived multiple lifetimes. We have all experienced every facet of being human.

We are now not just healing our wounds from this lifetime, we are doing Karmic settlement on a massive scale, at a very accelerated rate."

"The term "old-soul" refers to the stage of consciousness evolution an individual has attained by this lifetime - it does not mean better than, or farther along than, those who do not have to do the healing. There is no hierarchy in the Truth of a Loving Great Spirit. Those who appear to have low, or no, consciousness in this lifetime are simply doing their healing in another space-time illusion parallel to this one. All old-souls are born at a heart-chakra level of consciousness and therefore have more sensitivity, and less capacity for denial, than other people. In other words, the gift of having access to Truth and Love carries with it the price of greatly increased emotional sensitivity." - Christ Consciousness

(One of the problems of writing something like this, is that I have to write this as if this may be the first thing a person reads on my web site. I can't take for granted for instance, that they know what I mean when I use the term old soul. Including all the quotes from other writings makes this article that much longer - and I am going to try to limit the quotes for the remainder of this one.)

In regard to past lives, my information is that all old souls have lived in the neighborhood of 150 lifetimes on this planet in this Creation Dream. Someone I respect recently shared with me some information that he was getting through a person that was accessing the Akashic Record under hypnosis. This person believed that he has had 19 past lives. My interpretation of this is that those are the major lives in relationship to either Karmic settlement and/or the issues that need healing in this lifetime - not the total number of lives.

(Again, anyone serving as a channel is interpreting through their own paradigm - even if it is not a conscious paradigm. And the Akashic Record in my understanding is not only the record of everything that has ever happened on the planet - but also includes the energy of every word spoken and every thought! A lot of information in other words. And I am not sure it is indexed all that clearly. ;-)

When you do the math, you can see that 150 lifetimes - even if you figure an average life span of 35 years, which is highly unlikely due to death in childhood and the reality that for much of the history of the planet life expectancy was in the 30s - you are still talking about only a little over 5000 years out of 66,000. So, it seems to be a reasonable and logical number to me.

And I mention this number now because it relates to my understanding regarding the phenomena of twin souls and soul mates.

"From my earliest memories in this lifetime I had experienced her occasional presence in my dreams. I have never been able to retain a clear visual image of her upon awakening, but the echo of the memory of how it felt to be with her has been with me always. I very rarely brought it to conscious awareness, or spent time thinking about her, but the sensation of her haunted me. I would catch myself looking for her as I walked down a street or shopped in a store - anywhere and everywhere. The looking was seldom a conscious process - it was almost as if some part of my deepest being was always watching, always waiting.

When I began my recovery process, my healing, it had been necessary for me to become conscious of the dysfunctional attitudes I had learned about relationships in childhood. That was when I became aware that on some levels my "looking for her" was about the 'princess and frog' syndrome. That is, the false belief that I needed a princess to love me before I could be whole. It was society's reversed perspective on life that had led me to believe that someone outside of myself was necessary to full-fill me. That attitude is dysfunctional because it is a set-up. As long as I was giving other people the power to make me whole, I was doomed to be a victim.

Once I started to erase the 'old tapes' about needing some 'her' to make me okay, I started to awaken to the Truth that Spiritually I am a prince. I started to realize that only through healing my wounded soul could I become conscious of my wholeness. When I committed myself to Spiritual purpose and growth, and let go of the false belief that I needed some one else to 'fix' me, then I realized that only in health and wholeness could I Truly give myself in a relationship. Only by learning to access Love for myself could I share that Love with another person.

It was after I accepted that I was the only person who could 'fix' me, that I became aware of a deeper level from which the 'looking for her' impulse originated. I started to understand how humans have attempted to apply Spiritual Truths to physical existence, and how confused we had become because of this reversed thinking. That was when I realized that, although the levels of thinking that I had to find 'her' to be whole were dysfunctional, there was a deeper level where the impulse came out of Truth. That Truth was that my soul was looking for it's other half. The polarization of the lower mind, and subsequent reversal of the Earths energy field of emotional consciousness, had caused my twin soul and I to be torn apart sixty-six thousand years ago. I came to realize that an important part of the evolutionary process was the awakening of my soul to wholeness so that my twin soul and I could be reunited. And that our reunion was not necessary for becoming whole - but rather that becoming conscious of wholeness, of Oneness within, was necessary for that reunion to take place." - The Dance of The Wounded Souls Trilogy Book 1 "In The Beginning . . . ' Chapter 9

"What I know is that you two have been together many times before in other life times. You made a sacred pact to come together in this lifetime to help each other heal the wounds you need to heal - to serve as teachers and guides and support for each other as you go through this school of Spiritual evolution that we are all in.

It doesn't matter what you call that - twin souls, soul mates, whatever - what matters is that you honor the power of the connection that you feel." - Wedding Prayer/Meditation on Romantic Commitment

Now, to look at the vertical/Spiritual interaction dynamic of this Illusion which we are experiencing. I am not going to go into a detailed discussions of the different planes of existence in this article. I will just say that on the highest levels we are all ONE. The energy of consciousness is projected outward (downward vibrationally) from the Source. It passes through the level of Cosmic or Christ Consciousness as One emanation. We are all one in Christ Consciousness. It then is projected into the next level which is the Archangelic plane. The emanation becomes 12 different vibrational manifestations on the Archangelic plane. These are the 12 tribes of human kind.

The projection then proceeds downward into the Angelic plane where it again multiplies by a factor of 12. These are 144 tributary tribes. It keeps flowing downward in multiples of 12 - and that is enough about that, right now.

We are all one at the Highest levels. At the lower levels we are more closely related vibrationally to other beings who are extensions of the Source through the vibrational stream that is our tribe. We are even more closely related to those who are members/emanations of our tributary tribe.

As has been stated, all humans are our kindred spirits on multiple levels. For this particular discussion however, the term Kindred Spirit refers to those who are the closest relations to us vibrationally - on the same wave length - and of those there are 144.

Everyone is a member of a clan of 144 Kindred Spirits - related more closely to but still flowing out of the ONE Source that feeds all. Not only are we more closely related vibrationally to these souls - but they are the ones that have been present in multiple lifetimes in our Spiritual evolutionary process. Out of the 144 Kindred Spirits in your vibrational clan - 143 + you - there are 3 to 5 Kindred Spirits who you have spent a high percentage of romantic lifetimes with. These are your Soul Mates. (I believe that having 20 romantic lifetimes with another soul is a great deal.)

All old souls also have a Twin Soul who they were split from because of the polarization of the Energy Field of Collective Intellectual Consciousness / The Lower Mind. That Twin Soul also is part of a clan of 144 Kindred Spirits who are almost as closely related vibrationally to you as your own Kindred Spirits.

My information is that we have had very few lifetimes with our Twin Soul. I believe that I have had only 3 lifetimes in which my Twin Soul was in body with me - and we had a relationship to each other. So, meeting my Twin Soul will be a very different feeling from meeting a Soul Mate who I have had 20 lifetimes with. The feeling of familiarity will be quite different. (That is why, in my Romantic Adventure I thought the person might be my Twin Soul. She felt familiar in a very powerful way - but not familiar as in someone that I had known through many lifetimes.)

What matters is to start seeing life in a much bigger picture. When I started to understand how Karma worked, and how large a picture this puzzle of life is - that is when it became easier to forgive myself for my past. I could start really seeing (and believing / remembering / having faith even when I couldn't see) that everything happens for reasons in alignment with Divine Purpose. That there are no mistakes, no accidents, no coincidences. The God-Force/Goddess Energy/Great Spirit is so powerful that everything is unfolding perfectly - which means that ultimately everything serves Divine Purpose. And since The Universal Source is LOVE, and we are an Unconditionally Loved part of that Source - then everything ultimately serves Loving purpose.

We are on a journey home to Love. By honoring the power of the connections we feel, we become more aligned with our own growth process. It is very important to be healing the inner child wounds so that we can discern between energetic connections of vibrational kinship and the type of connection we feel when we meet someone who feels familiar because they are emotionally wounded in the way that makes them unavailable or abusive or whatever fits our pattern. It is very important because discernment will help us to follow the carrots/messages we are getting instead of hanging on to unhealthy situations so that the Universe has to use the stick on us.

Ultimately it doesn't really matter rather we can discern what kind of connection we are feeling because the Universe will lead us wherever we need to go. But the more discerning we become, the more clearly we see ourselves and our path, the faster we can let go, learn our lessons/settle Karma, and move on to the next lesson. The larger that our Spiritual belief system is - the easier it becomes to accept the things we cannot change so that we can relax and enjoy life in the moment while we are healing.

Sometimes a person is both a Kindred Spirit/Soul Mate and abusive/unavailable in alignment with our patterns. We do, after all, have a lot of Karma to settle with people from our past lives - and the patterns from our past lives are the reason we have the patterns we do in our present life. Our Kindred Spirits/Soul Mates, other Spiritual Beings who Love us, come into our life to help us remember to protect and take care of our self - by setting boundaries and enforcing them, by breaking off a relationship after two weeks instead of holding on, by standing up for our self and our Truth. (The "jerk" that you are holding a resentment against is on a Spiritual Truth level a teacher who came into your life out of Love to help you learn and grow.)

Karmic settlement can take place from an encounter that lasts minutes or hours as well as a relationship that continues over years. Because you feel a strong energetic connection with someone is not reason to abandon your self. Even if you are sure someone is your Twin Soul, you still need to be willing to let go of them. Perhaps you need to let go of them in this lifetime in order to reunite with them in the next.

Most all of us hope that this is our last lifetime because of the pain we have experienced being human in a hostile environment. In holding on to that type of thinking we are affirming and validating the illusion of separation and the pain of being human.

The shift we need to make in our relationship with life is to embrace it!

When we can enlarge our paradigm enough to see, and accept, the wholeness of life - the perfection of the balance of the Yin and Yang that appear to be polar opposites (darkness and Light, suffering and happiness, masculine and feminine, etc.) is when we will shift the paradigm enough to be free of the Illusion. By embracing and Loving our self and our life experience, we are owning our True Self and the higher reality which we Truly exist upon.

It is a process. A long gradual process. That is why it is so important to be focused on Love. Love for our self. The more moments of the day we can access Love in our relationship with ourselves - accepting wherever we are at, in whatever circumstances -

the more we own the Unconditional Love that is Truly ours. As we access Love for self, we access Love for all humanity because we are all connected - we are all ONE.

By learning to embrace our self and life in the moment for as many moments of the day as that is possible for us - we will free ourselves from the Illusion that we are separate from The Source. Through learning to forgive, accept, and Love the person we are - we will learn to Love our neighbors.

It is by embracing our human experience we will be liberated from it. And that is when it is really going to get fun.

"That is what this is all about! The second coming has begun! Not of "The Messiah," but of a whole bunch of messiahs. The messiah - the liberator - is within us! A liberating, Healing Transformational Movement has begun. "The Savior" does not exist outside of us - "The Savior" exists within.

We are the sons and daughters of God. We, the old souls, who are involved in this Healing Movement, are the second coming of the message of Love.

We have entered what certain Native American prophecies call the Dawning of the Fifth World of Peace. Through focusing on our own healing the planet will be healed."

"We who are doing this healing are about to graduate from the school of Karmic human experience. Any minute now . . . or any lifetime.

What graduation means is that we can be released from the Karmic merry-go-round, from the Karmic dance that was necessary because of polarization and "reversity." It does not mean that we will cease to exist; that would be a pretty hollow victory indeed.

What I believe it means is that when peace prevails, when the thousand years of peace begins, when a balanced, harmonious, Spiritually-aligned world evolves, then we can come back and play with all of our friends.   With our Kindred Spirits and our Soul Mates, and in union with our Twin Soul."

Chapter 35 - Energetic Attraction - emotional familiarity or Karmic connection?
"If you meet someone who feels like your soul mate - watch out"

"Western Civilization (in reaction to earlier ages when it was out of balance to the other extreme of allowing superstition to rule) does not acknowledge that multiple levels of reality exist and as a result, has been way out of balance towards the left brain way of thinking - rational, logical, concrete, what you see is all there is. . . . . Because emotional energy could not be seen or measured or weighed, and was not sanctioned by the AMA, emotions were discounted and devalued."

"It is because there is more than one level of reality that life is paradoxical in nature. What is True and positive on one level - selfishness out of Spiritual Self, can be

128

negative on another level - selfishness out of ego-self. What a caterpillar calls the end of the world, God calls a butterfly.

Humans have always had expressions that describe the paradoxical nature of the life experience. Every ending is a beginning. Every cloud does have a silver lining. For every door that closes, another door does open. It is always darkest before the dawn. Every obstacle is a gift, every problem is an opportunity for growth.

These are all expressions that refer to the paradoxical nature of life - the seeming contradictions that are a result of the multiple levels of reality. When we start to understand and recognize that there are multiple levels of reality, then we can begin to unravel the paradox and see how all of the pieces fit together perfectly." - Codependence: The Dance of Wounded Souls

There are multiple levels of reality that come into play in romantic relationships - including metaphysical levels. In this chapter I am going to discuss two of the most prominent and powerful levels of metaphysical reality that come into play in romantic relationships - emotional connection and karmic connection.

Metaphysical means beyond the physical - that is beyond the concrete three-dimensional reality that we experience, that can be seen and measured. So, this doesn't just refer to the type of metaphysical areas that involve past lives and soul mates and Karma - it also include emotions.

One of the reasons that emotions have been so discounted in Western Civilization has been because it is not possible to take an x-ray and see that we have unresolved grief from the past that is knocking our system out of balance and causing us to be depressed. Emotions have also been discounted in Eastern Civilization although the Eastern approach to medicine and science is much more Holistic in general and does acknowledges the existence of energies of a metaphysical nature.

"What is so sad to me - and sometimes makes me angry so that I rant and rave - is that it is not just traditional mental health professionals that discount emotions, but also New Age and alternative healers and spiritual teachers. New Age is in many ways a synthesis of Western and Eastern beliefs and practices. What too many of the people involved in New Age don't understand is this: the reality that both traditions discount emotions is a symptom of a larger dysfunction caused by the planetary conditions that dictated the course of human evolution on this planet.

Eastern beliefs though more holistic in general and accepting of the metaphysical energies that are the focus of acupuncture (to name one example, Feng Shui, Chi, etc.), have also discounted emotions - as something that one should rise above. In order to become "enlightened" it was thought that one must rise above being human and feeling messy human emotions.

Both Western and Eastern beliefs are out of balance and codependent in my belief.

"All civilizations are dysfunctional to varying degrees, as are subcultures within those civilizations. They just have different flavors of dysfunction, of imbalance.

As an example: In much of Asia the individual is discounted for the good of the whole - whether that be family or corporation or country. The individual takes his or her self-definition from the larger system. That is just as out of balance and dysfunctional as the Western Civilization manifestation of glorifying the individual to the detriment of the whole. It is just a different variety of dysfunction.

The goal of this dance of Recovery is integration and balance. That means celebrating being a tree while also glorying in being a part of the forest. Recovery is a process of becoming conscious of our individual wholeness and our ONENESS with all."

"As I pointed out in the online book I wrote explaining my perception of the September 11th terrorist attack as a manifestation of the human condition of codependency, both Western and Eastern Civilization have been out of balance.

"The dysfunction in Western Civilization has evolved to be more focused toward a left brain, masculine type of view of reality - concrete, rational, subdue the planet and multiply. Eastern Civilization has tended toward more feminine, abstract, contemplative - detachment from the concrete, a perspective with more detachment from the Illusion. But Eastern Civilization, though based upon a more intuitive perspective, did not, for the most part, manifest that in the treatment of women." - Attack on America: A Spiritual Healing Perspective & Call for Higher Consciousness Chapter 4

Eastern Civilization also did not manifest any balance emotionally. Whereas Western Civilization has tended towards allowing righteous male anger and aggression to drive civilization's evolution, Eastern culture has in general tended more towards denial of all emotions - a stoic role model for appropriate emotional behavior." Codependency Recovery: Wounded Souls Dancing in the Light Book 2: A Dysfunctional Relationship with Life Chapter 11: Codependent Counselors / Therapists / Healers

When I am working with people, teaching them my approach to inner healing, I always asked if they have been involved in Eastern meditation practices. The reason that I ask that is to be able to tell them that when I talk about how important the observer perspective is to codependency recovery I am not talking about the passive observer that is taught in meditation practices. The type of observer perspective I teach people is pro-active and intervening - not just passively observing thoughts and feelings but actually taking action to change the internal programming that we do have the power to change.

"By cultivating this detached perspective - detached from our ego experience of being human - we can observe both the mental and emotional levels of our being from a more discerning perspective. It facilitates changing the intellectual programming and taking some of the terror out of healing the emotional wounds. It allows us to set internal boundaries within, and between, the mental and emotional levels of our being.

When I speak of a detached observer perspective, I am not talking about the kind of observation that is taught in some spiritual meditation practices. Many people use that type of observation as a way to avoid feeling the feelings. That type of detachment from emotions is what some people experience on anti-depressants. Some people use chanting and meditation as anti-depressants. Chanting and meditation can be invaluable tools but applied in an imbalanced manner can, like positive affirmations, be used as tools to deny feelings.

Just observing the feelings does not heal them; does not fundamentally change our relationship patterns; does not make our fear of intimacy go away. We need to feel, experience, and release the emotional energy in order to heal the wounds and take power away from them." - Co-Creation: Owning your Power to Manifest Love

I teach people to develop an observer / witness perspective that is pro-active and intervening, that actually becomes our Recovery Control Center / our Conscious Recovering Adult Observer perspective - so that we change how we are relating to our own internal process instead of just reacting to old tapes and old wounds." - The Metaphysics of Emotions - emotional energy is real

In my book Codependence: The Dance of Wounded Souls I use principles of Quantum Physics and Molecular Biology to explain my Spiritual belief system - and my understanding that this human experience is a dance of energy governed by vibrational energy interaction dynamics and patterns.

So, what does this all have to do with romantic relationships, you are probably asking. Everything actually. There is literal vibrational Truth to such expressions as being "on the same wave length" with someone. There are people whom we have a closer vibrational relationship to than other people - people who we can feel closer and more connected to within a few hours of meeting them than we do to people we have known our whole life. The people we connect with in these ways are Kindred Spirits, and they are members of what could be called our vibrational tribe or stream - as I talked about in the last chapter. A few of those Kindred Spirits are soul mates with whom we have been involved romantically in past lives. In addition, we all have a twin soul that we have been separated from because of the condition of polarity that has dictated the human condition for tens of thousands of years.

Polarity being the "Tree of Knowledge of Good and Evil" - and the story of Adam and Eve being not an account of what caused polarity but a twisted symbolic interpretation of planetary conditions as humans were experiencing them.

"It is somehow appropriate - in a sick, twisted, kind of way - that Earth Day and Mother's Day are so close together. Civilized society has been raping our mother Earth for as long as it has had the technology to do so. Women have been raped, not just physically by men, but also emotionally, mentally, and spiritually by the belief systems of "civilization" (both Western and Eastern) since the dawn of recorded history.

Those belief systems were the effect of planetary conditions which caused the Spiritual beings in human body to have a perspective of life, and therefore a relationship with life, that was polarized and reversed. This reversed, black and white, perspective of life caused humans to develop beliefs about the nature and purpose of life that were irrational, insane, and just plain stupid.

As just one small but significant example of this stupid, insane belief system, and the effect it had on determining the course of human development - including the scapegoating of women, consider the myth of Adam and Eve. 'Poor' Adam, who was just being a man (that is, he just wants to get in Eve's pants) does what Eve wants him to and eats the apple. So Eve gets the blame for Adam not having boundaries. Now is that stupid or what? And you wondered where Codependence started.

The stupid, insane perspectives that form the foundation of civilized society on this planet dictated the course of human evolution and caused the human condition as we have inherited it. The human condition was not caused by men, it was caused by planetary conditions! (If you want to know more about those planetary conditions you'll have to read my book.) Men have been wounded by those planetary conditions just as much as women (albeit in quite different ways.)" - Mother's Day

What is so vital for us in recovery is to start to learn to have discernment in sorting out what levels of energetic connection we are feeling when we meet someone. Because we were raised with fairy tales of the Prince and Princess living happily ever after - an archetypal energetic imprinting which resonates with all of us because of having been separated from our twin soul - we believe such powerful feelings of connection are a sure sign that we have reached the door step to happily ever after.

This is very much not true. There are many different levels of energetic connection but the one which has been most powerful in shaping our lives is the one I talk about in the quote from my book I have used in several places in this book, the one below - the feeling of familiarity with someone who vibrates on an emotional energetic dynamics level - "on the same wave length" - with the emotional dynamics from our childhood. In other words, people who feel familiar because they are some how like our parents in their internal emotional dynamics.

"In our disease defense system we build up huge walls to protect ourselves and then - as soon as we meet someone who will help us to repeat our patterns of abuse, abandonment, betrayal, and/or deprivation - we lower the drawbridge and invite them in. We, in our Codependence, have radar systems which cause us to be attracted to, and attract to us, the people, who for us personally, are exactly the most untrustworthy (or unavailable or smothering or abusive or whatever we need to repeat our patterns) individuals - exactly the ones who will "push our buttons."

This happens because those people feel familiar. Unfortunately in childhood the people whom we trusted the most - were the most familiar - hurt us the most. So the

effect is that we keep repeating our patterns and being given the reminder that it is not safe to trust ourselves or other people."

There is a good reason that I make a point by saying - in both my writing and my work with people individually - that it was important for me to realize that if I met someone who felt like my soul mate I had better watch out. As long as I was not in recovery from my codependency - as long as I was not actively involved in the process of healing my inner child wounds and changing my subconscious ego programming so that I was learning how to have the wisdom / discernment to recognize when a feeling of attraction was mostly coming from the codependent familiarity of feeling abused, abandoned, and betrayed - then I was doomed to keep repeating the same relationship patterns over and over again. It was only when I got into recovery that I could start learning the lessons that I needed to learn and developing the discernment to be able to start changing my relationship patterns.

There are always multiple levels of reality, of vibrational energy dynamics, involved in this human experience we are having. It is vital to start seeing our own internal dynamics more clearly in order to start practicing discernment in our relationships. The Truth is that someone can feel familiar in a way that recreates our wounding with our parents / patterns - and be a soul mate also. In fact, it is inevitable that when we do meet someone who is our soul mate - or even more powerfully our twin soul - there will be Karma to settle. Which means no happily ever after in this body in this lifetime - though such a connection can certainly help us access great Joy and Love.

As I said above, I needed to realize that when I met someone who felt like my soul mate I needed to watch out. That doesn't mean that I need to run away necessarily. As I talk about in Chapter 15 when talking about my April Fools Day lesson in falling in love, running away would be going to the other extreme. We are looking for some balance in the middle ground.

There are multiple levels to feel attraction to someone - many of them codependent and dysfunctional, based upon our wounds and programming. But there are also "right on" reasons for that attraction.

"What I have found is that in many instances even though the levels that I can see, that I am conscious of, are mostly dysfunctional - arising out of the false beliefs and fears of the disease of Codependence - on deeper levels there are "right on" reasons for behaviors for which I was judging myself. . .

. . . As another, more universal example, when I started to learn about Codependence, I used to really beat myself up because I found that I was still looking for "her," even though I had learned about some of the dysfunctional levels of that longing.

I had learned that as long as I thought that I needed someone else to make me happy and whole I was setting myself up to be a victim. I had learned that I was not a frog who needed a princess to kiss me in order to turn into a prince - that I am a prince already, and just need to learn to accept that state of Grace, that princeness.

I had come to understand that those levels of my longing were dysfunctional and Codependent - and I judged and shamed myself because I could not let go of the longing for "her."

But as my awakening progressed I realized that there were "right on" reasons for that longing, for that "endless aching need" that I felt.

One of those "right on" levels was that the longing was a message concerning my very real need to attain some balance between the masculine and feminine energy within me - which begets dysfunctional behavior when it is projected, focused, outward as I had been taught to do in childhood.

And on a much deeper level I came to understand that I am - and have been, ever since polarization - looking for my twin soul."

The key is to pay attention to whether that other person is doing their own healing. If they are that can give us the gift of being able to explore love and emotional intimacy with someone else who is learning to explore love and emotional intimacy. That can give us the opportunity to experience an incredibly wonderful, immensely valuable, probably excruciatingly painful at times, opportunity for emotional healing, Spiritual growth, and Karmic settlement. A real E-ticket ride as it were.

It is very important to be in recovery paying attention to the lessons being presented to us to make the most of an opportunity that can potentially be the greatest, most sublime gift we have ever received on our path. Working through the issues and Karma involved can take us to a level of emotional intimacy, of opening our hearts to Loving and being Loved, that can allow us to regularly touch the Sacred and Divine. A union of two beings in body with such an energetic connection creates an transcendent energetic connection with The Source more powerful than any single being can access individually. Truly a magnificent gift to be grateful for - and well worth going through the emotional healing to create.

Chapter 36 - Fear of Intimacy - Relationship Phobia
"I always had someone unavailable that I was obsessing over"

"Codependence is a disease which involves the being's emotional defense system being dysfunctional to the extent that it breaks our hearts and destroys our ability to Love and be Loved, wounds our souls by denying us access to our Spiritual Self, and scrambles our minds so thoroughly that it causes our minds to become our own worst enemies." - Codependence: The Dance of Wounded Souls

For most of my adult life, I effectively had a relationship phobia. The extremes I learned in childhood were completely unavailable (my father) and completely enmeshed (my mother.) In my first sexually and emotionally intimate relationship (not any true emotional intimacy because I was incapable of it then - more accurate would be to call it emotional attachment) I got completely enmeshed with a woman I met in college. She was the one who really initiated me into being sexual. We got engaged to be married. I caught her in bed with my best friend - literally, caught them in bed.

I realized in retrospect in recovery, that she had almost certainly been the victim of incest from a young age - and was a sex addict. The pain of that experience, was to say the least, incredible. I was so much in denial of my feelings, and so codependent, that I stayed engaged to her for another year and a half.

I did not again in the next twenty years, make the mistake of getting involved with someone who was available enough to have the power to hurt me like that. I pursued only unavailable women. I always had someone unavailable that I was obsessing over, trying to figure out how to get her to see how wonderful we could be together. (This was completely unconscious and something I only realized looking back at my patterns in recovery.)

"One of the most ridiculous forms that obsession used to take for me, would involve me actually writing out the script of a conversation with a woman who was unavailable to me in some way. I would write pages and pages. I would say this, and then she would say that, and then I would say, etc., etc. This conversation would build to a the climax where I would say just the right words and suddenly she would understand. She would see the light and rush into my arms in overwhelming gratitude as she awakened to how good I was for her and how much I loved her. And then we would live happily ever after.

The trouble was, she never had the same script I did." - Obsession / Obsessive Thinking Part 2

The other extreme for me, was allowing myself to get physically involved with a woman who was chasing me that I did not really want to be with, a woman I did not feel a strong attraction / energetic connection to. Then I would be the unavailable one.

It was actually less painful for me to be alone, obsessing about someone who was unavailable, then it was to be the unavailable one. In those interactions, the evidence seemed to indicate that I was incapable of loving. The other person would often accuse me of exactly that. Being able to blame someone else for my feelings of abandonment and betrayal was less painful than blaming myself for being defective. More bearable than the pain of that little boy who felt he had failed in his responsibility for his mother's feelings and well being.

It was my emotional incest issues that really dictated my emotionally intimate relationships. Obsessing about someone who was unavailable, feeling betrayed by their inability to see our potential, feeling abandoned when they rebuffed me, was the less painful of the two extremes that my spectrum in relationship with romantic relationships involved. The result which would have been more devastating - in my subconscious emotional perspective of the options available to me - was getting into a relationship with someone who was available and being revealed for the shameful, unlovable being that I felt I was.

I was terrified of being responsible for another persons feelings, for their happiness. I had failed in my responsibility to my mother - and was certain (subconsciously) that I would fail again, because something was obviously wrong with me. Any woman who felt available, was someone to run away from, or push away. I was terrified of being smothered, of being engulfed, by a woman's emotional needs - and then being betrayed because of my defective being. This is one of the effects of emotional incest.

"I came from a traditionally dysfunctional family, in that my father was the emotionally unavailable angry person while my mother was the martyr with no boundaries. I so hated how my father behaved that I became a martyr like my mother. I was a martyr because I did not speak my Truth or set boundaries - I avoided confrontations, and tried to please the other person to keep her liking me.

In my first relationship in my codependence recovery, I realized that for me, setting boundaries in a romantic relationship felt to my inner child like I was being abusive. The very thing I had sworn to myself I would never be - like my father. I had to constantly be alert to that child's feelings and let that wounded part of me know that it was not only OK to set boundaries and say no - but that it was not Loving to do otherwise.

I discovered that there was a 4 or 5 year old age of my inner child who felt overwhelming shame that I could not protect my mother from my father. I thought that was my job. To make my mother happy.

I thought that I was not worthy of Love because I had been unable to do my job. So, in my adult life I was attracted to emotionally unavailable women who were verbally abusive. To my disease, it was better to be in relationship with someone like my father, than to fail to do my job in a relationship with someone who was available emotionally.

I had a relationship phobia that for the most part kept me from getting into relationships because I felt I was defective in my ability to be responsible for another person happiness.

Until we do some healing of our childhood wounds, it is impossible to really understand our adult patterns. If we have never experienced ourselves as independent emotional beings separate from our parents, we can not truly be present for a relationship in our adult lives.

Emotional incest is a violation and invasion of our emotional boundaries. It is not sexual abuse, nor is it sexual in nature - although sexual incest is often accompanied by emotional incest. It can however cause great damage to our relationship with our own gender and sexuality. Emotional incest, along with religions that teach that sexuality is shameful and societal beliefs that one gender is superior to the other, fall into a category that I call sexuality abuse - because they directly impact our relationship with our own sexuality and gender.

Our parents were our role models. We learned how to be emotional beings from their behavior and attitudes. We learned what a man is, what a woman is, from their example. We cannot undo that programming without being willing to heal those emotional wounds. We cannot know who we truly are without separating ourselves on the emotional energetic level from our parents." - Emotional Incest Issues

The excruciating pain of finding my fiancé in bed with my best friend was the proof of, and felt like punishment for, that unworthiness. It was only in recovery when dealing with my emotional incest issues, that I realized how my mother had betrayed me. She always told me how wonderful I was, how special and gifted - she acted as if the world revolved around me. But she never protected me, or herself, from my father. My mother was my first love. She was my Goddess. The fact that she allowed my father to terrify and traumatize me - she who was perfect in the eyes of that little boy - obviously meant there was something wrong with me.

I got in touch with the fact that my mother betrayed me early in recovery - but it was only a few years ago in processing about my fear of intimacy issues that I saw the connection between the two betrayals. My fiancé's betrayal was just a repeat of my earliest experience of loving a woman. Both situations involved betrayal by the primary woman in my life, and the primary man. The excruciating pain I experienced as a young adult was only a fraction of the devastation felt by that little boy. That poor little boy. His first experience of love, the first loves of his life - his God and Goddess - punished him. Terror of intimacy is a pretty appropriate response.

The result of my relationship phobia, my terror of intimacy, is that for the next 35 years after breaking up with the woman from college, I spent a total of 3 years living with someone in a relationship. One year at 25 and 2 years at 43. In 2005 at 56 I got involved in the relationship I am in now as I finish this book in August of 2012.

Chapter 37 - Codependent Defenses ~ The Gatekeeper
"A relationship with no conflict is an emotionally dishonest relationship"

"Some people, when they first get into Recovery, when they first start on a healing path, mistakenly believe that they are supposed to take down their defenses and learn to trust everyone. That is a very dysfunctional belief. It is necessary to take down the dysfunctional defense systems but we have to replace them with defenses that work. We have to have a defense system, we have to be able to protect ourselves. There is still a hostile environment out there full of wounded Adult Children whom it is not safe to trust.

. .

. . . The process of Recovery teaches us how to take down the walls and protect ourselves in healthy ways - by learning what healthy boundaries are, how to set them, and how to defend them. It teaches us to be discerning in our choices, to ask for what we need, and to be assertive and Loving in meeting our own needs. (Of course many of us have to first get used to the revolutionary idea that it is all right for us to have needs.)"

"Codependence is a disease which involves the being's emotional defense system being dysfunctional to the extent that it breaks our hearts and destroys our ability to Love and be Loved, wounds our souls by denying us access to our Spiritual Self, and scrambles our minds so thoroughly that it causes our minds to become our own worst enemies." - Codependence: The Dance of Wounded Souls

Gatekeeper is a term I first remember encountering over 20 years ago in relationship to archetypes. It is one that I have come to associate in my mind with the ferocious battle our codependency can put up when we are at a place when we are attempting to open our hearts to Loving and being Loved - when we are attempting to open up to allowing good things to happen in our lives instead of sabotaging ourselves.

Mythologically there are both positive and negative usage's of the term Gatekeeper - but in my use, in reference to codependency and fear of intimacy, I think of it as a negative term. In fact, I used to think of the Gatekeeper as some kind of elemental, primal, reptilian presence that emerged from the primordial swamp of the collective unconscious to strike terror into my heart. It was my Gatekeeper that caused me to have the relationship phobia that I described in the last chapter. My issues around opening up my heart went way beyond fear - terror of intimacy was the much more accurate term I often used.

That is why it was such a monumental / transformational shift for me early in 2004, to be able to get past my terror of intimacy and Truly open my heart to myself - and another human being to an extent I never had previously. That of course, doesn't mean my Gatekeeper went away completely - although I easily slipped back into wanting to believe that, because it is easier to see things as black and white and to think that the other person's gatekeeper is the problem because I am past all of that (this is called denial.)

I used to always associate the term - in my negative image of it as being behavior that certain codependents exhibited (not a nice guy like me of course;-) - with the type of defense that caused a person to strike out in a venomous manner. This was related to how my father raged - and the programming that resulted from that verbal abuse. I realized at a certain point in my recovery that I had a pattern in my life of having at least one person in my life who was very critical and shaming. This would usually be some kind of pseudo authority figure - acting teacher, coach, boss/supervisor, older roommate, etc. Having someone in my life that was very critical and shaming was comfortable for me (on an unconscious codependent level) because it was familiar from childhood.

That pattern didn't really manifest itself for me in relationships until I got healthy enough to get past my relationship phobia so that I could get into a relationship. Really! I had to get healthy enough to get into a relationship before the person in the relationship could become that abusive "authority figure." I got into a relationship in the early 90s when I was 7 years sober - and it was the first time I had lived with a woman in a relationship (as opposed to as a roommate) in over 15 years. The only other time I had lived with a woman was the result of a drug and alcohol induced marriage in my mid 20s that lasted for a year.

The relationship in the early 90s lasted 2 years and was an invaluable learning experience. It was in that relationship that I learned how to fight. The combination of not doing relationships that lasted any length of time, with my patterns in regard to relationships had resulted in me not ever really having had the experience of arguing and fighting with a partner in a relationship.

As I mentioned in the Relationship Phobia column: "The extremes I learned in childhood were completely unavailable (my father) and completely enmeshed (my mother.)" If I was interacting with a woman who was somewhat available my fear of enmeshment would come up and I would run away. The only kind of women that I could get involved with had to be emotionally unavailable enough that I would feel deprived and abused - because that was what my codependency was comfortable with. The deprivation would cause me to passive aggressively (because I was programmed in childhood to manipulate since it was not okay to communicate directly and honestly and have boundaries or needs) push to get my needs met, which would result in the woman becoming critical and shaming as some point. That is when I really knew I was "in love" with her because she was treating me in the way I felt I deserved to be treated.

This is really sick stuff, these codependent relationship patterns. I realized as I was writing this, that the relationships where I was "in love" with an unavailable woman were relationships that I ran away from in a passive sense. What I mean by that is, I would set it up so they rejected / threw me away - self fulfilling prophecy - so I wouldn't have the responsibility of ending the relationship. Pretty fool proof way of staying out of relationships.

The toxic shame at the core of my codependency caused me to have major issues about receiving. No matter how much consciously I wanted positive validation and love from other people, I could not accept it when I got it because deep down inside I didn't feel I deserved it - and it did not feel comfortable or familiar. In one the Update Newsletter for my web site I described this in a way I like, as part of a discussion about learning to be open to positive validation and love from others.

> "My resistance to opening up to receive Love would cause me to minimize positive feedback by telling myself that the other person wanted something from me, or was just being kind, or whatever. I spent several years in recovery practicing saying just plain "Thank You." Instead of minimizing (oh it was nothing), joking it away, turning it back on them (oh you are really the one who ___), or dismissing it because I suspected the other persons motives or mental health. The feeling deep within was that if someone was loving and positive towards me, it was either a sinister plot or there must be something wrong with them." - Joy2MeU Update October 2000

In my family of origin, I hated how my father treated us - "like dirt" was the phrase that used to come to mind. He was the perpetrator and my mother was the self sacrificing martyr victim. I did not want to be anything like my father so I ended up becoming like my mother - being a victim martyr with no boundaries because of my fear of confrontation and abandonment.

In the relationship in the early 90s, I realized that my wounding caused me to feel like a perpetrator if I set a boundary in an intimate relationship - the very thing I promised myself I would never do, be like my father. In that relationship I learned how to fight. How to stand up for myself and know that a fight didn't mean the end of the relationship. I had to work at it - telling my inner children that it was okay to say no and set boundaries, that it was okay to be angry and express it. It did take a lot of work to overcome that programming. I sometimes liken the experience to someone who has spoken in a real quiet voice all their life - when they start speaking in a normal voice it feels to them like they are yelling. Someone who has been a people pleaser to avoid confrontation in intimate relationships like I was, will feel like they are being abusive when they start standing up for themselves and owning their anger.

In the relationship in the early 90s, the person I was involved with was wounded in such a way that she had a gatekeeper that was vicious and mean. She didn't observe "fair fighting" rules. One of those rules is that you never say the really mean, cruel, soul wounding types of things that cannot be taken back. The really vicious attacks on the other persons being or body or masculinity/femininity or whatever. She would lash out viciously when she felt scared and cornered.

I was able to hang in there and learn to fight with her, without saying those kinds of things back to her. Something I was really grateful for - both that I didn't get abusive in that way, and that I learned that it was okay to get angry and fight. It was very important in my recovery to realize that emotional intimacy includes anger. That the message that I learned from my mother - that it was not okay to be angry at someone I love - was a false message. Avoiding conflict denies intimacy - we cannot be emotionally intimate with someone we can't be angry at. Conflict is an inherent part of relationships - and working through issues is how intimacy grows. Conflict is part of the fertilizer that is necessary for the growth of emotional intimacy. A relationship with no conflict is an emotionally dishonest relationship - and the other extreme of the codependent spectrum from relationships that have constant conflict. Both are unhealthy.

Although I had not gotten involved in any relationships that had lasted any length of time since that two year relationship, the women who I had romantic experiences with for brief periods of time (in 1998 and 2003) since then had a gatekeeper that could be mean and vicious. That was one of the wonderful things about the relationship experience that I had in 2004 - that actually started in December of 2003.

The woman I was involved with that year was a quantum leap forward in terms of my patterns. She was not mean and abusive. When her gatekeeper kicked in she could be cold and distant - and sometimes would behave in ways that felt kind of cruel or mean, but she was not mean and vicious in the things she said - even in the times when her pent up rage was triggered. It was actually great progress that she was able to access that rage - and our relationship was the first time she had ever had someone who was safe enough to really be able to express her anger to. She has been a people pleaser in her life, and part of the ironic perfection of our relationship is that the times when I would react out of some codependent insanity actually helped her to learn to own her anger and set boundaries. Her patterns were similar to mine in that she was either people pleasing and being deprived and abused or running away - so the fact that she hung in there with me so long and was willing to confront issues and work through them was great.

In that relationship experience in 2004, I went from the unavailable one to the one who was available because of a breakthrough in processing about my fear of intimacy issues. Then the woman that I opened my heart to Loving became the unavailable because of her fear of intimacy and betrayal issues. That caused her to react to her issues by getting involved with another man - which left me feeling abandoned and betrayed. A wonderful opportunity for growth.

August 2012 - In this article that I wrote in 2004, I say that I Truly opened my heart in the relationship in 2004 - and that may have been true as far as I was capable of it at the time, but it was really nothing compared to where I have gone since then. In fact, my Higher Power had to trick me into believing the person I was involved with in 2004 was my twin soul in order to prepare me for the relationship that I am in now. I am going in the next chapter of this book share some of the emotional pain I went through in relationship experiences in 1998, 2003, and 2004 that helped to prepare me for this relationship. In the chapter that follows the next one, I will share some of my journey in healing my fear of intimacy issues. I have done enough healing to get past my relationship phobia so that I am no longer spending my time living alone as I did for most of my life.

Chapter 38 - Deprivation issues drive relationship addiction behavior
Sharing my experiences and emotional healing process

The Joy2MeU Journal is a body of work online in a password protected part of my website that is only accessible to subscribers who really resonate with my work. My regular website provides over 250 web page - millions of words - free to anyone with an internet connection, in other words plenty to read without needing to subscribe to anything. In that Journal - which is itself close to 100 web pages - I share some books in progress / unpublished that I have written along with the story of my recovery and Spiritual Path. Included in the sharing I do of my story is a personal journal of my recovery process over a period of 5 years. Starting in the spring of 1999 and continuing through the end of 2004 I shared in this Journal a personal journal where I was processing through my fear of intimacy issues. That very painful process resulted in getting me to a place where I am now in a relationship and don't have time to write any more.;-)

Although my most intimate - and far out metaphysical - writing was confined to my Joy2MeU Jounal in the early years, I eventually started sharing on more and more intimate levels in my Update Newsletters - which I would post as webpages online and then send an announcement email with a link to the Update to all the people on my e-mail list. I am going to use a combination of some my writing from those Updates and my journal to share an overview - and some specifics - of my personal history in dealing with my fear of intimacy for this book because I think you might find it helpful to know that I felt crazy and wanted to die and went through lots of intense pain. I have found that sharing my recovery process - and role modeling that it is okay to not be perfect and is okay to be a wounded human being - can help other people to forgive and accept themselves and their own process. A considerable part of this chapter is taken from my April 2008 Update Newsletter and will include quotes from other Updates and my journal within it - and I have added other quotes and excerpts in editing and expanding it for this book.

Sharing my emotional healing

I have recently been working with a few people who were dealing with relationship addiction issues - and hearing about quite a few others. All of us have a desperately needy, desperately lonely age of the inner child within us. It is that young child part of us that feels like it is life threatening when we don't hear from the other person and wants to send numerous text messages or e-mails or call the other person constantly. Before I got into recovery, I used to say that I couldn't stand to be around needy people - and it was because I couldn't stand the needy part of me. I needed to own - and learn to have compassion for - that wounded, desperately needy part of me in order to stop letting that part of me have so much power.

I described this Deprived, wounded, lonely child in my article The Inner Children that need Boundaries.

"Desperately needy, clingy, wants to be rescued and taken care of, doesn't want to set boundaries for fear of being abandoned - very important to own, nurture, and Love this part of ourselves because relating to this part of our self out of either extreme can be disastrous.

Allowing this desperate neediness to come out in our adult relationships can drive someone away pretty fast - no one outside of us can meet the desperate needs of this child. We can love this part out of the Loving compassionate adult in us and keep those needs from surfacing at inappropriate times by owning how wounded this part of us is and taking steps to validate and nurture this inner child.

Not owning that part of us can be just as damaging - being terrified of letting ourselves feel the woundedness and neediness of this part of our self can cause us to shut down our ability to be vulnerable and open to emotional intimacy. If we cannot own how deprived we were emotionally as children and instead try to keep this part of us shut away we cannot Truly open our heart and be vulnerable as an adult. People who tend to be counterdependent and can't stand being around needy people are terrified of the needy part of themselves - and because of that will keep picking emotionally unavailable people to be in relationship with, or will run away if someone is emotionally available because it will feel like neediness to them.

When this emotional deprivation is associated with a teenager within us it can cause us to act out sexually to try to get this emotional neediness met. The fact that we have in the past acted out sexually in ways that we are ashamed of - or found ourselves very needy, vulnerable, and powerless to suppress the emotional neediness in sexually intimate relationships - can cause us to shut down to our sensuality and sexuality out of fear the loss of control we experienced in the past."
- The Inner Children that need Boundaries

Codependency is doubly traumatic. We were deprived in childhood and then our ego adapted a codependent defense system that caused us to be deprived as adults. So, we have deprivation issues from our adult life as well as from our childhood.

"My thinking, in relationship to a relationship, is much healthier and more balanced than it used to be - but it still tends towards the extremes within the spectrum of what is possible. It feels more natural for me to completely let go of the idea of having a romantic relationship or to think in terms of what it is going to be like when we are living together then to think in terms of getting to know someone gradually. Kind of like, either pretend the water isn't there, or dive into the deep end without looking first to see what may be just under the surface.

It is easier for me emotionally to not even consider going in the water than to gradually ease myself into the shallow water - because if I am even looking at the water it gets me in touch with grief about being alone. The abyss of wish-to-die pain and desperate loneliness from my childhood - the deprivation issues that I spent so much of my life either denying or allowing to run my life - do not have anywhere near the power they used to because of the healing I have done. It is relatively easy now for me to separate out the childhood feelings of loneliness - and they do not any longer have a life threatening feeling of desperation to them. But I also have been very deprived in my adult life - of Love, companionship, affection, touch, sexual fulfillment, etc. - because of the patterns caused by my fear of intimacy. So the grief around those deprivation issues still has some power because the deprivation is still happening." - Emotional Honesty and Emotional Responsibility part 4: Discernment in relationship to emotional honesty and responsibility 1

This quote is from a series of articles on Emotional Honesty and Emotional Responsibility that I wrote in 2001. When I wrote the above paragraph it was true that the healing I had already done on my deprivations issues had taken a lot of power away from those issues - but there was a lot more healing to be done on them (as you will see in the excerpts below.) I was at that time, actually in the middle of a 4 year period of not being in any relationship because my fear of intimacy still had so much power.

In my March 2007 Update Newsletter I got into processing about my fear of intimacy issues. That resulted in an additional page of processing in which I shared a Personal History in relationship to fear of intimacy issues (which I will share in the next chapter.) It was an update of the previous time I had shared about those issues in August 2004 - and included my realization that the terror of intimacy defenses that were defending my heart were so powerful, that it was necessary for the Universe to guide me into the delusion that the person I got involved with in 2004 was my twin soul.

I will share some of that Personal History in the next chapter, but will include here a version of the addendum that I added to some of my articles in which I refer to my "latest" relationship experience.

"In my latest relationship experience I went from the unavailable one to the one who was available because of my breakthrough. Then the woman that I opened my heart to Loving became the unavailable because of her fear of intimacy and betrayal issues. That caused her to react to her issues by getting involved with another man - which left me feeling abandoned and betrayed. A wonderful opportunity for growth." - Chapter 37 Codependent Defenses ~ The Gatekeeper

I had a relationship experience in 2003 - my first in over 4 years - that was a long distance relationship that included two short visits by the woman to Cambria and one trip by me to her home on the East Coast - and was about 95% fantasy and 5 % reality. Starting in December 2003 and lasting - in my mind at least - through 2004 was an excruciatingly painful relationship with my "twin soul" delusion, which was about 80% fantasy and 20% reality. Those two experiences prepared me for the reality of the relationship that started in 2005. We have been living together for over 7 years now and got married in January 2011.

If I had not gone through the agony that I did in 2004 to take more power away from those deprivation issues and remove some of the blocks - that my fear of intimacy defense had erected to keep me out of relationships - I would not be in the relationship I am in now. So, I wanted to share some excerpts from places in my writing where I was dealing with these issues, in the hopes that it might be helpful to anyone out there who has recently, or is, experiencing this kind of experience. It is kind of embarrassing to reread these for me - but important to not buy into the shame and judgment the critical parent voice wants to beat me up with about them. It is so important to not blame ourselves for our own wounding and deprivation. It was not our fault that we were wounded and deprived in childhood - nor is it our fault that we were powerless to keep from acting out as adults. Blaming and shaming ourselves just feeds the relationship addiction. We need to learn to have compassion for ourselves - and recognize that the power those issues have is directly related to how much we were wounded and deprived.

> *"As long as we are judging and shaming ourselves we are giving power to the disease. We are feeding the monster that is devouring us.*
> *We need to take responsibility without taking the blame. We need to own and honor the feelings without being a victim of them."*

Hopefully, some of you will find this helpful in forgiving your self so that you can be open to crating healthier relationship opportunities in the future.

some excerpts from processing about relationship experiences

From An Adventure in Romance - Loving and Losing Successfully 1999

"Is she my Twin Soul? Or an Angel sent by my Twin Soul to prepare me for our reunion. Will it happen in this lifetime? Or the next?

I don't get to know right now. I just know that I have to Let Go. And Let Go - and Let Go again.

I told her good-bye. I told her that I could not be in her life anymore as long as she was running from her issues and punishing me as a symbol for all of the sins of unkind men.

And now I cry every day.

The pain is primal - cellular. The sobs come from someplace so deep as to be ancient. I can't write a line without sobs bursting forth from my heart chakra - such an old wound, such a deep trauma.

But is it about the woman I have just told good-bye or has that woman touched off the old grief for "Her" - Is she Her??

More will be revealed. I just have to Let Go and Let Go and Let Go some more.

And I cry every day - and the Joy is right behind the pain because I have never felt SO CLOSE TO HOME!!!"

Romantic Relationship 2003 (the one that was 95% fantasy and 5 % relationship)

"The grief is right near the surface. All I have to do is consciously breathe into it, and the sobbing starts coming, the tears start flowing.

What comes out of my mouth is, "I don't want to lose her." Sobbing. Crying. Hurting.

And then I tell myself, this can't all be about her. All this grief is not about the possibility of losing this specific person. I need to separate out the levels here. The intuitive message I have gotten for years, what I tell the people I am working with, is that, about 20% of what we are feeling in a moment of intense grief is about what is happening now - and about 80% of it is unresolved grief from the past.

This doesn't feel like childhood grief though. I am sure some of it is connected to issues from my childhood, some of it is childhood wounds being triggered - but this doesn't feel like inner child wounds.

And then I get it. This is adult grief about being alone. This is about how deprived I have been in my adult life. Sobs bubbling to the surface in a continuous stream of burp like little explosions (not a very elegant description, but graphically accurate:). Tears seeping from my eyes.

This is about being so alone for so long as an adult. This is about being deprived of companionship, of affection, of romance, of touch, of sexual expression. This is grief from my adult life that I am feeling now.

"These deprivation issues bring up a great deal of sadness for me. It is not old grief from my childhood that I can release and take power away from. These are ongoing issues that I need to release grief energy about, but then more builds up. This is grief about now - and the recent past.

When these issues are triggered, I need to just feel the sadness - to acknowledge it, honor it, release what I can. I need to accept them as a perfect part of my path somehow, so I don't fall into a victim place of self pity about them. I can feel sad for myself, affirm that I need and deserve affection, touch, Love, companionship, sexual fulfillment - and then let go of buying into the belief that I am a victim because those needs are not being fulfilled today.

This is one of those internal boundary areas that I have found so important to practice discernment about in recovery. I need to feel and honor the feelings - the feeling of being deprived, the feeling of being the victim of both my fear of intimacy and the Divine plan - but it is vital for me to not buy into the belief that I am a victim in relationship to my Spiritual Path. Buying into the belief in victimization is what creates the artificial emotional state that is self pity." - Dance 12 written June 23, 2002

This is really good. This grief is really important to feel and identify because it will help me to see things more clearly now.

This is why internal discernment is so vital to me and my process. I always initially identify the feelings coming up with the most recent thing that has triggered it - thus my first reaction is that what I was feeling was all about losing her."

At this point in my writing on the morning of October 7th about what happened yesterday afternoon, I got off into a discussion of the dynamics of my internal processing, of discernment, and of the disease dynamics as it manifests in romantic relationships. It is a really valuable discussion but it belongs elsewhere, so will be in a few chapters. Here is a quote from that writing:

"By being in my observer consciousness and telling myself the Truth, that this is not just about her - I am able to start identifying what it is really about. I recognize that part of the anguish I heard in my voice when I said, "I don't want to lose her!" is being caused by my disease.

Anguish and grief are two different things. Grief is pure emotional energy flowing. Anguish is caused by the mental filter / perspective that is dictating how I am relating to the emotions. Anguish is grief sifted / examined through a filter of fear, shame, blame, and black and white thinking."

"It **feels** like it is all about her. It **feels** like I am losing her. It **feels** like I will never have another love like this.

Those are feelings - they are not telling me facts, are not telling me the whole Truth.

"Just because it feels like you are being punished does not mean that is the Truth. Feelings are real - they are emotional energy that is manifested in our body - but they are not necessarily fact.

What we feel is our "emotional truth" and it does not necessarily have anything to do with either facts or the emotional energy that is Truth with a capital "'T'" - especially when we our reacting out of an age of our inner child." - Codependence: The Dance of Wounded Souls

Hearing the anguish in my voice as I was crying and sobbing, saying, "I don't want to lose her" was an immediate tip off to me that the disease was in play - was putting a negative, victim based spin on what I was feeling in the moment.

So, I pulled myself into my observer consciousness, my recovery control center, and started looking at what was happening from the perspective of the empowered adult on a Spiritual Path. I started using the tools from my codependency recovery tool box.

The tone and anguish in my voice did go back to an inner child wound. The genesis of the wound was in my childhood. It feels like it is probably real connected to the incredible pain, to the loneliness and feelings of isolation, that the 7 year old who tried to commit suicide must have felt.

But I have substantially healed that 7 year old's wound - it has next to no power in my life any more. This is about the effects of that wound - about the layers that were piled on top of it. This grief about how the defenses - that I adapted to protect the part of me that wanted to die - created my relationship phobia / terror of intimacy as an adult. This grief is about the deprivation I suffered as an adult because of the childhood wounding.

"I also know that there are layers of grief from the emotional trauma I experienced. There is not only trauma about what happened back then - there is also grief about the effect those experiences had on me later in life. I get to cry once again for that little boy as I write this. I have been sobbing for that little boy and the emotional trauma he experienced - but I am also sobbing for the man that I became. . . .

. . . . . I have been going through a transformation one more time in my recovery. Each time that I need to grow some more - need to surrender some more of who I thought I was in order to become who I am - I get to peel another layer of the onion. Each time this happens I get to reach a deeper level of honesty and see things clearer than I ever have before. Each time, I also get to release some of the emotional energy through crying and raging.

Through clearer eyes, and with deeper emotional honesty, I get to look at all of my major issues again to heal them some more. I used to think that I could deal with an issue and be done with it - but now I know that is not the way the healing process works. So recently I have gotten the opportunity to revisit my issues of abandonment and betrayal, of deprivation and discounting. My issues with my mother and father, with my gender and sexuality, with money and success. My issues with the God I was taught about and the God-Force that I choose to believe in. My patterns of self-abusive behavior that are driven by my emotional wounds - and the attempts that I make to forgive myself for behavior that I have been powerless over. And they all lead me back to the core issue. I am not worthy. I am not good enough. Something is wrong with me.

At the core of my relationship is the little boy who feels unworthy and unlovable. And my relationship with myself was built on that foundation. The original wounding caused me to adapt attitudes and behavior patterns which caused me to be further traumatized and wounded - which caused me to adapt different attitudes and behavior patterns which caused me to be further traumatized and wounded in different ways. Layer upon layer the wounds were laid - multifaceted, incredibly complex and convoluted is the disease of Codependence. Truly insidious, baffling and powerful." - Chapter 29 Grief, Love, & Fear of Intimacy

To say that what I am going through now feels like a major transformation is an understatement of epic proportions.

Yesterday when I was going through the grieving, I wasn't doing all this analyzing. I was just working my program as I have learned to work it. This is part of the gift of this writing for me - and for you hopefully - is that in writing about my process, I end up breaking it down into an understandable (hopefully) explanation of the underlying dynamics." - Joy2MeU Journal The Path of one Recovering Codependent ~ the dance of one wounded soul My Unfolding Dance 19 (October 2003)

This is another excerpt from that same journal installment:

"**Oh crap!!** It is going to be one of those kind of writing frenzies! Interruption - inner eruptions - of my writing for grieving. I just came home from the CoDA meeting (Thursday Oct. 2nd) sobbing and moaning as I drove - crying because of an issue that got triggered in my sharing. Not something I was expecting today. Not an issue that I was aware was part of the emotional eruptions going on right now. But here it is bubbling up in a string of sobs breaking the surface like air bubbles in a fish tank. The animal like moans of a wounded beast leaking out from deep inside of me like some gas under pressure or something.

I wasn't sure there was even going to be a CoDA meeting today - more than half of the Thursdays in the last 6 weeks had not had enough people show up for a meeting. Today we did. Still I sure wasn't going to share the stuff I am sharing here - too deep and powerful, too frightfully intimate for the level of recovery in these meetings locally.

The meditation in Melody Beattie's Language of Letting Go today was about family and making choices about interacting with family. One of the regulars led off the sharing, and since no one else was speaking up I went second. I was talking about how important it was to realize my family couldn't hear me - didn't understand the language of the Spirit and recovery that I speak. And then because there was a new person there, I started talking about how my parents couldn't see me when I was a kid. How they could only see their projections and through their fear and shame, through their idea of who I should be to make them feel good about themselves. I said that they have never been able to see the True me, not as a child and not now. And then I said - getting choked up immediately before I could get the sentence out - "I have spent my whole life trying to get people to see me."

That is what brought up the grief - trying to get people to see me. To see me and to Love me. To see me and still Love me."

"Grieving Sunday morning

Sunday October 5th.

Crying this morning. Spent the last 3 hours or so, reading through e-mails between us from early in relationship. So many feelings. So much has changed so profoundly because of this relationship. Inside of me, in my relationship with myself so much has changed.

To connect with this very special woman was such a gift in my life. She helped me connect with lost parts of myself. I don't want to lose this connection. My heart aches at the thought of losing this connection.

The last few days I have been reviewing, rereading, processing. Haven't been sure what I was going to share here - that is, in terms of details of how it all unfolded.

I will share some, not sure yet how much. What is so clear to me this morning, is that the special lady was a perfect part of my path - was a Divine, Blessed gift in my life.

Crying. Intermittently sobbing. Tears flowing. Heart aching. Soooo Grateful. Sooo sad - and yet there was / is such great Joy. Such a gift." - My Unfolding Dance 19

"I have been having to work real hard at certain times - some periods for hours - on my internal boundaries to keep from being in the kind of energy that drives relationship addiction. The feelings of desperation, panic, and terror that the wounded inner children feel about losing a source of love. The feeling of energy out of control in my body so that I am not comfortable in my own skin - so that I feel like I am jumping out of my own skin. The life and death urgency, desperate neediness to be reassured that my love is not going to go away.

I have, of course, recognized these inner child place for what they are, and have continued to talk to them and try to calm them down - reassuring them that everything is going to be okay. That does not mean telling them that she will come back, that she won't go away. It means telling them, that if she does go away it will be what is best for us. That if she goes away it will be part of our Higher Power's plan. That maybe our Higher Power brought her into our life to break through the barriers and learn about Love because there is going be another woman in the future who will be able to be more available and willing to commit to the adventure." - My Unfolding Dance 21

This talking to my terrified inner children to calm them down, is an example of setting internal boundaries so that I don't allow the feelings of the wounded child to define my adult experience. I also set boundaries with the critical parent voice that wants to blame me or the other person for my pain. Boundaries within both the emotional and mental allow me to see myself and the situation with more clarity.

It is invaluable to me to have learned how to have some discernment internally so that I can separate the levels of the grief that I feel about losing a specific relationship (about 20% of what I am feeling when I am having a very powerful intense emotional reaction) from the unresolved grief from my past (about 80% of that type of reaction.) To be able to separate my grief about losing the dream / fantasy of what I hoped the relationship would be, from the grief that is actually about losing a specific person - makes it easier for me to let go of that person. (The great majority of the grief we feel at the end of a relationship is about the loss of the dream / illusion we invested in, rather than the actual reality of relating to that person.)

I believe that it is necessary to do our inner child healing work (which is an ongoing relationship not something we do and are done with) to be able to set internal boundaries and learn to have internal discernment. I believe that doing this work is what will help me one day to have the ability to have a healthy, lasting romantic relationship. The old way of allowing the romantic within and the desperately needy child and the magical thinking child and the wounded teenage horndog, etc., to dictate and control my relationships certainly did not work.

Romantic Relationship 2004 (the one that was about 80% fantasy and 20% reality and included twin soul delusion)

Some excerpts from My Unfolding Dance 31 (March 2004)

"I am in incredible excruciating pain. From the depths of my heart chakra come the sobs. I cannot imagine going on living right now.

I sent her the link to the Update at 11:32 pm last night. I am sure she is with him. Haven't heard anything back - she hasn't been online. The thought today is that perhaps she is going to end all contact completely. If she does it might be best in the long run if she absolutely certain that she is never coming back to me - but I do not know how I can survive it.

I cannot imagine ever being with another woman. I cannot imagine getting to know another woman - I can't even imagine wanting to meet anyone for a very long time. I do believe we were so perfect for each other and that she is my Twin Soul.

I am hurting sooo horribly. Oh God. What did I ever do to deserve such a cruelty from God - such an absolutely horrifying punishment. That may be old message from childhood but it feels like message from lifetimes of this hell of being human and not having Love in my life. The moans are coming again, the wounded animal sounds. aaaaaaaaaaaaaaaaaaaa!"

"Good Morning Sports Fans. Welcome to Robert's mad hatter ride. The question we are addressing this morning is Robert's mental health and emotional well being.

Have I finally had the psychotic break that I was worried about over 15 years ago when I first started writing the Trilogy? . . . .

. . . . So, No! I do not believe I am insane even if dysfunctional society would think me crazy. I have faith in my Truth, in my message, in my beliefs about my path. I stand firmly in my Truth.

Have I been acting insane in certain ways lately? Has my life felt insane in recent weeks?

A resounding Yes! to both of those questions.

Why have I been feeling and acting insane recently? - you ask. Would you be surprised if I were to tell you it was because of a romantic relationship?" - Joy2MeU Journal The Path of one Recovering Codependent ~ the dance of one wounded soul My Unfolding Dance 31 (March 2004)

Some excerpts from My Unfolding Dance 36 (April 2004)

"On my short mountain walk right now. Am in huge pain. I thought I had experienced hell. I thought that I had been through hell and that I had survived it. But the hell that I have experienced up to now is a meek small shadow of what I am feeling now. . . . . THIS IS HELL!!!!!! THIS IS HELL!!!!!! There can be no devastation to match this. There can be no pain that approaches what I am feeling. I cannot think of any reason to even want to survive this. I can only experience terror at the thought of the weeks and months and years to come living in the HELL of separation from Her. I cannot imagine a reason to want to continue living in this kind of pain. . . . . . FUCK YOU GOD. YOU FUCKING SADISTIC CRUEL UNSPEAKABLY COLD BASTARD!!!!

I keep going to the anger to pull me out of the pain. Anger at God. Anger at the disease. I will not take the easy way out of this by turning my anger at her. There will be some anger at her, but what is happening is not her fault or her doing. This was a set up - and I am ENRAGED by the CRUELTY of this emotional experience. . . . . .

. . . . . . I cannot express to you the pain I was in. . . . . . What an incredible process! What a focused, concentrated, intense, compressed, pressurized, hothouse, petrie dish, cyclotronic accelerated atom smashing molecular structure transmuting diamondizing thermonuclear fusion producing explosion of growth and transformation.

I am in the cocoon being torn apart and put back together again. I hope to fuck I am being put back together again because I sure as Hell am being torn apart.

I am in the Black Hole having the life sucked out of me by hurricane force cyclonic pressures that threaten to tear me limb from limb, mind from body, heart from soul - even as I am polished and compressed by unspeakable pressures in this transformation that will vomit me forth a brilliant diamond of crystalized refractive hardness and ineffable power.

That is, if I live through the next couple of weeks. I mean, rather I live through the next couple of weeks or not, I will come out a diamond, a butterfly, a beautiful swan - I am just not sure if it is going to be in this body or not.

I am in HELL!!!!!!!!!!! The pain is unfuckingbearable. I must find release from this pain! I will not be able to endure this magnitude of pain for much longer. It is not humanly possible to endure this much crushing agony." - Joy2MeU Journal The Path of one Recovering Codependent ~ the dance of one wounded soul My Unfolding Dance 36 (April 2004)

Some excerpts from Mini-Newsletter 8 September 2004

"There is obviously still some terror and shame at the heart of my fear of intimacy that was causing me to sabotage the relationship. My ego defenses caused me to behave in ways that pushed for the destination my disease wanted - that is to be rejected ("thrown away" was the term that kept coming out of my mouth.) To my disease that would be the inevitable conclusion, so better to get it over with then deal with the fear, the anticipation, of knowing it was going to happen eventually. It was the fear of being rejected for being unlovable and unworthy - and losing my Twin Soul again - that was creating so much fear of the outcome for me, because on some really deep level I felt like the outcome was inevitable.

"It was the terror in anticipation of losing her - combined with the pain of lifetimes of heart rending grief - that caused me to think that death would be preferable to living with losing her. As it so often proves to be in this human experience, the anticipation of pain is often worse than actually experiencing the pain. Now that I have lost her - and I do believe that we are not going to be able to be together again in this lifetime - I am in great pain, but the terror of anticipating the grieving is gone." - Joy2MeU Update August 2004

I hate this!!!! My fear of the outcome caused me to behave in ways that made that outcome inevitable. SHIT!!!!!"- Joy2MeU Journal The Path of one Recovering Codependent ~ the dance of one wounded soul Mini-Newsletter 8 September 2004

These excerpts can give you an idea of what was going on emotionally for me during this period of time - but I am going to interrupt what I wrote in that Update to put the spotlight on some of the behaviors that feeling those feelings caused in me. The following is from an article that I published on October 31st 2004 - and I am going to include within it something I talked about in an earlier Chapter in this book to make a point.

"I have stated in numerous places in my writing that I believe that romantic relationships are the greatest arena for Spiritual and emotional growth available to us - because they are the ones that push all of our emotional buttons, trigger all of our deepest wounds. I have been in conscious codependency recovery for many years, but I have had relatively little experience in romantic relationships because of the relationship phobia I talked about in Fear of Intimacy - Relationship Phobia

It was because of that relationship phobia that I didn't understand my fear of intimacy defenses - had not had the opportunity to work through the layers of the defenses in an actual relationship experience - enough to be able to stop them from causing me to sabotage the relationship that began in December of last year.

"I recently had the gift of being involved in a romantic relationship that helped me to open my heart in a way that I had never before been capable of doing in this lifetime. Unfortunately, when we first got involved I was still reacting to old tapes that I hadn't yet been able to stop giving some power to. Those old tapes caused me to sabotage - and then end - the most Loving and nurturing relationship I have ever been involved in. . . . It was only after ending it that I was able to get in touch with the fact that what needed to change was me. Recognizing what I had done was the shock to my system that I needed to look at and start changing the old tapes that were blocking me from opening my heart. I was then able to open my heart to Loving myself and the other person in Truly magnificent ways." - June 2004: Emotional Intimacy - A romantic tragedy / a Spiritual Transformation

It was Truly magnificent, amazing, and awe inspiring to me, for me to open my heart to Love in a way I had never experienced in my life. To break through what I thought were the most formidable, entrenched blocks to intimacy - to opening my heart to another human being - is the single most powerful and transformational experience I have had in my life. I was Truly in awe of what I discovered about my own capacity for Love, for Loving.

That was when the truly insidious nature of my codependency really kicked in. Once I had gotten past the huge, obvious defenses to intimacy, the more subtle and deeper levels of my wounding started to cause me to behave in ways that would sabotage my ongoing relationship with her. That is, that after my fear of intimacy defenses against opening my heart to another person had caused me to sabotage and end our original relationship, then the core wounding / the toxic shame caused me - even after I had opened my heart to her - to sabotage the possibility of reconnecting with her on a romantic level.

"In this relationship, I started out in the role of counterdependent with her being the codependent - and then it switched. . . . . . My dysfunctional "destination thinking" kept me reacting from a place of thinking that if she could just open her heart in the way I had, then we could be together in a wonderful way - a version of happily-ever-after. I would fall into pushing - campaigning - for the destination I wanted which would sabotage being able to be present and enJoy what we had in the moment because it would push her into her counterdependent reaction of running away and thinking she needed to banish me from her life." - July 2004: Enjoying the Journey - a Birthday Miracle

I fell into a horrible codependent trap. I was behaving towards her in ways that were not Loving in order to try to convince her of how much I Loved her and how wonderful we could be together if she could get past her fear of intimacy.

In Chapter 15 of this book - Falling in love as a choice I talked about my April Fools Day lesson about falling in love. In it I said, "I am choosing to go into the emotional place that she will lead me to learn lessons about my self. I will not buy into the belief that she is victimizing me. When I am hurting because: she is not doing what I want her to; when she is not opening up to the potential of how wonderful we could be together; when she is reacting to her fears and wounds; I will always remember that I choose to venture down the path this way and that any feelings that result will be my responsibility - they will be the consequences of my choice. They will not be her fault. She does not have the power to hurt me unless I give it to her - and I am choosing to give her some power over my feelings."

I understood that in 1990 and here I was in 2004 falling into feeling like a victim. That is how powerful the codependency is - not because I am stupid. I did recognize it somewhat at the time, but was still powerless to stop the behavior. As I say in the next paragraph, she was available as long as I was unavailable - this is the point where I would have let go of the relationship if I had been healthier. (And of course, I didn't end it in a healthy way because I was supposed to sabotage that relationship to learn the lessons I needed to learn to be available for my present relationship.)

"She however, who had been totally committed to the relationship as long as I was still somewhat emotionally unavailable, was afraid of my new capacity to Love. She hadn't opened her heart to herself yet, so she was afraid of me being available to Truly Love her in healthier ways that she had ever known - in healthier ways than I had ever been capable of. In the attempts we made to reconnect, she kept reacting to her old tapes that told her that she was not deserving of my love, that she would fail me if she gave me another chance to be in relationship with her." - June 2004 Emotional Intimacy - A romantic tragedy / a Spiritual Transformation

What I said in this quote from my June article is the truth - she was reacting to her own fear of intimacy and betrayal issues, and to the toxic shame at the core of her relationship with her self. And I could see that in her clearly - and kept trying to help her understand. But in that June column I was still not seeing my self clearly - was not owning my responsibility in what was happening.

I was behaving in ways that gave her good reason to pull back - so that at the same time she was reacting to her wounds, she was taking care of her self by pulling back from my unhealthy behavior. I got past the gatekeeper that was guarding my heart from opening to another being, but then the gatekeeper that was guarding me from opening my heart to my self caused me to focus upon and blame her gatekeeper for keeping her unavailable to me in the ways I wanted her to be available. As I said in one place in my processing about all of this, it is like I pushed her into a corner and then in effect judged and blamed her for being in a corner.

Even though I was starting to see my part in things more clearly in July, I was still primarily blaming her gatekeeper when I wrote my first article about the Gatekeeper in August.

She did react to her wounds and run away - but she was also responding to unhealthy and imbalanced behavior on my part. Underneath the gatekeeper that was guarding my heart to protect me from being hurt by others, was the toxic shame that was a deeper level of my gatekeeper - that was keeping me from opening my heart to myself on the kind of powerful and transformational levels that were in balance with the magnificent way I had opened my heart to Love another. Truly insidious and baffling and powerful is this condition of codependency.

But my codependency recovery has helped me to keep stripping away the levels of dishonesty - the rationalization and denial and justification - that the critical parent voice creates to hide the real reason I was behaving the way I was. It helped me to stop focusing so much on her and her part in things, and bring the focus back to me and my part in things - so that I could take responsibility for my side of the street and uncover the real reasons for my codependent behavior." - Codependent Defenses - Part 3 My Gatekeeper

Here is the rest of what I had to say in that Update Newsletter from April 2008.

As I said above, it is kind of embarrassing to reread - and to share here - those feelings I went through. Those women were not people I had much in common with - nor was I even very attracted to them (physically, emotionally, in any way really - I think I have sometimes tried to convince my self I was attracted to someone because they were attracted to me and because I had those deprivation issues.) But these relationships were a necessary part of my recovery journey.

This was a long excerpt - with some additions & editing - from the April 2008 Update Newsletter of the Joy2MeU.com website. I have moved a chunk of what was originally included in that Update (and in this chapter) to the end of the next chapter because it is about my present relationship and really belongs there instead of here.

Chapter 39 - Personal History in relationship to fear of intimacy
"deep down, all I have ever really wanted was a simple life with a good woman"

Most of this chapter is an excerpt from an addendum to my March 2007 Update Newsletter in which I gave an overview of my journey through healing my fear of intimacy enough to have gotten into the relationship that I am still in now in August 2012 as I prepare this book for publication. (With the information from the April 2008 Update Newsletter following the overview.)

"I started my first web site on Silcom.com in February of 1998 - and Joy2MeU.com in February of 1999. Even before starting Joy2MeU.com I had started to do some processing about my issues in writing for the web site. I had already gotten enough of a taste of the power and promise of the internet to recognize that it was a vehicle which could allow me to share my recovery in a way which was helpful to other people around the world.

"I guess it is pretty weird to be processing here on my computer and then sending it out for the world to read - but that is what I do. The Truth is so powerful and wonderful and by doing the process work we get to start being allies with the Spirit where Love lives instead of with the disease where fear rules." - Update - Joy to You & Me November 1998

That November 1998 Newsletter was one in which I talked of my fear of being too visible - of becoming a target for closed minded people who would want to burn me at the stake again for making controversial statements. And I stated that since I had decided that I wanted to get all my Karma settled and was willing to be burned at the stake again, maybe I was even ready to start looking at my fear of intimacy. That being willing to be burned at the stake was easier for me to contemplate and potentially accept, than dealing with my fear of intimacy - tells you something about how much terror is involved for me in opening up to Love.

It was interesting to me, that in my latest Intensive workshop (March 24th 2007 - as I said, this chapter is primarily taken from an addendum to my Update Newsletter for March 2007) I ended up talking about the challenge that I issued to the Universe in that November 1998 Update Newsletter. I hadn't talked about that in depth in any of the previous Intensives. I am going to include - and reread for myself - a long excerpt from my August 2004 Update that includes that challenge that I first issued in November 1998 - it was a challenge that the Universe answered immediately the first time I issued it. The very next day after I challenged the Universe to bring on whatever lessons I needed to learn, I started a relationship experience. And it answered it fairly quickly on the other times that I stated my intention and commitment here in writing on my site for the world to read - which meant to me, shouting out loudly and clearly for the Universe to hear.

(Within the March 2007 overview of my relationship history, I used a long excerpt from my Update Newsletter of August 2004 that I updated and clarified in that March 2007 Newsletter. In that 2007 Update on my website I used different colored type to add comments of clarification and additional explanation. In this chapter I am going to use italics for the excerpt from the August 2004 Update - but not for the quotes within that excerpt - as a way of trying to clarify where it is coming from without using different colored type. (And there are no quotes from my book in this chapter so any italics will be from the August 2004 writing.) The comments that I added at that time I am going to put within parenthesis - and I will be indenting them just a small amount. I will do any updating to those comments that I feel will be helpful for this chapter - as well as adding some additional information as the Spirit moves me. That updating or additional material will be only slightly indented and will not be in parenthesis. In some places there are comments within the article in parenthesis because I was correcting or updating something.)

"My priority for many years now has been my work - what I believe is my mission as a mystical messenger in this lifetime. My brief romantic adventure at the end of 1998 and into early 1999 - where I got to experience that I could do a romantic relationship without my self worth being involved - taught me that it was possible for me to Love and lose without being devastated by shame and blame and feelings of failure. I even said in that article, that now I know I have nothing to fear from intimacy.

"I have learned:

That when I know who I am and have my self-esteem rooted in my Spiritual connection then I have nothing to fear from intimacy. I can be hurt for certain because I will be choosing to give some power away over my feelings - but hurt is part of life and well worth the adventure of Loving and Losing.

That it is Truly possible to do enough healing to be able to open my heart to someone and then not take it personally when the other person "rejects" me - because I Truly know in my gut that she is just reacting to her wounds not to some inherent flaw in my being.

That I can have my worst fear of abandonment and rejection appear to come true and not give it any power because I do not have to buy into the disease telling me that it is my fault - that I did something / said something / am something that is wrong / a loser / a mistake / unlovable / unworthy. This is such a gift - to know that I can keep the critical parent shut up and out of the game is Truly an Amazing Miraculous reward for being willing to do my healing." - An Adventure in Romance - Loving and Losing Successfully

Knowing that I have nothing to fear from intimacy and getting past my fear of intimacy turned out to be two entirely different things. I did not come close to a romantic relationship for over 4 years after that Adventure in Romance ended. I kept chipping away at my fear of intimacy issues whenever the Universe prompted me to look at them, but I didn't take any action to put myself in the arena.

(In several places in this excerpt I refer to the "arena." That refers to something I quoted earlier in that Update, a statement I make in many places in my writing - and which the title of this book is take from - "I believe that romantic relationships are the greatest arena for spiritual and emotional growth available to us.")

The biggest breakthrough for me in my personal process in relationship to being willing to deal with my intimacy came when I wrote my October 2000 Update. What came up in that Update processing scared me so much I went into denial about looking at my intimacy issues until the Universe pushed me into more processing while I was writing my May 2001 Update.

What pushed me into the processing in May 2001 was something I said to a friend after an NA meeting. This is the first paragraph in my May 23, 2001 Update Newsletter

"Hi everybody. I hope you are finding some moments of Joy in your life adventure today. I am having a heaven of a good time myself. I have really been enjoying my life this last few months. In fact, someone in my home group here in town - which is a Narcotics Anonymous meeting - had heard me talking about how much I was enjoying life and how grateful I was, for so many weeks that she made the assumption that I was in love. She asked me on the way out of a meeting a couple of weeks ago how my relationship was going. I said, "Are you kidding me! I have been talking about how much I am enjoying life - would I be doing that if I was in a relationship?"

Hearing my self say that was a prompt from the Universe to do some processing about my fear of intimacy issues.

That led to 3 pages of Newsletter processing, followed by 3 more pages in my journal within the Journal. That processing caused a major breakthrough in my recovery process in 2001.

"One of the things that I am realizing in the processing that was set off by this latest breakthrough in my process, is that I seem to just now be reaching - on a personal level - the level of consciousness that my book was written out of. It has been over 10 years now, since I wrote the core of what was to become Codependence: The Dance of Wounded Souls - over a period of 48 frenzied hours of writing, to be able to give a talk that I had scheduled months before." - Joy2MeU Update - August -2001

That was followed with more processing about my fear of intimacy issues in my journal in June of 2002 and then in November of that year. It was in that November 2002 processing that I got in touch with how comfortable that I had become with being alone and isolated.

"Because it is not a simple issue, because my road truly has gotten much narrower, because I have been busy in my life, it was easy to slip into just accepting isolation - and not take any action to change that condition of isolation. I have actually been quite happy and content with living here in isolation, able to devote my time and energy to my work. ;-)" - Joy2MeU Journal My Unfolding Dance 17 November 2002

"I had slipped into a black and white place of just accepting my isolation - a very comfortable rut. . . . . I am starting to take some actions to change it - some risks that involve peeking out of my comfortable rut." - Joy2MeU Journal My Unfolding Dance 18 November 2002

I did start taking some action to stick my toe into the arena at that time. I took some actions to sow some metaphysical seeds out into the Universe affirming that I wanted a romantic relationship in November of that year. One of those actions was to join an online personals service - not because I thought I would meet anyone that way, but as a metaphysical exercise in putting my intention out there. Nothing really came of joining that service for over a year until November 30th 2003 when I discovered the profile of my Twin Soul and sent her a message.

(My terror of dealing with the fear of intimacy defenses that were defending my heart was so powerful, that it was necessary for the Universe to guide me into the delusion that the person mentioned was my twin soul. In the excerpt from my August 2004 Update I was still thinking that the woman was my twin soul.)

During the time between the brief relationship that ended in January of 1999 and March of this year (2004) - over 5 years - my number 1 priority in my life was my work. I was totally focused upon, and somewhat obsessive compulsive about my writing. The result is the huge web site that you see. I wrote some wonderful stuff during that time - and it was a perfect unfolding of my path and mission to be so focused on my writing for that time. I am very proud of the body of work on this site. And everything I wrote was in some way related to what was going on in my personal growth process and recovery - was a part of my gradual peeling away of the layers of my fear of intimacy issues.

As I said earlier, it had never even occurred to me that anything but my work would be the first priority in my life. I was quite content with living in isolation with my writing in a place I love - living Joy-fully relating to nature without any messy emotional intimacy in my life. The transformation I went through in February of this year, after breaking up the relationship I had with the woman whom I believe is my Twin Soul, led to me opening my heart to her and changed my life - "changed my relationship with life and Love forever" as I said in my March Update.

I was writing furiously for my journal during this transformation time - trying to sort out and get clear on what is happening. I was going through a rapid and intense transformation that was revealing new facets of the "new me" almost daily in March of this year. On the morning of March 18th I realized that the relationship was now the first priority in my life. This is what I said in an e-mail to her that day.

"In doing that however another shift occurred in my perspective. My number 1 priority has always got to be myself, taking care of myself, doing what I need to do for my recovery and healing. And part of the commitment to myself is to my mission, which is an inseparable part of my recovery and Spiritual Path - an internal thing not an external thing. My mission isn't some external thing I have to be committed to - it is part of being committed to myself, it is part of me. I think maybe this new level of compassion for myself has made me more whole - more integrated than ever before.

What I realized the thoughts about wanting to be there for you this morning meant - what on one level I called wanting to be your sanctuary - is that Loving you has become my number 1 priority externally, That you have first call on my time and energy any time you need it." - Joy2MeU Journal My Unfolding Dance 32 March 2004

One of the things I realized then was that I have plenty of material written already - more than most of you will probably ever read. That doesn't mean that I won't keep writing - I have enough writing projects in the works to keep me busy for the rest of the year - but I will never again allow my writing to be an excuse to short change someone I am in relationship with. I did that when I was actually in a romantic relationship with my Twin Soul from December until the beginning of February when I broke up with her. I will never again let my work damage a relationship!

(Comment added in 2007: "My priority since getting into my present relationship has been the relationship and taking care of the family that came with it. The only real writing I have done in the last year and a half has been for my Update Newsletters. I am okay with that - as I said there is plenty on my site for people to read. My life is much more complicated now, but also richer and fuller - more grounded in the reality of the human experience, in experiencing life. It is much simpler and easier to live in a beautiful isolated place writing about metaphysics and intellectual theory about how to relate to other human beings than it is to actually relate to other human beings.;-)"

One of the reasons that I had been so comfortable in my isolated rut is because I had gotten so good at accepting whatever the conditions were in my life and making the best of them by choosing to focus on the part of the glass that was full instead of letting my codependency cause me to focus on the part of the glass that was empty so that I felt like a victim. I had really gotten very good at acceptance - and at letting go - which was what allowed me to have a lot of Joy in my life no matter what areas of my life I was experiencing deprivation in. I was able to learn to Truly be present in the here and now and be happy with what I had.

"We need to be willing to let go of everything.

In my particular case: I need to let go of ever having very much money in my life; of ever having much success for the book; of ever publishing more books; of ever having another romantic relationships; of ever having the kind of nurturing, comfortable space I would like to live in; of everything that I want.

I need to let go of trying to write the script so that the Universe can give me what I need.

It may, and often does in my experience, turn out that once I have let go of something - let go of trying to dictate to the Universe my idea of what I need in my life to be OK - then the Universe says "OK, now that you have surrendered, you can have what you wanted."

Because when I let go, I also open up to receive. As long as I am holding onto something, I am blocking the energy flow of the Universe. I have to let go and open up in order to allow the flow.

The catch is, that the letting go has to be real. I have to accept on a gut level that I can be happy and peaceful and fulfilled without: money; a relationship; whatever. There is no tricking the Universe into thinking I have let go when I am just pretending to let go so that I can get." Joy to You & Me and Joy2MeU Update 2-4-00

The thing is, that we can go out of balance with anything - including acceptance. In one of the articles in my Recovery Process for inner child healing I quoted something I originally wrote for a question and answer page on my original web site.

"We can go out of balance with anything. I can use acceptance as an excuse for not taking action or responsibility. I can use forgiveness as an excuse for not standing up for myself - to avoid confrontations. I can say I am taking care of myself when I am really isolating and indulging in instant gratification." - The Recovery Process for inner child healing - emotional balance

I was using acceptance to find serenity and Joy in my life in a really wonderful way - but I was also using acceptance as an excuse for not taking action to put myself in the arena. I had given up on my dreams coming True in the name of letting go. I was not taking responsibility as the co-creator in my life for doing my part in making my dreams come true.

"That is part of the paradox of recovery. It is very important to know that it is Ok to have dreams, to affirm and visualize our dreams coming true, to take action and plant seeds to make them possible, to open up to receiving all of the abundance of the Universe - and then we need to let go of believing that we will not be Ok until, or if, those dreams come true. We need to let go of the future and be present today. And know that we are Unconditionally Loved today - and every day, rather we reach our goals or not." - Joy to You & Me and Joy2MeU Update 2-4-00

I had spent so much energy on learning to let go of the future, of not allowing my destination thinking to cause me to feel like a victim today because I haven't reached the destination - that I forgot to do my part in making my dreams come true. . . . . I have had huge deprivations issues in my life because of the relationship phobia created by my fear of intimacy issues. I had to work real hard to learn how to stop giving those deprivation issues the power to pollute how I related to women. In fact, in my journal processing of June 2002, I got in touch with some shameful behavior that manifested in my relationships with women after I got into recovery - because I was actually feeling the fear for the first time. Because those deprivation issues had so much power, it was easier for me to go to the extreme of not getting involved in physically intimate relationships.

"It was so important for me to learn to let go of any wants of mine that weren't being met. Certainly I want a romantic relationship, on some level I am starved for support and companionship, for affection and touch, for Love - but there is no one in my life today who can fill that role for me so I have to let go of the illusion that I am not OK today without it.

It was so liberating for me to learn to stop being the victim of not having what I wanted - and start focusing on being grateful for what I had. Wishing things were different just made me a victim, and when I am focusing on the part of the glass that is empty I am creating a victim space for myself where I am generating feelings of self pity. It was a miserable way to live life.

"It was wonderfully liberating in recovery to start learning that I could start to see life in a growth context. That I had a choice to focus on the half of the glass that was full instead of giving power to the disease which always wants to focus on the half that is empty. When I focus on what I have, and have been given, that I am grateful for - instead of just focusing on what I want that I don't have - it helps me to let go of the victim place my disease wants to promote.

What works for me is to remind myself of the difference between my wants and my needs. My Truth is that every day that I have been in recovery all my needs have been filled - and there has not been a single day that all my wants have been met. If I focus on what I want that I don't have then I feel like a victim and make myself miserable. If I choose to remind myself of what I have and how far I have come then I can let go of some of the victim perspective." - Gratitude

A part of my Karmic mission in this lifetime was to learn how to not be a victim. By not focusing on my wants that have not been met, I don't create victim feelings for myself. I am OK today without those wants being met. If I start thinking that I will never have a relationship, or about the future at all, then I am not being present today. As long as I am present today, I can accept wherever I am at, and whatever my reality is by owning my power to choose where I focus my mind. . . .

. . . . . Human connection, companionship, affection, touch, etc., are legitimate "needs" - but I classify them as wants, because that is what works to help me find some peace and serenity today. Different definitions for the same word in different context, from a different perspective.

I do not have to let go of wanting a romantic relationship. What I learned to let go of, was buying into the belief that I am not OK **today** without one. And I learned to not focus on the future and feel deprived about what might be - or might not be - going to happen then." - Joy2MeU Journal My Unfolding Dance 12 June 2002

I did such a good job of focusing on enjoying the journey that I forgot that I had some responsibility for making my dreams come true. I had experienced having my hopes and dreams crushed so many times that it was easier to stop hoping and dreaming. I made my mission my life - and accepted that I wasn't going to have the type of relationship I wanted in this lifetime. I really accepted that part of the price I had to pay for being a teacher and messenger was to be deprived of a romantic relationship for the rest of this lifetime.

"My Truth is that I do believe I am a mystical messenger on a Divine mission - that is my reality. How can another person really understand that? It is a pretty hard thing to get one's mind around. Why would someone want to live with a person who is either: A. that delusional; or B. an actual mystic? Anyone who knows and sees me in person has ample evidence that this messenger is very much human - flawed, imperfect, learning and growing, a wounded soul in recovery. How does one relate to a recovering codependent that is also a mystical messenger?

I have spent years working on peeling away the levels of my fear of intimacy issues. The writing for this Journal and my site have been so valuable in that process. I think that because of my mission the process has seemed to unfold very slowly for me - so that I would share it in my writing. One of those good news bad news things again. But I have come so far - I am now much more open to being a "receptacle for Love to flow into" as well as being a "channel for Love to flow through."

"Anytime I have a chance to speak my Truth, to share the beliefs and knowledge which I so passionately embrace, I get to touch the Divine. I get to be a channel for Love to flow through. (One of the things I want to talk about in this Newsletter is that it can be easier to be a channel for Love to flow through than a receptacle for Love to flow into.)" - Joy to You & Me and Joy2MeU Update10-20-2000

(It was writing this line in the October 2000 Update that led to the processing in part 2 of that Update Newsletter about my fear of intimacy. It was the stark Truth that was revealed to me when I wrote how much easier it was for me to be a channel than a receptacle - that forced me to open up the Pandora's box that processing my terror of intimacy felt like to me.)

As I say, I think I have been, am being, successful in this mission of being a messenger, and that it will continue as long as I am in this body.

However, deep down inside, all I have ever really wanted was a simple life with a good woman - with a woman who I can Love and who Loves me." - Joy2MeU Journal: Miracles 2 Leap of Faith ~ Publishing The Dance part 2

NO MORE! I will no longer accept that I can't have a romantic relationship in my life. On August 18th, as I was getting ready to go to one of the CoDA meetings here locally that I started and continue to serve as secretary for, I had an insight. It was one of those slight shifts in perspective that suddenly shine a new Light on some issue, situation, event, whatever. This insight brought me great Joy - and some of that sobbing and crying again.

The insight had to do with realizing what the adjective is that most describes my experience of 2004 thus far. That it has been a very difficult and painful time - perhaps the most painful time - in my recovery is something I have been writing and talking about for some time. But, as I noted above in the writing I did a couple of weeks ago, it has not been the most difficult time. I also could not say that it was the most Joyous - although there has been a lot of Joy mixed in with the pain. And then yesterday the adjective came to me.

The year of 2004 has been for me, the single most EXCITING period of time in my life. It was exciting because I was given the opportunity and gift of developing some deep emotional intimacy with another human being. I opened my heart to another human being for the first time in my adult life - and though I got my heart broken, it was a glorious adventure. It was exciting because I was Alive in a way that can only come with involvement in an emotionally intimate relationship with another being . . . . .

(2004 was exciting - but it was mostly in my own mind that the excitement (and the intimacy) occurred. The 2 years since I got into my present relationship have been more exciting, and contained much more intimacy in reality. The processing I did in 2004 was in reality about getting more intimate with myself.)

. . . . I believe what I said in my March Update - that I quoted above:

"What I believe has been revealed in recent days and weeks is that - though the mission of spreading the message will continue on some level as long as I am in my present body - the primary focus of my life in the future has shifted to Loving and experiencing being Loved in an the intimate union with my Twin Soul (or soul mate if that is to be - hopefully the Universe has not helped me open my heart without having someone in the wings waiting for me to Love.) I believe, I feel very strongly, that I am finally ready for the life partner I have been seeking forever - and that my days of wandering in the wilderness in isolation on a personal level are about to end." - Joy2MeU Newsletter March 2004 - Opening to Love

It appears that my focus now is going to be finding the Soul Mate that I believe is out there. I am going to do what it takes to find the woman who is going to be willing to explore emotional intimacy with me. That is of course easier said that done because it cannot happen with just any woman. It has to be someone that I have some physical attraction to for one thing - but even more important it has to be someone who I feel a strong vibrational connection to, an energetic attraction to/relationship with. I don't believe that my Higher Power has arranged for me to learn to open my heart without having a plan to allow me to have the type of relationship that I have always wanted. I want to be with someone who Loves me and cherishes being in relationship with me - who will give me the chance to be a "receptacle for Love to flow into" - and who has done enough healing that she will be open to allowing me to Love her. I believe that one of my Soul Mates whom I have not yet settled all my Karma with - is in body at this time, and hopefully has been preparing to be reunited with me. Finding her is going to be a priority in my life now.

(It turned out that not only did I not have to go looking for the next relationship, but when it appeared suddenly and unexpectedly in my life the type of feelings of Karmic attraction / soul mate / vibrational connection I was talking about here were not part of the equation - physical attraction definitely was involved, but not the instant recognition / vibrational connection / "this is my soul mate" type of feeling of familiarity. The Divine Plan presented me with a scenario I could not have imagined - one that not only brought me a beautiful life partner, but also included a precious little baby and a marketing director to help me spread the message.)

. . . . . So, I am going to wrap up this Update now. But first I am going to make a declaration about my future and the direction that I am heading in. I am actually going to repeat a declaration I first made in my November 1998 Update. The day after I published that Update I met the woman who I had the Adventure in Romance with in December of 1998. (Who showed up in the matches sent to me on Match.com last week - my Higher Power's cute sense of humor again.;)

I then repeated this declaration in my November 2002 Update. That was followed by a relationship experience in the Spring of 2003. It was a long distance relationship that included two short visits by the woman to Cambria - and was about 95% fantasy and 5 % relationship. (As opposed to the relationship in 2004 with my "twin soul" delusion, which was about 80% fantasy and 20% reality.) It was very important however because it opened me up to being willing to take the risk of getting involved with someone who did not fit my "Dream Woman" image. My "Dream Woman" image - of what I thought my Twin Soul would look like in this lifetime - was revealed in my processing in the journal the early part of this year, to be the biggest block / defense my ego was holding onto to keep me from getting into a relationship.

As I got in touch with how much of that long distance relationship was a fantasy, I repeated the declaration in my September 2003 Update. (At that time I was also trying to raise the money to keep my book in print.)

"If the relationship adventure that is in my life now continues as one of the ways I am getting to learn about Love - that will be great. If it doesn't, then I hope I do not have to wait 4 years for my next opportunity. If my book goes out of print and I have to let go of this web site - it will be very painful and sad to me, but I am willing to accept my path as it unfolds with faith in a Loving Higher Power. Whatever it takes, however it unfolds - I Know a Loving Divine Plan is unfolding. So I will paraphrase again what I said in those two November Updates:

Screw the fear, bring on the Love. I once again reaffirm my commitment to being an ally with the Spirit where Love lives instead of with the disease where fear rules. Whatever is in store for me on my path that will help me learn about - and reconnect with - Love, I welcome. Bring it on Universe!

So, this Update- and my Donations page - is my way of planting some seeds. More will be revealed about what grows." Joy2MeU Update September 2003

That planted the seed for me to meet the woman I found in the online personals on November 30th (2003). Because I was open to getting involved with someone who did not fit that image, I was able to get involved with the woman (who I would later realize - delude myself into thinking - was my Twin Soul) in December. That Dream Woman image was a major reason that I did not get invested in that relationship - and eventually ended it - because my Twin Soul does not fit that Dream Woman image in many ways.

It was letting go of the Dream Woman image - on one level by admitting to myself that it looked a lot like my mother when she was 19 and I was a baby - that helped me break through my fear of intimacy defenses and open up my heart to Loving her.

[Letting go of that Dream Woman image - and so much of the other emotional turmoil / insanity that I went through in 2004 - was the Universe preparing me for the relationship I am in now. I would not have been able to even begin this relationship if I had not gone through the experiences I had in 2004. (I don't mean that I needed to experience insanity to prepare me for this relationship - although this one has certainly had it's moments.;-) What I mean is that working through my fear of intimacy defenses caused me to feel insane at times while I was being led to let go of various parts of the armor plating that was protecting my heart by keeping me unavailable to experience a relationship that didn't meet all the preconceived notions I had about what would be necessary for me to do that.]

So I have made this declaration 3 times - and it was always followed within a relatively short time with a relationship experience. I am going to make this declaration here today and have faith that the Universe will answer my challenge by either creating a miracle that causes my Twin Soul to open her heart to me and realize we belong together - or that the Soul Mate that I still have Karma to settle with will come into my life. And I have faith that whichever of these things happens, this will be my last relationship of this lifetime and will last for the rest of this lifetime.

So I originally challenged the Universe in the Joy to You & Me Newsletter IV - November 22, 1998. I then repeated it, using the same wording, in November 2002:

> **"So, I once again reaffirm my commitment to being an ally with the Spirit where Love lives instead of with the disease where fear rules**. I Joyously, with tears running down my cheeks and sobs of Joy bubbling up my throat, proclaim and declare to you; to the Universe; to my Higher Power; to The God-Force, Goddess Energy, Great Spirit, Holy Mother Source Energy; to all that is blessed and holy; **Fuck the fear I say - full speed ahead in the direction of Love.**
>
> I trumpet and broadcast proudly out into the Universe: my commitment to my recovery journey; to my Karmic mission; to speaking my Truth; and say: "Bring it on Bubba baby!" Because it is so worth it! Every second of suffering and pain, terror and loneliness, is worth being able to access the Truth of Unconditional Love. Amen. So be it. So it is. Blessed be.
>
> Should be interesting to see what happens now, don't you think. ;-)" Joy to You & Me and Joy2MeU Update Newsletter November 2002

I declare here today, August 30th, 2004, that I am ready to meet any challenge the Universe wants to throw at me that will serve my quest to reconnect with Love. I believe that the greatest service I can do to my own healing and recovery process - and to the Planetary Healing process - is to explore emotional intimacy in a Loving romantic relationship. If it is part of the Divine Plan for my Twin Soul to awaken to our connection and decide that she wants to be my partner in this journey that would be wonderful and a True gift of Grace. If however, it is not possible in the Divine Scheme of things for us to be reunited until our next lifetime, then guide me to the Soul Mate that is to be my next teacher and partner in this quest for Love. Full sped ahead in the direction of Love is the theme and the direction!!!

Once again I reaffirm and declare my commitment to being an ally with the Spirit where Love lives instead of with the disease where fear rules.
Bring it on Universe!!!! Whatever it takes!!!!
Screw the fear - I Demand to be Guided to Love!!!!

Thank You for the Wonderful Relationship that is Manifesting in my Life Now!" - Joy2MeU Update August 2004

(That declaration in August 2004 took until January 12th 2005 to produce results - something I first shared in my March 2005 Update. In August 2012, I am adding some additional information to this excerpt from the March 2005 Update that was not in that Update when published - including an excerpt from an article that has never been published on my site that is within this excerpt.)

"A major goal for me in 2005 is to be more involved in life. I have taken steps to be more Alive and involved with other human beings this year. My time of living in isolation in a beautiful place I Love, focused on my writing, was a wonderful, wonderful chapter in my life. But I entered this year knowing that I wanted to be more involved in the experience of living from now on, than in writing about it from an intellectual, theoretical perspective. . . . .
. . . . . The woman from last year, that I believed was my Twin Soul is no longer in the picture in any way. I don't know if she is in fact my twin soul or not. I can't really know that with certainty. What I know is that she was a catalyst for the greatest single period of growth I have ever experienced. I will be forever grateful to her for that.
In writing the last article in the sub series about that relationship experience that I published at the end of December, I talked of how far I had come in the process of letting go of her - of letting go of my dream of what she and I could be together. I shared how she had run away from our relationship 6 times - and had come back 5 times.

"I am glad that she came back 5 times, because that gave me the opportunity to clean up my side of the street. I am very sorry that she is still powerless to stop her ego defenses from causing her to go into reaction to the extremes. I am very sad that she is not at the point in her recovery / Spiritual path where she is willing to do the healing to make amends to her self and to me for her reactions. I have accepted that she is not going to be in my life again
As I finish up this series of articles, as I come to the end of the incredibly transformational year that 2004 has been for me, I remember something that I

was told in probably the first 48 hours of being in treatment 21 years ago next week. Insanity is doing the same thing over and over again and expecting different results.

It was not insane to allow her - to welcome her - back into my life 5 times, because there were more layers of my issues to peal, more to be learned from this particular teacher. Letting her back in a 6th time would most likely be insanity. She probably has a long ways to go before she can overcome her powerlessness over her codependency - and she will do it at a perfect time and in a perfect way for her Spiritual Path. I accept now - and it is very sad to me - that her path and mine are probably not going to cross again in this lifetime. I am profoundly grateful for the lessons I learned from interacting with her. I will always treasure the special moments we shared. But I am moving on. I deserve to have someone in my life who is capable of Loving and allowing themselves to be Loved. I deserve to have someone in my life who is willing to keep communicating and to make a commitment to working through issues instead of reacting by running away from them and stopping all communication.

One way that I can prove to myself that I deserve to be in a relationship that is nurturing and growing and Loving is to say no to a relationship that isn't. It is time for me to take responsibility for protecting myself against her codependency by Knowing that I am not willing to do the same thing over again with the same result. I am moving on, and looking for the soul mate that has been preparing herself for our reunion. It is time for me to meet her again so that I can learn more about Loving and being Loved. I have reached the point where I have bid goodbye in my heart to the woman who was my teacher in 2004." - Codependence Recovery - Taking Responsibility Part 2

I had gone most of the way to letting go of her when I wrote that article. And then something happened that I have never experienced so powerfully previously. A communication from her about that article - and an e-mail that she sent me on January 2nd (my e-mail response to that one was the last communication between us) - opened my eyes to some facets of the relationship experience I had not seen clearly before. I read that e-mail through one time - and I was completely done with the relationship. Instantaneously it was over for me absolutely. In writing this today I realize that what happened in the moment of my reading that e-mail, was that any ties / chords of energy that were still in place from me to her were completely severed. Never before have I experienced such a clear and clean and complete closure of anything in my recovery process. (This shift occurred because she communicated with me in such a way that it helped me wake up to the fact that she was bi-polar and had told me that she had gone off of her medication when we first met - a red flag I had ignored. Realizing this helped me to recognize how much of her behavior was caused by that condition and helped me let go of taking anything that had happened personally. That helped me let go of the relationship completely and magically.) It was a blessed gift and a miracle.

And of course, it was perfect timing in the Cosmic Scheme of things. Because 10 days later I was contacted for the first time by someone who just might be that soul mate I stated that I was going to be looking for in the August Update and December article.

The Universe answered my prayer / affirmation / challenge by bringing a new teacher into my life to help me do some more work on healing my relationship with myself - healing my fear of intimacy issues. And my Higher Power arranged that I would be completely through with the last experience before this one appeared in my life. Very cool.

Rather this person is someone / the soul mate, that is going to be in my life long term or not I do not know at this time. It is possible that she is a brilliant flaming shooting star who is flashing through my world to illuminate some things / issues that I needed to see with more clarity - a catalyst of growth and awakening. Perhaps I will get to once more experience a broken heart and the grief that goes with it. I don't get to know that right now. What is important is that I am willing to take the risk - and the Universe has brought a very special lady into my life to help me learn. I am hoping that she is the special woman who will be willing and able to surrender to opening her heart to me, to surrender to the experience of Loving me - while I surrender completely to the experience of Loving her, to opening my heart to her. More will be revealed about how this newest adventure is going to unfold.

So anyway, I thought this was going to be a pretty short Update - but as usual, I got a bit wordy. Oh well. It has helped me get some more clarity. If it proved of value to you, that is very cool. 2005 is going to be another interesting and exciting year. Hopefully it won't be nearly as painful as last year - but whatever it takes, wherever I am led, that is where I am willing to go in my Quest to experience Love." - Update March 2005

(In my June 2005 Update, I shared how events unfolded to bring Susan into my life - and wrote the following about the intuitive message that I clearly heard after spending time with her on January 23rd 2005, the day we first met in person.)

"During the course of the time we spent together that evening I got a glimpse of her True Self. Because of her childhood wounding and life experience, she had developed a defense system that to me - in our communication up until that night - had already seemed to be waving a lot of red flags warning me not to get involved. I was pretty stand offish despite the fact that I found her to be a very beautiful woman. Once I got a glimpse of her True Self, I knew immediately that this was a woman that I had to get to know.

What I saw was a woman with a beautiful heart and soul - with a huge capacity to Love - underneath the defenses that she had been forced to adapt to protect herself in her life journey. There was no doubt in my mind after that night, that no matter how many red flags I was seeing, I needed to surrender to experiencing whatever my Higher Power had brought her into my life to experience.

Her defenses were perfectly designed to push my buttons - to trigger some of my deepest wounds and reactions. And of course, my defenses pushed her buttons as well.

That night I surrendered to whatever ride the Universe had in store for me with this woman. That night I realized that I needed to ignore the red flags, let go of any preconceived boundaries or expectations, and go wherever this adventure led me." - Joy2MeU Update June 2005

The following is the excerpt from the April 2008 Update Newsletter that I moved to this chapter .

"The relationship experiences in 2003 and 2004 were a necessary part of my recovery journey.

"It was necessary for me to buy into the delusion that the person I met in December 2003 was my twin soul - in order to delve into my issues as deeply as I did in 2004. It was going through that experience that brought me to a place where I was available for my current relationship.

The Universe completely ambushed me with this relationship - and did it in such a way, that I had to throw out all the romantic fantasy stuff. There was no feeling that I had met a soul mate or twin soul - or that there was some powerful vibrational or Karmic connection in this relationship. I don't even think in those terms any more.

And it is not that there isn't romance in my relationship with Susan - there is. But there isn't a delusional romantic fantasy involved. I didn't get involved with her because I thought she was a soul mate or my twin soul or anything. And I didn't have to delude myself that there was a karmic connection after getting involved with her in order to justify that involvement - as I did in the fantasy relationship of 2004. I recognized that the Universe had brought her into my life as a teacher - and that I needed to surrender to the experience. That she is a gorgeous babe was a definite plus in helping to make that surrender. (And that isn't to say there isn't some karmic connection between us - there must be or we wouldn't be so deeply involved in helping each other grow.)" - Update on My Fear of Intimacy - an addendum to the Joy2MeU March 2007 Update

My deprivation issues caused me to buy into the delusion that the woman in 2004 was my twin soul so that I would try to hang onto the relationship. It caused us both a lot of pain but hopefully also facilitated a lot of growth for both of us. It did for me anyway, I Truly hope it did for her also.

As I shared with my yahoo e-mailing list in January, there was indeed a powerful karmic connection for me in this relationship - with a little baby named Darien. Susan's grandson who became my godson and step grandson was about 4 month old when I first met him.

"January the 23rd marked the 3rd anniversary since Susan and I met. A record for me for sure. I am so grateful that Susan came into my life - and this relationship sure has drastically changed my life. In my June 2005 Update I explained how "It took a cosmic "coincidence" of pretty monumental proportions for us to even connect at all" - and how on the evening of January 23rd 2005 I got a clear message from my Spirit that I was supposed to surrender to the experience of whatever my interaction with her would entail.

"That night I surrendered to whatever ride the Universe had in store for me with this woman. That night I realized that I needed to ignore the red flags, let go of any preconceived boundaries or expectations, and go wherever this adventure led me.

It has been a real e-ticket ride so far. I have thought it was over a multitude of times. She would react in ways that pushed my buttons - and I was sure it had ended. But then it would begin again.

The key factor is that she is actively in recovery, dedicated to getting healthier." - Joy2MeU Update Newsletter June 2005

And it is certainly true that Susan is very actively in recovery, and that without that we would not have had a chance for a relationship to last this long. But even with that, I think my fear of intimacy would have sabotaged the relationship long ago except for the factor that I really didn't know anything about at the time I wrote that June 2005 Update. That unknown factor is Darien.

We moved in together in June of 2005 - and until that time I didn't really have a relationship with the little boy. It was after we started to live together that Darien and I were drawn together. I mentioned in my August Update last year that I had just recently realized that he and I had a powerful Karmic / Soul connection.

"In late April or early May this year I had one of those light bulb going on / aha kind of moments of insight where I realized that Darien and I had a soul contract. That our souls had agreed to meet up at a certain point in this lifetime to be teachers and helpers to each other on our Spiritual Paths. Despite the powerful connection I feel to him - and that he obviously feels to me - this had never occurred to me before. When I mentioned my insight to Susan, she kind of looked at me funny and said something like, "Well duh, of course. You didn't know that?"" - Joy2MeU Update August 2007

Our concern and love for Darien got us through many rough passages in our relationship. He helped us to not take ourselves and our wounded ego button's so seriously, and to lighten up at times when we really needed to lighten up. Many times when I thought it was over, it was Darien who brought us back together. We have had a successful relationship in large part because we weren't just focused on the relationship - we weren't really free to allow our respective fear of intimacy to sabotage us because we both love that little boy so much. Our focus was larger than just the relationship between the two of us. That was true even before we became his primary guardians - which essentially started at the time of the April (2006) Intensive in San Francisco (the first time I offered my Intensive Training Workshop - something that was Susan's idea), even though it didn't become official until June of that year.

He continues to bring so much Joy to both of us, and the direction of our lives continues to be greatly impacted by our desire to take care of him. My fear of intimacy is still keeping me from opening my heart completely to Susan in some ways - and to myself also of course (the fear of shining too brightly I mentioned in my last post here) - but our Higher Powers unfolded our paths perfectly to put us together with Darien so he could help us both learn about Love. Susan and I are learning a great deal from each other - and the common ground of our love for Darien is helping our love to evolve." - Yahoo Mailing list January 2008

I got choked up and teary today rereading the quote above - and recognizing how the Universe orchestrated my path so that I could get past the shame and the terror of intimacy enough to be present for the relationship I am in today.

"So today, I am grieving once more for the eight year old who was trapped, and for the man he became. I am grieving because if I don't own that child and his feelings - then the man will never get past his terror of allowing himself to be loved. By owning and cherishing that child, I am healing the broken heart of both the child and the man - and giving that man the opportunity to one day trust himself enough to love someone as much as he loved Shorty." - Grief, Love, & Fear of Intimacy

I can see clearly now that Darien is the first human being - since my parents when I was an infant - that I have ever opened up my heart to completely. Because of my Love for Darien, I am gradually opening my heart to Susan.

Recovery is really an incredible journey - I highly recommend it.;-)

Be kind and compassionate for your self today - it is not your fault that you are wounded and have been deprived." - Joy2MeU Update April 2008

In my final preview of this chapter I felt the need to add something extra - and ran across what felt like just the right notes in August 2009 Update.

"A few days after posting the latest additions to my Darien page, towards bedtime he was fooling around behind me on the couch. He started trying to take things out of my pockets - and then I did let him take some folded up flyers out of my back pocket. They were flyers for my next Intensive that I carry around in case I meet someone that I think might be interested in my work. When he opened the flyer and looked at it, he says "It's you!" - because my picture is on the flyer.

Then he got this look of, like wonder on his face, and he gushed - gush is the word that most accurately fits the tone of voice and emotional content of his expression (not a way of expressing himself that I have ever heard from him before) - "I Love you!" And then he said, "You do this for the whole world." And he repeated both of those things several times after that.

I have no idea what was going on in his 4 3/4 year old brain - what he thought the flyer was - but it felt like a communication directly from his Spirit.

. . . . It felt as if the Great Spirit was speaking to me through him in that moment." - Joy2MeU Update August 2009

My Darien page is a page on my website that I put up to share pictures and stories about this little boy who has taught me so much about love.

"The mugging goofball pictured here is my partner Susan's grandson Darien. Before he could even walk or talk, before he even could crawl, I had started calling him Mr. Personality because of how expressive he was. He is my godson and step grandson - and his presence in my life is one of the greatest blessings of my recovery - one of the greatest gifts in my life. He is a precious, sweet, beautiful Spirit in a little boy body. He has brought great Joy to my life - and has taught me much about Love. He is a treasure.

The idea of of putting up a web page dedicated to him had been coming up in my mind for awhile because I want to leave him some evidence of how special he is to me. I don't know that I will be around long enough to see him grow up completely - and the thought of that makes me very sad. In fact now, when I think of how much longer I might live, it is always in the context of how old Darien will be by that time." - http://joy2meu.com/Darien.html

Chapter 40 - Romantic Relationships and Valentine's Day 2010
"This is not the relationship I was asking for, wanted or expected - but it is perfect."

On February 14th 2010, I posted an article with the above title as part of my page dedicated to my precious and beautiful godson and step grandson Darien. In it I shared the story of a remarkable breakthrough that Susan and I had made in our relationship. It was a breakthrough that led to our getting married in January of 2011.

For this chapter I am going to make additions to that article to include more details about our relationship, how it has unfolded, and some of the challenges and rewards that are a part of the gift that is this relationship.

I started the article on January 12th, 2010 when I wrote the following.

"On this day 5 years ago my life changed. I got an e-mail that was the result of "a cosmic 'coincidence' of pretty monumental proportions" - it was an e-mail from Susan.

The first mention I ever made of Susan in my writing, was in my March 2005 Update Newsletter - at the end of which I wrote:

"Rather this person is someone / the soul mate, that is going to be in my life long term or not I do not know at this time. It is possible that she is a brilliant flaming shooting star who is flashing through my world to illuminate some things / issues that I needed to see with more clarity - a catalyst of growth and awakening. Perhaps I will get to once more experience a broken heart and the grief that goes with it. I don't get to know that right now. What is important is that I am willing to take the risk - and the Universe has brought a very special lady into my life to help me learn. I am hoping that she is the special woman who will be willing and able to surrender to opening her heart to me, to surrender to the experience of Loving me - while I surrender completely to the experience of

Loving her, to opening my heart to her. More will be revealed about how this newest adventure is going to unfold." - March 2005 Update

It is now 5 years later - 3 years longer than my previous relationship record - so it has been long term for me, and Susan has been a brilliant flaming star illuminating issues in my life, definitely a catalyst for growth and awakening. But it has taken some time for some of the lessons to sink in, for some of the issues to become illuminated."

For this chapter I am going to add the story of the "coincidence" and some other information that I included in my June 2005 Update and some snapshots of the evolution of the relationship in other Updates - along with a couple of new sections I am writing now - one section before and one after sharing the rest of the Valentine's Day 2010 article.

Here is a long excerpt from my June 2005 Update.

"My lady and I are a most improbable, surprising coupling in many ways. We had been living very different life styles with divergent priorities - and an almost 14 year age differential. It took a cosmic "coincidence" of pretty monumental proportions for us to even connect at all in the first place. I had taken down my profile on the online dating services for a period of time because I didn't anticipate getting involved in another relationship in early January. I was still processing through the lessons I had learned in the relationship experience I was gifted with in 2004 - and because the shift I mentioned in my March Update had taken place at the very beginning of the year, had not made the profile visible again as yet. (This is the passage that I expanded upon in the last chapter.)

"And then something happened that I have never experienced so powerfully previously. A communication from her about that article - and an e-mail that she sent me on January 2nd (my e-mail response to that one was the last communication between us) - opened my eyes to some facets of the relationship experience I had not seen clearly before. I read that e-mail through one time - and I was completely done with the relationship. Instantaneously it was over for me absolutely. In writing this today - because of the digression above - I realize that what happened in the moment of my reading that e-mail, was that any ties / chords of energy that were still in place from me to her were completely severed. Never before have I experienced such a clear and clean and complete closure of anything in my recovery process. It was a blessed gift and a miracle.

And of course, it was perfect timing in the Cosmic Scheme of things. Because 10 days later I was contacted for the first time by someone who just might be that soul mate I stated that I was going to be looking for in the August Update and December Suite 101 article. " - Joy2MeU Update Newsletter March 2005

The coincidence had to do with a phone counseling client on the East Coast. I had shared with her that an important part of me opening up to becoming available for a relationship experience had been putting up a profile on some online dating services. (I originally did the online dating thing thinking nothing would come of it, but rather as a symbolic action - as I mentioned in an earlier chapter - to put my desire for a relationship out to the Universe.) She had decided to take my advice that she try out the experience - and in communicating with me about the profile she had put up, asked me if she could see my profile. So, I made my profile viewable for a period of less than 24 hours. During that time the woman who I am involved with now contacted me. She happened to do a search that night for men who lived in Cambria. She has always been drawn to the little coastal town I live in - and had even gotten married here some years earlier. She had dreamed for years of moving to this area - and on that night her frustrations with living in San Diego had driven her to repeat a search that she had done previously without seeing my profile because it wasn't available.

So, on the night of January 12th I received a communication from her. I was not really interested in a long distance relationship, and though she was very attractive it didn't look to me from her profile as if we were interested in the same types of things - so I didn't respond for a few days. We exchanged a few e-mails and she told me that she was going to be in the area soon - but I really had no expectations that anything would come of our connecting.

She did not contact me when she had told me she probably would - and I had pretty much dismissed the possibility of meeting her from my mind that weekend. When I did hear from her on Sunday afternoon the 23rd of January, it was unexpected and on the phone number I use for counseling which I do not get other calls on normally. I was actually kind of rude when I first answered because I thought she was someone else that should have known better than to call me on that line. Despite my rudeness, she was compelled to drive to Cambria to meet me that night.

During the course of the time we spent together that evening I got a glimpse of her True Self. Because of her childhood wounding and life experience, she had developed a defense system that to me - in our communication up until that night - had already seemed to be waving a lot of red flags warning me not to get involved. I was pretty stand offish despite the fact that I found her to be a very beautiful woman. Once I got a glimpse of her True Self, I knew immediately that this was a woman that I had to get to know.

What I saw was a woman with a beautiful heart and soul - with a huge capacity to Love - underneath the defenses that she had been forced to adapt to protect herself in her life journey. There was no doubt in my mind after that night, that no matter how many red flags I was seeing, I needed to surrender to experiencing whatever my Higher Power had brought her into my life to experience.

Her defenses were perfectly designed to push my buttons - to trigger some of my deepest wounds and reactions. And of course, my defenses pushed her buttons as well.

That night I surrendered to whatever ride the Universe had in store for me with this woman. The intuitive message I got that night was very clear - that I needed to ignore the red flags, let go of any preconceived boundaries or expectations, and go wherever this adventure led me.

It has been a real e-ticket ride so far. I have thought it was over a multitude of times. She would react in ways that pushed my buttons - and I was sure it had ended. But then it would begin again.

The key factor is that she is actively in recovery, dedicated to getting healthier. Thus though her reaction was to run away from me - her pattern has been to leave relationships before she could be left - she did not run away for long. I had my deepest wounds around abandonment, betrayal, and rejection pushed - and kept coming back for more because that is what I had surrendered to doing back on January 23rd. I kept throwing out any intellectual, rational conclusions about what was going on, about the red flags that kept appearing - and surrendering to following my intuitive guidance to go wherever this ride took me.

One of the most unusual things about the experience to me, is that she was resistant to my writing from the beginning. What has been a normal occurrence for me in recent years, is that women who fell in love with my writing and my message would think they were my soul mate or something and want to get to know me. She didn't much care for my writing - has still not completely read my book - but was interested in me anyway. She saw something in me that she was very attracted to, that was not the result of what I do or the message I have been given the gift of carrying.

She had no interest in me being her teacher - and in fact, thought that it was me that needed her as a teacher. She was, of course, accurate in that assessment in multiple ways. She has been the catalyst for amazing growth for me - and is continuing to teach me daily. I had to let go of my role as a teacher in relationship to her - and really start learning about being a man in a relationship separate from my identity as a messenger and teacher.

This is not a relationship that I am going to be writing about in any detail as I have with past journalizing about my fear of intimacy issues - and my journey to learning to open my heart. I am only going to share in the most general kind of way about this amazing adventure the Goddess has gifted me with.

What has unfolded in recent months, is that she is now living here in Cambria - and I am moving in with her in the next couple of weeks. I have not only been given the blessing of having the opportunity to share my life journey with a dynamic, exciting romantic partner - I have inherited a whole family in the process. The brood includes her 17 year old daughter, her daughters boyfriend and their 7 month old baby - soon perhaps to be joined by her 20 year old son. I am getting the Joyous and amazing opportunity to be a step grandfather to the amazing little baby - and am sooo grateful for the opportunity. The family also includes 2 dogs, 2 cats, a rat, and a chicken named Jack. (And now a 3 month old pygmy goat named Pixie.)

The way the events unfolded - which included her getting a job in the area that fell through and being forced to move with very little in the way of financial resources - has allowed me to do something which I have never done before. I was able to step up to the plate and take financial responsibility for this whole brood. I have always had a problem just providing financially for myself, and have never felt capable of taking on that kind of responsibility.

That is what has put me into a precarious financial position - supporting my new family (along with plane trips to see my father before he died, and to go to his funeral.) When I got to the point of giving notice on my apartment in anticipation of moving in with my lady and her family, I still wasn't sure that the relationship wouldn't blow up and cause her to run away in reaction to her counterdependent defenses - leaving me in a position where I had no money and no place to live. But I took the risk anyway because that is what my Spiritual guidance told me to do - because I could see that there was potential for a great reward, a pot of gold at the end of this rainbow, if things worked out between us.

I am so very very grateful I have done this. I am today, June 27th, feeling very secure in the relationship - having grown to a place where I am giving less and less power to my reactions and hers - and really believe this is going to work out in very wonderful ways.

The growth I have made in surrendering to the adventure and not letting my inner child wounds have so much power, has created the space for her to grow in tremendous ways. She has been able to accept my help and develop a trust in me - two things that her wounding caused her to be very very resistant to - that has helped her to open her heart to me in amazing ways. She has learned to get past her defenses and be vulnerable - and we are developing a delicious and magnificent emotional intimacy. The experience of being Loved by her as she opens her heart to me, is exquisite. For the first time in my life, I am Truly being given the opportunity to receive an abundance of the Love I have been starved for all my life.

I have faith that the financial needs will be met somehow and that we are going to get the chance to explore this wonderful intimacy that we are creating between us. I do believe that what I intuitively wrote about in that Wedding Prayer over 7 years ago is now present and happening in my life.

(The following is one of several excerpts in this final chapter, that includes a long section that is part of another chapter of this book. I am leaving this here for a specific reason - it is a very good thing for you to review as you finish this book to help you remember what is important, and what is necessary, to have a chance to be available for a romantic relationship that will work for you to have some love and intimacy in your life instead of feeling like a victim of romance not being what you wanted or expected it to be.)

"You will need to Let Go. And Let Go, and let go again. On a daily basis. Let go of believing that the other person has to be in a good mood or has to like the same things or wants to do things at the same time. Let go of expecting that they can be there for you in the way you want all of the time. They can't. They are human. No one can meet all of another person's needs.

You each need to have resources / friends outside of your relationship. You each need to have parts of your life that aren't dependent upon the other.

You will hurt each other, scare each other, make each other angry. Which will then give you the gift of being able to work through those issues to a deeper level of emotional intimacy.

You have got some stuff to work through - that is both the bad news and the good news. Because as you reach those deeper levels of emotional intimacy your love will deepen and grow in ways in which you can't even imagine. You are boldly going where neither of you has ever been before. And you have a friend and a partner who is willing to make a sacred commitment here today to go on this adventure with you.

Celebrate that!! It is an incredible gift!

Grab each moment you can and be present with it.

By being willing to be present to feel the difficult feelings - hurt, sadness, anger, fear;

by being willing to walk through the terror of embracing life - the terror that this commitment to intimacy can bring up;

by being willing to take the risk of being abandoned and betrayed - to take the risk of completely exposing yourself to another being; you are opening yourself to Joy and Love to depths and on dimensions that you have only had the slightest taste of so far.

BE each other's sanctuary. Be patient and kind and gentle whenever you can make that choice.

The more you do your healing and follow your Spiritual path the more moments of each day you will have the choice to Truly be present the moment.

And in the moment you can make a choice to embrace and feel the Joy fully and completely and with Gusto.

In any specific moment you will have the power to make a choice to feel the Love in that moment as if you have never been hurt and as if the Love will never go away.

Completely absolutely unconditionally with fearless abandon you can embrace the Love and Joy in the moment.

Glory in it!

Loving is the Grandest, most sublime adventure available to us.

Lets your hearts sings together.

Let your souls soar to unimagined heights.

Wallow in the sensual pleasure of each others bodies.

Roar with the Joy of being fully alive.

Go for it!!!!" - Chapter 20 Meditation on Romantic Commitment

I now have the friend and partner who is willing to go on this adventure with me. It is an exquisite, blessed opportunity. This year has already been the most Joyous of my life - and it keeps getting better!!!!!!! What a blessing! What a gift! " - Joy2MeU Update June 2005

In my Update for October of that year, I shared what was developing.

"Last night there was a perfect moment in my life - a Kodak moment. I was lying on the couch looking at my "step" grandson sleeping in his stroller, while above him in the loft his grandmother - my significant other - was working on her computer. I took a mental snapshot of the moment as one that I always wanted to remember. In close proximity to two people that I Love very, very dearly - a moment of domestic bliss if you will. It brought tears of Joy and gratitude to my eyes, as I thanked my Higher Power for the opportunity I have been given to Truly open my heart to some other human beings in a magnificent and profound way.

The adventure I am experiencing in my life right now is Truly a blessed and awesome gift. The baby is now 11 months old - and just the most precious, beautiful, incredible little boy. Never had I imagined myself changing diapers and taking care of a baby - and Loving every moment of it. I have become Mr. Mom - doing the shopping and the laundry and taking care of the baby for periods of time - while my lady goes into work in San Luis Obispo every week day. Definitely not what I had imagined in my future only a few short months ago.

What is going to evolve in the coming months is a mystery right now - in the more will be revealed realm. There are numerous challenges, as there are with any new relationship - with such major changes in one's life. The pygmy goat had to go because of the noise it made - and that combined with a problem caused by one of the dogs has made it necessary for us to be looking for a new place. My mate is trying to establish herself in a new area in a business where contacts are vital - and the market is slow. I have been trying to generate more income to support this new family of mine, and it has been a major challenge.

As I mentioned in the June Update, my significant other is a magnificent teacher for me. The payoffs for being in the relationship have been enormous - and have led to many, many of the snapshot type of moments of domestic bliss, of romantic Love, over the course of the last 4 months. It is Truly the ride of my life.

It is now possible that we will need to move out of Cambria. I am having to consider multiple options to deal with the financial issues - including getting another job to help support this wonderful brood of a family. When things are stressful, my significant other feels like maybe she needs to move back to San Diego where she has the contacts to bring in more income. We are considering moving back there together - and she at times, feels like she needs to leave the relationship and move back there herself. That would Truly break my heart. I am so hoping that this relationship ending is not part of the Divine Plan.

We are considering moving to other towns in this area - but at the present time do not even have the finances to accomplish that. Truly a time when more will be revealed. She Loves living here in Cambria, as I do - but the housing situation here is very restricted. When one is looking for a large house that also takes pets, the choices are very slim.

It is a time when a lot of faith is required to be able to live one day at a time while also trying to create the abundance necessary to have choices. . . . . the reminder to have faith in the future while enjoying the journey one day at a time, is very timely and appreciated. As I was saying to my Lover yesterday - as we took a walk through the magical forest behind the house we want to rent - it is important for us to remember to not give so much power to fear of the future, and instead to "take time to stop and enjoy the baby." This time of experiencing her Love for me growing, our Love for each other growing - and sharing with her the experience of watching him grow - is the most amazing, Joyous time I have ever experienced. I am so grateful for this last few months no matter what the outcome of the situation turns out to be. I hope this adventure between us can continue for the rest of my life. ~ Robert October 17, 2005

. . . . My path has Truly been blessed with some amazing miracles over the years. There have been many times when the guidance I got from my intuition caused me to say "No way Jose!" to my Higher Power. This relationship experience is one of them. In the very beginning - and at times since then - I have thought I was crazy to think this relationship could work out. But my intuition told me to keep surrendering to the experience - and I am soooo grateful for the faith I have shown in following where this has led me. I have faith that the future will hold more miracles - although of course, I have no way of knowing what those will look like. I do hope and pray that this relationship will continue. I Know that a Loving Divine Plan is unfolding - and more will be revealed about what the future holds. In the meantime, I am going to enJoy this wonderful experience of Loving and being Loved by an amazing woman - and going to take time to enjoy the beautiful baby - while moving forward with faith that more miracles are just around the corner. ~ Robert 10/18/05" - Joy2MeU Update October 2005

In a Newsletter attached to my March 2006 Update I shared about the evolution of the relationship under the headline: **"freedom is just another word for nothing left to lose."**

"The line from the Kris Kristopherson / Janis Joplin song about freedom that is the topic heading for this section, is one I always resonated with - probably in part, as a rationalization for my deprivation.

To my ego defenses, it was better not to take the risk of succeeding - of opening to Love and success and abundance - because then I would just be setting myself up to lose something I valued. That to my damaged ego, would be worse than never having anything worth losing.

I have written in several places about my resonance with the song The Rose including the second Newsletter page of my June 2003 Update.

"It's the heart afraid of breaking that never learns to dance,
It's the dream afraid of waking that never takes a chance."

Since my ego defense is set up to protect me from the lie that I am inherently defective, that there is something shameful about my being, it operates from a place of believing it is better to not love, then to love and lose. My codependency is trying to protect me from opening up to abundance - of all types - as a way of trying to keep my shameful, defective being a secret.

It doesn't want me to take a chance, to really go for it.

The work I have done to open up to Love brought me to a place where I was willing to surrender to the relationship experience that I am gifted with today. That relationship has been a challenge to my ego from the very start. I knew the first night I met her, that she was a teacher who had come into my life to teach me about surrendering - as I mentioned in my June 2005 Update.

Susan, my significant other (who is now the Marketing Director for Joy to You & Me), has challenged my ego defenses in relationship to multiple levels and issues - but lately, most especially in regard to the limitations in the 2 areas I mention in the long excerpt about my fear of intimacy issues above: money and health.

In relationship to health, her presence in my life spurred me to lose over 30 lb. last year - and to get much healthier in many ways. She continues to challenge me to go the next level, in terms of working out and changing some habit patterns that are not healthy.

In regard to money, she has been pointing out how my fears have kept me in deprivation financially. How I am spending so much time and energy in counseling people one on one in my telephone counseling, when there are so many people out there who desperately need to hear what I have to share with them.

Once she saw me in action, speaking at the CoDA conference in San Francisco in October, and saw how dynamic and passionate I am in teaching people what I have learned - she started pushing me to set up more workshops / appearances. It was that appearance that really helped her to understand that what I teach people is how to radically change their relationship with self and life into a more Loving experience - and that what I do has very little to do with traditional counseling or therapy.

As I talked about in the Update portion of this Newsletter, the formula for integration and inner healing that I developed is the missing piece that so many people have been looking for. I knew that when I published the book, and that is why I thought it would be a best seller. When it wasn't - and I ended up in such a desperate situation financially, I guess I got gun shy.

I have never charged enough for workshops, or my counseling services. I have always come from a place of fear. Each of the several times I raised the telephone counseling rates, I have been afraid that I would lose all of my clients. Each time I have set a price for workshops, I have set it very low. The exception to this was the retreat I did on Ibiza last year - and that price was set by the people who organized it there.

When I say, I haven't charged enough - I don't mean charging what the teachings are worth. I don't think it is possible to set a price tag on what I teach people. Helping a person completely change their relationship with self and life is something that is invaluable. Many people have told me over the years, that it wouldn't possible to pay me enough for how much I had helped them improve the quality of their life. (An incident comes to mind that happened several years ago in an airport. I ran into a person who had been a client of mine in the early 90s when I was doing inner child healing groups with people. I had not seen her in 7 or 8 years probably - and the first thing that she said to me was, "Thank you for my life!" She had done the work with me before I published my book, and years before I had a website - before I had really refined the approach as much as I have in recent years.)

What I mean, is charging enough so that I can start having a little more financial freedom. In my October 2000 Update, I spoke about how it was much easier for me to be a channel for Love to flow through, than a vessel for Love to flow into.

> "Anytime I have a chance to speak my Truth, to share the beliefs and knowledge which I so passionately embrace, I get to touch the Divine. I get to be a channel for Love to flow through. (One of the things I want to talk about in this Newsletter is that it can be easier to be a channel for Love to flow through than a receptacle for Love to flow into.) - Joy2MeU Update October 2000

This beautiful teacher Susan has come into my life to help me learn to be a vessel for Love to flow into - not only on a personal intimate relationship level, but also in terms of helping me break out of the limiting ego boxes that have restricted my ability to carry the message that I have been given to carry. She is a teacher who has come into my life to help me learn how to respect and honor my self/Self and my gifts more fully.

The next step is to start setting some prices for what I do that will allow me to have some more freedom financially to keep spreading the message - that demonstrates that I do honor and value what I do, and that I do have faith that I deserve more abundance in my life. Thus the Intensive Training Days that I have started. I have set a price for them that I believe is reasonable and that will bring more financial abundance in my life if they are successful. I have set them up as an affirmation of the value of what I have learned, of the work I have put into nurturing the gift of being able to communicate and teach others what I have learned - and as an attempt to open up to allowing more financial abundance to flow into my life.

They are also an attempt to spread the word, and to facilitate future appearances to carry the message of Love and Joy that has been given to me to share. As Susan has pointed out to me, I can be of service to a great many more people doing these workshops than I can by putting so much of my time and energy into speaking to people one on one on the telephone.

I have never been good at marketing myself. My new Marketing Director put it this way, "you are the kind of artist that a manger gets so frustrated with while trying to get them to promote themselves."

When I self published the book and was marketing it myself, I did have some experiences where I lost money on workshops. That has been the evidence my ego has been using to hold me back for years - that I couldn't afford to invest the money to set something up if there was a chance I would lose money on it. Now I am attempting to break out of the limiting box my old tapes have had me trapped in.

I set up the Intensive and have been praying that this first one will work so that it can become a series of events around the country - and overseas also, one of these days. I have now had enough people sign up that the expenses are covered. That is great news! How many more people will sign up is in the More Will Be Revealed category right now.

My job is to plant the seeds and take the action - the outcome is in my Higher Power's hands. Hopefully my Marketing Director's prodding will help me to open up to new ways to carry the message, and to being a vessel for the symbolic money energy to flow in a much more abundant way." - Joy2MeU March 2006 Update Newsletter Part 2

Susan's Transformation

Susan's attitude towards what I do changed radically after we started living together. It was quite an interesting transformation with Susan going: from being someone who didn't want to hear anything about what I could teach her about codependency recovery; from the beginning when she was very critical of my book and called it the Dance of the Wounded Ducks; from being someone who mocked attempts on my part to set boundaries and the whole idea of codependency; to being my biggest proponent wanting to share what I teach with everyone. She has ADD and thought my articles were much too long and would usually skip over large parts of them if she did try to read them. And it was a few years before she completely read and understood my book.

But she did get it. Almost by osmosis - it seemed. She overheard my side in telephone counseling sessions. She heard me share at the CoDA convention I mentioned and a few other places - and also in meetings. Because the first time I did the Intensive workshop we had Darien with us - and we became his primary guardians after that - she wasn't able to be present for a whole one of my workshops for several years. But she was able to get it. And she really came to understand how important and vital my work is for helping people change their lives for the better. She basically carries my message everywhere she goes.

And she goes a lot of places. She goes to lots of 12 step meetings - AA, CoDA, Al-Anon. She is the only person I have ever known personally that got court ordered to go to Al-Anon - although we were together for some years before she started attending regularly even though she had been court ordered to go several years before we met. (I used to tell her that it was a measure of how very codependent she was that her Higher Power got the world's leading expert on codependency recovery assigned to her case.)

She is also very involved in Landmark Education and through her involvement there got involved in promoting events to raise money for homeless children - which led to booking bands and shows. She is very social, has a passion for music, and loves dancing.

It is one of the ways that we are different. I am much more a stay at home kind of person - while she is always wanting to be on the go. This has actually worked out very good for us - very functionally, because I am happy to stay home with Darien while she is out and about.

I am a farm boy from the Midwest and she is 100% Southern California babe. There are numerous ways in which we are at different extremes of the spectrum - and this is something that I am seeing a lot these days. Two people get together who - in certain areas - are very different from each other. One person being out of balance to one side of an issue or area - and the other person to the other side. I think that is part of the Cosmic Plan in this Age of Healing & Joy that we are experiencing - pairing people who can help each other to get more balanced, move more to the middle ground.

This is not the relationship I was asking for, not the one I thought I wanted or expected - but it is perfect. I learned from my experience in this relationship that it is very important for people to be willing to let go of preconceived notions and expectations so that they can be present to learn from, and enjoy, the relationship the Universe has brought into their life today. Be careful about holding out for what you think you want. If I had held on to "dream woman" image, I would never have gotten into a relationship - it was a perfect defense by my ego to keep me unavailable for a relationship.

We don't always get what we want - but we do get what we need. Be open to recognizing that someone has come into your life to be a catalyst for your growth even if they don't fit your idea / fantasy of what you want your relationship to look like.

The very important thing is that we have both been clear from the beginning that our relationship was about something larger than just the two of us - that we had been brought together by our Higher Powers as part of our Spiritual Growth process. We are committed to living our relationship in a Recovery / Spiritual / Transformational context. When things get really hard, we pray together. We hold hands and I say my prayers and affirmations for both of us.

In the November 2006 Update I shared about the next turn of events in our journey together.

"At the end of my August Update Newsletter I mentioned that it was possible we could be moving.

"There is a chance that Susan, Darien, and I will be moving to San Diego. (On August 30th Robert did announce he and his family are moving to San Diego.) It is possible that being there (where Susan would be near her kids, and have more opportunity career wise) would help us in spreading the message and bringing in more income." - Joy2MeU August 2006 Update

We did move in mid September. We are now in Encinitas California - a community in Northern San Diego County sandwiched between Carlsbad and Oceanside to the north, and Solana Beach and Del Mar to the South. We live in a house that is about half the size of the one we had in Paso Robles - with an ocean view from the back yard that is astroturf. (The front yard is also astroturf - something that seemed pretty strange to us at first, but is actually very nice with a 2 year old running around.)

So, now we are in a big city. It doesn't really feel like it to me most of the time however. I have pretty much limited my movement to places in the immediate vicinity - and try to stay off the freeways as much as possible. So far, because Susan is working and we are not at a financial position to put Darien in daycare yet - I have been primarily a nanny. Which is an ongoing, and special gift, in my life.

Being a primary caregiver to Darien - who will be 2 on the 10th (probably a few days before I get this published) - continues to be one of the great miracles and surprises of my recovery. Never could I have imagined being in the position of taking care of a baby at this stage in my life and recovery. The Joy and wonder of watching this precocious, precious little man grow up from the tiny baby I first met in March of 2005, to revealing himself to be a uniquely charming and delightful character who captures the heart of anyone who gets to experience his personality, fills my heart to overflowing with such Joy and contentment. There are times: when he is laying with his head on my chest gazing into my eyes; or when he curls up in my arms with his head laid on my shoulders; or when he burrows in beside me when he is sleeping with us; or just listening to him jabber or watching him run and play - moments that I feel a sense of Blissful Love that is sublimely exquisite. Such a gift!

It brings to mind once again something I have shared in past Updates - that GRATEFUL is not nearly a huge enough word to describe my feelings about what a gift my recovery has been to me. It is not a big enough word to describe how grateful I am for having the courage to work through my fear of intimacy issues to the point where I was willing to surrender to getting into a relationship with Susan, or to describe what I feel about all the richness and abundance of Joy and Life this relationship with her has brought into my recovery adventure - which includes, of course, my precious step grand-son, God-son, Darien. I am very, very, very, grateful that I am having the opportunity to experience this special little man in my life.

So, this has been a good move. Susan is much happier here where she is closer to family and the many friends and meetings that were so vital to her early recovery. Her oldest daughter actually lives just up the street - and it was in visiting her that Susan discovered this place with the astroturf yard. She also found work that is fulfilling and makes her happy - so that is very good.

I haven't found a lot of time yet to get very grounded in the community and develop new relationship with people and meetings, because I am spending so much of my time taking care of Darien. We have found a Montessori school nearby which we think will be a wonderful - and affordable - place for him to develop and grow and free up more time for me to focus on getting established here myself. I have real mixed feelings about that, because though I need the time to focus on myself, I will miss spending so much of my time with him. He is such a cool kid - and this time of being with him so much is such a special, special time in my life. I am profoundly GRATEFUL for the abundance of Love and Joy that I am experiencing in my day to day life right now." - Joy2MeU Update November 2006

Here is the continuation of the article in 2010 that I was able to publish on Valentine's Day.

"February 12th 2010 - hopefully for publication on Valentine's Day
On Christmas I wrote the following to my Yahoo mailing list:

"I posted the newest pictures on my Darien page earlier this month, but haven't had time to tell the stories yet. I am going to be sharing about a huge breakthrough Susan and I have had in our relationship in that writing for the Darien page - but not sure when I am going to get it done. Hopefully before the start of the new year." - Friday 12/25/09 9:25 PM "Merry Christmas to my Yahoo mailing list"

Although I have worked on this page intermittently since then, it is only now that I am nearing the finish. Last fall our relationship made a quantum leap in intimacy - and I have now opened my heart to Susan as much as I have to Darien.

In my early writings about the relationship, I talked about how I had opened my heart to her in a way I had never done to another person - and how I was able to Love in the moment in the way I described in my Wedding Prayer / Meditation on Romantic Commitment in reality and not just in theory - and those things were true to the extent I was capable of loving at that time. But the level to which I had opened my heart and was capable of Loving then was minuscule in comparison with where I am at now. I have tried to think of analogies - like the difference between a drop of water and all the water in the pond; a grain of sand to all the sand on the beach; being in preschool as opposed to getting my third Ph.D.; my level of consciousness at 30 days sober compared to at 26 years in recovery, etc. Obviously I am trying to convey that there has been a huge, quantum leap into dimensions and depths that I have never experienced before.

This was a major, huge, incredible breakthrough for me - and unfortunately the Universe need to use a big stick on me to get me to wake up.

"The way I think of it is that my Higher Power works with the carrot and stick approach: like a mule driver trying to get a mule moving, he can either dangle a carrot in front of the mule and get the mule moving after the carrot, or he can take a stick and beat him until he gets moving.

It is a lot easier on me to follow the carrots that my Higher Power dangles in front of me than to force the Universe to use a stick to get me moving. Either way I am going to get to where the Universe wants me - but the carrot method is a lot easier on me.

The more that I do my healing, the clearer I get on receiving the messages - the more I get to follow the carrots instead of experiencing the stick. The dance of Recovery is a process of starting to Love ourselves enough to start changing life into an easier, more enjoyable experience."

It was an incredibly painful experience - as opportunities for growth often are, especially when the stick is used. When Susan gave me my 26 year token at an AA meeting she said that us standing up there together was proof of the miracles possible when two people are in recovery. She said that "we went through hell" this last year and now our relationship has never been so good - or something to that effect. (The part in quotes is a direct quote.) The people in the room could feel the Love we have for each other now - and it was a very cool experience.

The "hell" part was not fun - but it was a major load of fertilizer for both of us. I don't know if we could have reached the level of Love and intimacy that we are at now had I been willing to follow the carrots. I don't think so sitting here today. I think we needed to go through what we went through as a perfect part of our individual spiritual paths. A few weeks ago, when I started writing this, I was really beating myself up - judging and shaming myself for not following the carrots. I told her that I was so sorry - that it was like I was in a black out for a couple of years. But that isn't true. I was doing the best I knew how I at the time. And the things that she went through - that I, in a way, set her up for - were a perfect part of her growth process. Some deep issues that she needed to get in touch with - just as I needed to get in touch with the issues that were driving my behavior.

There were plenty of carrots that told me something wasn't right in how I was behaving - but it wasn't yet time for me to uncover the source of those fears, of that defensive behavior yet. Up until last fall, I was still very defended in my relationship with her. This was something I recognized and mentioned in my writing - but that I was not able to overcome until a few months ago.

At the beginning of the Darien page I quoted my April 2008 Newsletter:

"My fear of intimacy is still keeping me from opening my heart completely to Susan in some ways - and to myself also of course (the fear of shining too brightly I mentioned in my last post here) - but our Higher Powers unfolded our paths perfectly to put us together with Darien so he could help us both learn about Love. Susan and I are learning a great deal from each other - and the common ground of our love for Darien is helping our love to evolve. . . . . I can see clearly now that Darien is the first human being - since my parents when I was an infant - that I have ever opened up my heart to completely. Because of my Love for Darien, I am gradually opening my heart to Susan." - Joy2MeU Update April 2008

And it was gradually that I was opening my heart to her. I wasn't ready yet to break through in a major way because I wasn't aware of where my resistance was coming from. I knew that I wasn't comfortable with the way I was keeping her at a distance, the way my fear of intimacy was still operating to keep my heart mostly closed, but had not uncovered the cause. In some writing I did in January 2007 I was forced to look at my fear of intimacy issues again by some things that came up as I was writing an appeal for help in keeping my book in print. That caused me to do some processing in my March 2007 Update about what I had written - although I ended up sharing what I had written in an addendum to that Update rather than in the Update.

"And that is what I am seeing right now - that my terror of intimacy has risen it's ugly head and has been doing a number on me. I have been allowing myself to focus upon the "stress" of the financial situation as an excuse to be distracted and not present in my relationship with Susan. And I have been using my precious step grandson / God son Darien as part of my camouflage for doing that." - My Fear of Intimacy revisited again 2007

So, as far back as January 2007 - over 3 years ago now - I was aware that I was focusing on Darien, not just because of my Love for him - but also as a way of keeping some distance between us. In that March 2007 Update I shared that I was going to be writing about my fear of intimacy, and also about my issues with my own masculine energy which I thought was a key to opening up my heart to Susan. Then I wrote the addendum page just quoted - and basically talked about the history of my processing through my fear of intimacy issues. That left the actual issues I needed to look at for another extra Newsletter page - a page which I never finished. Obviously it wasn't time yet to make the break through.

Ultimately those issues had to do with my father. Those are issues that I still need to do some processing about, and I plan on doing that processing in my next Update Newsletter which I will try to get finished this month. The issues that I had with my father - resentments of how he treated me (which I had done some work on, but not enough) and betrayal issues from early childhood that I had not even known were there - were what was causing me to keep up walls with Susan. I was discounting and invalidating her, withholding my love and affection and attention because of buttons that she pushed in me because of my issues with my father. And I set her up to react out of issues she had with her father who abandoned her. Her abandonment issues caused her to revert to an old pattern of hers - seeking attention and validation from men.

I am not going to go into the processing I need to do any more here. I will be sharing about those issues with my father and the behaviors they caused in the upcoming Update. I am going to wrap up this section with an answer I gave to someone who sent me a question in a message on Facebook - and then include some pictures from our trip to Cambria on the 5th anniversary of our first meeting.

Q: "hi. im curious what you think...do you think that a codependents relationship with someone that they have chosen out of their codependency COULD ever work? and what if when that relationships trust has already been destroyed? i think i know the answer to be no, but im am struggling with my feelings and thoughts on this and thought maybe you could give me some insight/advice. thanks."

A: "Yes ___, it can work if both people are working on their issues so that they can stop reacting and start seeing things more clearly. That includes seeing that the violation of trust that occurred was not personal - just the other person reacting to their own issues. So blind trust cannot be restored - but trust based on the reality of who the other person is today can be built.

I hope that makes some sense. It is really a very complicated process sorting all of this out - and involves owning and grieving for the old wounds that have been triggered in the latest situation."

The key ingredient in choosing to go forward with exploring a relationship with Susan back in January 2005 was that she was dedicated to her recovery. She is often more dedicated to her recovery than I am able to be to mine - and she challenges me on that when I am being lazy and complacent. It is vital to be able to work through issues in a relationship - and the magic that happened when we were able to work through our issues a few months ago Truly does make this relationship a priceless gift that I treasure and cherish, as I spoke about in one of my theoretical articles on healthy relationships that I wrote over 10 years ago.

(This article is Chapter 12 in this book and this is one of two long excerpts I am leaving in this final chapter because it would be good for you to read as you finish this book, to remind you of the single most important factor to look for in a potential relationship.)

"It is vitally important to make healing and Spiritual growth our number one priority so that we can look to the other person for help and support - not expect them to rescue us and give us self worth. Healing is an inside job. My issues are my responsibility to work through, it is not the other persons job to compromise her self to accommodate my fears and insecurities. If I am choosing wisely when I enter into a relationship then I will choose someone who will be compassionate, patient, and supportive of me while I work through my issues.

And no matter how wisely I choose, or how much healing and recovery the other person has had, she will still be a human being with her own issues to work through so she will not always be able to be patient, compassionate, and supportive. For one person to expect another to always be there for them, to always have the space and time to be available to us, is another insane expectation.

We do want to choose someone who is willing to work through issues. When another person is willing to do the work with us, a relationship can be an incredibly nurturing, magical space to explore what True Love means - some of the time. It can not be that all of the time. There might be periods of time - days, weeks, even months - where things are going beautifully and it feels like we may have reached "happily ever after". But then things will change and get different. That is how the life process works - it will not be someone's fault. It will be a new opportunity for growth for both people.

Two people who are working through their issues and are willing to do the grief work, can turn an argument about some stupid, mundane life event into some mutual deep grieving. That is True emotional intimacy.

When we are willing to own our power to be the neutral observer who can see our responsibility in whatever is happening without shame and judgment, and can also have the courage and willingness to hold the other person responsible for their behavior without shame and judgment - then the magic can really happen.

Two people who have negotiated some guidelines to help them in times when they are vulnerable and reactive - can transform an argument about some symptom into an opportunity to heal some core wounding. . . . . .

. . . . . . They can achieve a place of True emotional honesty and intimacy where they can get in touch with their individual wounds and grieve together. That is the kind of emotional intimacy which can form a very deep bond and be Joyously healing for both people.

To be willing to be conscious and emotionally honest with ourselves is a courageous act of faith that will allow us to progressively increase the number of moments in each day that we have the ability and freedom to be happy and Joyous in the now. To find another being who is willing to join us in this adventure, and to explore True emotional intimacy with us, is a priceless gift to be cherished and treasured." - Chapter 12 Partners in the Journey

I was able to get past my reactions - and separate the pain from my childhood from the pain in the now - to get a place where I was able to take responsibility for my side of the street - for how my behavior set her up to seek attention elsewhere. Her process unfolded perfectly in sync with mine in that the Love she feels for me helped her to hit a bottom in her old pattern that allowed her to reexamine some of the old ideas / attitudes and wounds driving her behavior and see her self more clearly so that she could get to a deeper level of honesty with herself and me. It was a True journey into intimacy and a gift (that felt like shit some of the time) - but I am very grateful for how things have unfolded because the place we are at now is a place neither of us has ever been.

It is still quite scary at times, being so vulnerable from having opened my heart to her so much - as I am sure it is also for her - but we are going forward enjoying this new closeness, this new much deeper intimacy, and this new more mature Love that comes from having worked through issues that would have destroyed most relationships. I am proud of myself, and very grateful and proud of her, for having the courage to reach the place we have in our relationship now. As I said to her on my Facebook page, "Thank you Sweetie for making my life so much richer. You are the Valentine that is the answer to my prayers!" - RB 2/14/10

It wasn't until June that year that I had a breakthrough in regard to the issues with my father - the ones that were affecting my relationship with Susan. I added the following processing to a page on my website that is an article entitled: God the Father, and my father.

"Today would have been my Father's birthday. June 14th. Flag day. He used to tell us they put the flags up because it was his birthday.

It never felt to me like my father loved me. He was never able to say "I love you" to me directly in his life. On his death bed I said "I love you" to him - and the best that he could do was say, "Same here."

I have said for years - and said again at a CoDA meeting last night - that I think I have more shame because my father was there the whole time I was growing up. If he would have abandoned us physically and not been there - then I could have made up stories about him loving me. But he was there every day - and it never felt like he loved me.

Thanks to the beautiful, courageously recovering woman I am in relationship with, I realized last fall that it was my father that I got sober for. It had never occurred to me to think that. And also, thanks to being in a relationship with someone who is in recovery, I got in touch with pain from when I was an infant about what felt like my father's abandonment and betrayal. What felt like was his rejection because I wasn't good enough - because I wasn't lovable. I always have said that I never felt loved by my father, but what I realized last fall was that there was a time when I felt like he loved me - when I was a baby. His first son. Then my parents left the college town where my father was going on the GI bill - he always said he had to quit college because of me - and moved on to the farm I grew up on when I was about 6 month old. That was the start of my father working very hard to support a family that eventually included 6 kids. My next brother was born 15 months after me - and I was no longer the center of attention - but by then, I had already lost much of my father's attention because he was working to support his growing family.

I did get in touch with this infant wounding last fall, but I hadn't really worked through it yet - which was causing me to react - out of that wordless pain and terror of an infant who feels rejected and betrayed by his father - to my partner. That happened yesterday - and again today. The part of me that is convinced that I am so unlovable that even someone who seems to love me completely will leave me - as it felt like I lost my father as a baby.

When I reacted yesterday, and my partner was able to respond out of her recovery instead of out of her old wounded defensive behavioral reaction, I was not able to get through it - I just turned it back in on myself and judged myself for my reaction. Today when it happened and she again was able to respond out of recovery, I was able to bring the focus back to myself in a healthy way - and that led to my breakthrough.

I have been saying to people for years that my mother taught me how to rationalize abusive behavior - both with her role modeling and with direct messages like: "Your father really loves you, he just doesn't know how to show it." And I did learn to rationalize from statements like that. What was different today, **was that for the first time ever**, I got it on a gut level that what she was saying was also the Truth (with a capital T.)

My father did love me - and was incapable of showing it. **My father did love me!!!!!!**

My father died in May 2005 - just a bit over 5 years ago. I didn't grieve for my father then. I said that I had been grieving for not having a loving father for years - and that was the truth. But I did not ever really grieve for my father. Today I am grieving for my father. My father who did love me, but was incapable of showing me. Maybe it is not too late to be a different kind of father to my son.

Owning that my father did love me is hopefully going to let me finally open up to receive the love from my partner that I haven't been trusting because deep down inside I didn't feel like I was lovable.

6/14/10 12:56 pm. I finished writing this and sent a copy to my partner Susan at 12:16 - 40 minutes ago. We got off the phone talking about it - and crying - only a few minutes ago. The miraculous, incredible gift that is a result of us both being in recovery, is that me getting on a gut level that my father really did love me, helped her for the first time to get on a gut level that her mother really did love her. Huge paradigm shift for both of us!!!!!!!!!

I am going to be expanding on this processing in the coming days, and hopefully by Father's Day I will have been able to process through it in more depth and breadth and post it on my site. Right now, I am sobbing and crying because this is a huge piece - for both of us.

As long as at the core of my relationship with myself, was the belief / feeling that my father had rejected and betrayed me as an infant, there is no way that I could open up to receive love unconditionally from another person. There was no way that I could truly be more Loving to myself in how I treat myself, in how I live my life. As I say in the article above, I have made huge progress over the years - but this shame and terror of rejection was at the core of my relationship with myself. Opening my heart to Susan brought it to the surface for me. Now maybe I can really open up my heart to my self.

My father really did love me!!!!!!! ~ Robert 6/14/10 1:13 pm" - God the Father, and my father

Since the beginning Susan has pushed some buttons that were installed by my father. This is something that I haven't written about specifically previously, although I share about it in my Intensive Training workshop and with phone counseling clients all the time.

Susan had a really hard childhood. She was subjected to what amounted to torture by her mother and step father. She rebelled and got thrown into Juvenile Hall at 13. Then she escaped from Juvenile Hall and lived on the streets for 6 months when she was 13. She had to get tough to survive. When I say that her defenses were perfectly designed push my buttons - I was not kidding.

"Her defenses were perfectly designed to push my buttons - to trigger some of my deepest wounds and reactions. And of course, my defenses pushed her buttons as well." - Update June 2005

When she gets scared or stressed, she reacts defensively with a style of communication that makes a Marine Drill Seargent look like a teddy bear. Very harsh, critical, barking orders in an abusive way. Just like my father.

This is definitely one of those areas where I teach best what I need most to learn. In an article in my Healthy Relationship series that I wrote in 1999 - that became Chapter 12 in this book - I wrote something that came from my intuitive knowing - something I had knew theoretically but had never really applied in a relationship because of my relationship phobia.

"It is vitally important to make healing and Spiritual growth our number one priority so that we can look to the other person for help and support - not expect them to rescue us and give us self worth. Healing is an inside job. My issues are my responsibility to work through, it is not the other persons job to compromise her self to accommodate my fears and insecurities. If I am choosing wisely when I enter into a relationship then I will choose someone who will be compassionate, patient, and supportive of me while I work through my issues.

And no matter how wisely I choose, or how much healing and recovery the other person has had, she will still be a human being with her own issues to work through so she will not always be able to be compassionate, patient, and supportive. For one person to expect another to always be there for them, to always have the space and time to be available to us, is an insane expectation." - Chapter 12 - Partners in the Journey

My issues are my responsibility! When she is in reaction and speaks to me in a harsh way, it is definitely important that I tell her that is not an acceptable way to speak to me - but it is also really important for me to work on not taking it personally. Realizing that she is reacting to her wounds, dancing with her issues - she is not consciously choosing to be abusive to me, she is reacting.

For me to expect her to stop a certain behavior because I don't like it is part of my codependency. Of course, I would prefer that she not talk to me in a certain way but if I expect her to change because I want her to, then I am setting myself up to feel like a victim. It is very easy to sabotage a relationship because the other person is not changing in the way we want them to change. My issues are my responsibility!

Yes I want to set boundaries with another person about what is an acceptable way to treat me. But if the other person is reacting unconsciously out of their wounds, then they aren't present in the moment - and aren't consciously doing something to violate my boundary, they are just reacting.

If I am in my recovering adult consciousness when she goes into this type of reaction, then I (at 6 ft tall) can look at her (5' 3" tall) and say to myself, "The chihuahua is yapping at me again." - and be amused by this petite person acting like she is a 6' 6" heavyweight.

If I react out of an inner child place - then I feel like the doberman is about to rip my throat out. It throws me back into the little boy whose father raged at him - and it feels life threatening.

It is my perspective that determines my emotional response / reaction - it is not her "doing something to me." My default programming is to react out of a victim place about what she is "doing to me."

By developing an objective empowered adult observer perspective, I have a choice (at least some of the time) to respond to her in a healthy, recovering adult manner - instead out of a wounded terrified child.

When I respond out of my recovering adult by saying something humorous, it relieves some of her fear and she can back down. When I respond out a child victim place, it just increases her fear which means she gets even angrier.

What an opportunity for growth.

Sometimes what we need isn't what we want. I wanted someone who would be kind and gentle and supportive - and who would definitely not be like my father. What the Universe - my Higher Power - decided was that I needed someone who was like my father.

In the beginning of our relationship I wanted her to read the article which is Chapter 30 in this book, the one in which I talk about how: "If someone loves you it should feel like they love you." What I realize now, is that in that Chapter I was being a little black and white in my perspective - this is right and this is wrong thinking. We are all wounded. We all have defensive patterns. We are all going to sometimes be abusive or controlling or manipulative or shaming - because that is the way we were programmed and conditioned. And where this shows up the most is in the relationships where our hearts are involved because those are the relationships that are the most important and threatening to us. That is why Romantic Relationships are the greatest arena for spiritual and emotional growth!

We aren't going to find someone to be in relationship with that doesn't push our buttons some of the time. They will trigger our childhood wounds. In this new Age of Healing & Joy, we are doing massive Karmic settlement. We have Karma to settle with the people that come into our lives, we have childhood wounds / emotional buttons that cause us to have explosive / implosive reactions. That is going to lead to conflict in relationships. If someone were to tell me that there was no conflict in their relationship and they feel loved by their partner all of the time, I would assume that they are being emotionally dishonest and were in denial.

"It was very important in my recovery to realize that emotional intimacy includes anger. That the message that I learned from my mother - that it was not okay to be angry at someone I love - was a false message. Avoiding conflict denies intimacy - we cannot be emotionally intimate with someone we can't be angry at. Conflict is an inherent part of relationships - and working through issues is how intimacy grows. Conflict is part of the fertilizer that is necessary for the growth of emotional intimacy. A relationship with no conflict is an emotionally dishonest relationship - and the other extreme of the codependent spectrum from relationships that have constant conflict. Both are unhealthy." - Chapter 37 Codependent Defenses ~ The Gatekeeper

What has happened is that as I am able to not go into my reactions so much, she has been able to change as well. She is much more compassionate and patient and nurturing now then she was when we got together. She has made great progress, but she still will react in a harsh way sometimes - just as I will react some of the time even though I have made great progress.

Because I learned from my mother it was not okay to be angry at someone I loved, I was set up to be passive aggressive in my relationships with women - to have the anger come out sideways. Her aggressive, bullying defense was actually more honest than my passively controlling behavior.

"Both the passive and aggressive behavioral defenses are controlling - they just employ different strategies. As I said in the last chapter, in talking about selfishness:

"Then I could start to see that the reason that I was being nice to someone was not just because I didn't want to hurt their feelings - it was much more about protecting myself. It was what I learned to do in childhood to: avoid confrontation; keep someone from getting angry with me; keep from being abandoned; try to earn love; etc. My defense system was set up to protect me from doing things that I thought would cause me pain - like: setting boundaries; speaking my Truth; asking for help; being vulnerable; etc." - Chapter 7: Multiple levels of selfishness

If I am not speaking my truth, not setting boundaries, as a form of manipulation to keep someone from getting angry at me, keep from being abandoned - that is controlling behavior. I would hold onto my ego self image of being a "nice guy" and judge those people who were aggressively controlling as being mean and heartless. I got ego strength from looking down from the moral high ground at people who were aggressively trying to get their needs met because I could not be honest with myself about how I was passively, indirectly, manipulatively trying to get my needs met. This is a form of emotional vampirism, nurturing myself emotionally by comparing myself to others and feeling "better than."" - Codependency Recovery: Wounded Souls Dancing in the Light *Book 2: A Dysfunctional Relationship with Life* Chapter 8: Codependents as Emotional Vampires

I needed to learn to be more direct and honest - and to stop taking her behavior so personally - in order to be able to be more loving in the relationship. If I had made that particular behavior a deal breaker in our relationship, I would have missed out on all the wonderful gifts I have gotten in this relationship over the years.

I feel loved by her the majority of the time now. Because we were dedicated to our recovery and spiritual growth process we have both grown in our capacity to be present and loving in the moment.

No relationship is ever going to be perfect. If you expect the other person to toe the line according what you think is acceptable behavior then you are being controlling and the other person is building up resentments. 95% of boundaries in a relationship are about negotiation (as I talked about in Chapter 17). We need to be willing to compromise in some areas in order to be available for a relationship.

The bottom line with anything, including a romantic relationship, is to ask your self, "Is the payoff worth the price." If the payoff for being in the relationship is greater than any price you are paying, then you have a relationship that is working on certain levels. Relationships are probably not going to work on all levels any of the time, let alone all the time. If a relationship is working on more levels then it is not, then it is a successful relationship to some degree.

We are not going to get to happily-ever-after. There is no happily-ever-after on this plane in these bodies. Being able to show up for a relationship and work through our issues is a goal in recovery. In order to have a partner and an ally in our journey through life it is necessary to have realistic expectations and perspectives of what a romantic relationship is in reality.

Seeing that romantic relationship are part of a spiritual and emotional growth process - being committed to living your relationship in a Recovery / Spiritual / Transformational context - can help you open up to nurturing love and emotional intimacy in your life as you develop an interdependent relationship with another recovering being. Recognizing that your partner is a teacher in this human boarding school we are attending, will help you learn the lessons you are here to learn at the same time you can have someone to enjoy the journey with.

"If we are living life in reaction to fear, we are being victims - and there is no chance of us being healthy in a relationship if we are making our choices in reaction to fear.

That is why it is so important to have a Spiritual Awakening - to raise our consciousness. By being in recovery, on a healing path, we are realigning our intellectual paradigm away from one that is driven by fear to one that is based on Love. In awakening to the possibility that perhaps there is a Higher Power that Loves us, we can start seeing life as a growth process rather than a test we can fail. Then the events and people in our life become opportunities for growth rather than instruments of punishment.

Life then becomes an adventure. One that can be painful and scary, can feel like a stupid game sometimes, but one that can also be Joyous and wondrous and full of miracles at times. By changing our concept of romantic love, we can also make romance a great adventure to be explored rather than some test we can fail.

As long as we are here in this big amusement park that is life in human body, it is better not to allow fear and shame to keep us from experiencing the most exciting rides.

"This is a playground, this is a wonderful summer camp. It is full of beautiful colors and wondrous sights, animals and birds and plants, mountains and oceans and meadows, whales and butterflies. It is full of tastes and smells and sounds and sensations."

Romantic relationships are the greatest arena for Spiritual and emotional growth available to us. They are the most exciting ride. It is well worth the risk to take a chance on love if we are viewing it as a learning experience that is a perfect part of our life adventure rather than the goal in, and of, itself. Romance is part of the journey, part of the experience - not the destination.

There is nothing wrong with wanting the prince or princess to come into our lives. What is important is to know that they will have issues to work through - and they will push the buttons of our issues so that we are forced to face them. Romantic relationships are hard work because of the dysfunctional programming and emotional wounding we experienced in childhood. It is necessary to keep working on them to give them a chance to be healthy." - Chapter 14 Romantic Love as a Concept

We got married on January 14th, 2011. I believe that this relationship is going to last the rest of my life. We are able to work through issues - to make progress in recovering and healing from the wounding and programming in our childhood - in ways that we never could have done on our own. Having the courage to venture into the Romantic Arena is definitely worth the risk in my opinion and experience.

I hope that sharing my experience, strength, and hope in this book will help you to open up to the possibility of a loving interdependent relationship in your life. We were set up to feel like failures in romantic relationships because of our childhood wounding and programming - that is the bad news. We can learn to take power way from our wounding and programming enough to be able to get past our fear of intimacy so that we can enter into the realm of romantic relationships - that is the good news. We have tools and knowledge and spiritual guidance available to us today that has never before been available in the history of humanity - that is very good news.

This healing process is why we are here in this body in this lifetime. And the greatest arena for emotional and spiritual growth is in romantic relationship. I am very grateful that I have been willing to do the emotional healing so that I could open up to the possibility of a romantic relationship. I am very grateful that Susan came into my life to be my teacher and lover and friend and playmate in this adventure that we are having in human body.

We are here to do this healing. We are here to learn about Love. We are here to learn to Love ourselves and to share Love with other people. The goal in recovery is to learn to be able to relax and enjoy the journey as much as possible while we are healing and settling Karma. It is very cool to have a companion and playmate, a partner and ally, a friend and lover on the journey. It is a much richer and fuller experience - to say nothing of less lonely. I highly recommend it. ;-)

"This healing process is why we are here!

The awakening to consciousness of our Spiritual nature and Spiritual purpose is why we are here at this time.

This is the age of awakening, of raising our consciousness, of becoming aligned with Divine Truth. This age is the time of atoning, of tuning into the higher vibrational emotional energy of Love, Light, Truth, and Joy. This higher vibrational energy is the homing beacon that guides us back home.

There is a reason that we never felt at home here. It is because we have felt disconnected, and then when we made all those attempts to reconnect, we were dialing the wrong number. We were looking outside for the answers.

This is not home. This is also not a prison. This is boarding school and we are getting ready for graduation. And it is all a perfect part of the Divine Script.

We are here to experience this human evolutionary process. The more we awaken to the Truth of who we are (Spiritual beings) and why we are here (to experience being human), and stop giving power to the false gods of money, property and prestige; people, places and things; the more we can celebrate being here!

Buddha had it half right: We need to let go of our attachment to the illusions of this Illusion. But as we stop giving power to the illusions, we can begin to celebrate being here, we can begin to enjoy our human experience.

This is a playground, this is a wonderful summer camp. It is full of beautiful colors and wondrous sights, animals and birds and plants, mountains and oceans and meadows, whales and butterflies. It is full of tastes and smells and sounds and sensations.

The gift of touch is an incredibly wonderful gift. One of the reasons we are here is to touch each other physically as well as Spiritually, emotionally, and mentally. Touch is not bad or shameful. Our creator did not give us sensual and sexual sensations that feel so wonderful just to set us up to fail some perverted, sadistic life test. Any concept of god that includes the belief that the flesh and the Spirit cannot be integrated, that we will be punished for honoring our powerful human desires and needs, is - in my belief - a sadly twisted, distorted, and false concept that is reversed to the Truth of a Loving God-Force.

We need to strive for balance and integration in our relationships. We need to touch in healthy, appropriate, emotionally honest ways - so that we can honor our human bodies and the gift that is physical touch.

Making Love is a celebration and a way of honoring the Masculine and Feminine Energy of the Universe (and the masculine and feminine energy within no matter what genders are involved), a way of honoring its perfect interaction and harmony. It is a blessed way of honoring the Creative Source.

One of the most blessed and beautiful gifts of being in body is the ability to feel on a sensual level. Because we have been doing human backwards, we have been deprived of the pleasure of enjoying our bodies in a guilt-free, shame-free, manner. By striving for integration and balance we can start to enjoy our human experience - on a sensual level as well as on the emotional, mental, and Spiritual levels.

As we learn the dance of Recovery, as we tune into the energy of Truth, we can reverse our emotional experience of being human so that most of the time it can feel more like a wonderful summer camp than a dreadful prison." - Codependence: The Dance of Wounded Souls

The End

Joy to You & Me Enterprises

Robert Burney formed Joy to You & Me Enterprises in order to facilitate the dissemination of what he believes is a vitally important and very Joyous message. **Codependence: The Dance of Wounded Souls** was the first project for this company in 1995. Until July 2011, when he used Amazon.com's CreateSpace to publish his second book **Codependency Recovery: Wounded Souls Dancing in The Light** *Book 1: Empowerment, Freedom, and Inner Peace through Inner Child Healing*, the financing had not been available to publish any additional books. Robert has however, published a wealth of information on recovery, healing, and spiritual topics on the internet. On his publicly available web site, Joy2MeU.com, he shares millions of words in articles, newsletters, and online books in which he discusses all facets of both the wounding and recovery process. In addition, he has 2 password protected web sites - the Joy2MeU Journal & Dancing in Light - in which he has published drafts of several future books and autobiographical information about the history of his recovery, emotional healing, and Spiritual growth process, as well as a personal journal about his recovery process over a period of five years. Since April 2006 he has been offering periodic day long Intensive Training workshops to train people in the Formula for inner healing and Spiritual Integration that he discovered and developed. He also has been doing telephone counseling since early 2000 and that has proven to be very effective in helping people apply his inner child healing approach in their lives.

Now in the summer of 2012, he is once again using Amazon's Create Space to publish his third book **Romantic Relationships ~ The Greatest Arena for Spiritual & Emotional Growth** *Codependent Dysfunctional Relationship Dynamics & Healthy Relationship Behavior* - with an e-book of the first half of this book published on Amazon Kindle in July 2012 and the second half e-book as well as the hard copy of whole book in September.

Copies of Joy to You & Me publications and news of Robert Burney can be obtained by contacting:

Joy to You & Me Enterprises
PO Box 235401
Encinitas CA 92023
Joy2MeU@silcom.com
http://Joy2MeU.com
http://www.facebook.com/robert.burney

29724568R00116

Made in the USA
Lexington, KY
05 February 2014